HORROR FILM
AND OTHERNESS

FILM AND CULTURE

FILM AND CULTURE

A series of Columbia University Press

Edited by John Belton

For a complete list of titles, see page 225

HORROR FILM
AND OTHERNESS

ADAM LOWENSTEIN

Columbia University Press
New York

Columbia University Press
Publishers Since 1893
New York   Chichester, West Sussex
cup.columbia.edu

Library of Congress Cataloging-in-Publication Data
Names: Lowenstein, Adam, author.
Title: Horror film and otherness / Adam Lowenstein.
Description: New York : Columbia University Press, [2022] | Series: Film and
    culture | Includes bibliographical references and index.
Identifiers: LCCN 2021054769 (print) | LCCN 2021054770 (ebook) |
    ISBN 9780231205764 (hardback) | ISBN 9780231205771 (trade paperback) |
    ISBN 9780231556156 (ebook)
Subjects: LCSH: Horror films—History and criticism. | Other (Philosophy)
    in motion pictures.
Classification: LCC PN1995.9.H6 L693 2022 (print) | LCC PN1995.9.H6 (ebook) |
    DDC 791.43/6164—dc23/eng/20211203
LC record available at https://lccn.loc.gov/2021054769
LC ebook record available at https://lccn.loc.gov/2021054770

Cover design: Milenda Nan Ok Lee
Cover image: From *The Babadook*. Credit: Atlaspix / Alamy Stock Photo.

For Irina
and for Simone,
with love ∾

CONTENTS

PART III. TRANSFORMING HORROR'S OTHER VOICES

ILLUSTRATIONS

ACKNOWLEDGMENTS

This book took shape in ways that made it an unusually personal project, a work of scholarship tied to my everyday life more intimately than ever before. I would not have dared to make the book as close to me as it is without the support of an extraordinary network of colleagues, students, friends, and family who believed in me, in the project, and in horror studies as the connective tissue between the two. Given the blurring between my personal and professional lives that characterized the creation of this book from start to finish, I cannot hope to thank everyone who contributed to its coming into being; each one of you has my deepest gratitude, and I hope you will see your inspiration reflected in the pages of this book.

Part of the joy in working on this book was experiencing its growth through a number of communal passion projects connected to horror studies that I have been lucky to be involved with in recent years. A Senior Faculty Fellowship from the University of Pittsburgh's Humanities Center allowed me to begin the collaborations with many individuals and institutions that commenced by honoring George A. Romero on the fiftieth anniversary of *Night of the Living Dead* in 2018. These collaborations have since grown in multiple directions, including the acquisition of the Romero Collection and the establishment of the Horror Studies Archive at Pitt; the founding of the George A. Romero Foundation; the creation of the Global Horror Studies Archival and Research Network through a Global Academic Partnership Grant from Pitt's Global Studies Center; the formation of the "Horror Genre as a Social Force" scholar community through Pitt's University Honors College; and the assembly of Pitt's

Horror Studies Working Group, which I have the pleasure of directing, as the umbrella collective that coordinates all of these efforts.

Needless to say, I must thank many valued friends, colleagues, and allies in conjunction with all of these projects as well as their precursors and offshoots: Stacey Abbott, Peggy Ahwesh, Terry Alexander, Richard Allen, Tanine Allison, John Amplas, Jonathan Arac, Jeff Aziz, Jessica Beck, Caetlin Benson-Allott, Don Bialostosky, Kathy Blee, Matt Blint, Livia Bloom Ingram, Aviva Briefel, Eugenie Brinkema, Marva Jones Brooks, Tony Buba, Paul Bullock, Jarrod Burris, James Cahill, Lori Cardille, Noël Carroll, Dan Chyutin, Robert Clift, Nancy Condee, John Cooper, Eric Crosby, Rusty Cundieff, Joe Dante, Jeremy Dauber, Nick Davis, Mario DeGiglio-Bellemare, Suzanne Desrocher-Romero, Bill Dotson, Tom Dubensky, Charles Exley, Lucy Fischer, Nicola Foote, Gloria Forouzan, Ed Galloway, Rosalind Galt, Ora Gelley, Shai Ginsburg, Bernie Goldmann, Michael Goodhart, Peter Grunwald, Tom Gunning, Barry Gutterman, Boaz Hagin, Steven Haines, Randall Halle, Franco Harris, John Harrison, Adam Hart, Wendy Haslem, Joan Hawkins, Tim Holland, Heidi Honeycutt, Chad Hunter, Sarah Joshi, Laura Kemmerer, Bridget Keown, Margee Kerr, Chika Kinoshita, Nathan Koob, Dan Kraus, Dan Kubis, Carl Kurlander, Marcia Landy, Sarah Juliet Lauro, Adam Leibovich, Carrie Fischer Lepore, Jen Lingler, Akira Lippit, Maria Loh, Roger Luckhurst, Sonia Lupher, Colin MacCabe, David Marshall, Dawn Lundy Martin, Jason Middleton, Sarah Minnaert, Philippe Mora, Joe Morrison, Laura Mulvey, Audrey Murrell, George Nama, Adam Nayman, Angela Ndalianis, Greg Nicotero, Dana Och, Ben Ogrodnik, Lisa Parker, Bill Peduto, Dave Pettersen, Marian Phillips, Erik Piepenburg, Greg Pierce, Isabel Pinedo, Dana Polan, Michael Prosser, Livia Rappaport, Adam Reinherz, Chris Roe, Jim Rogal, Gayle Rogers, Christine Romero, Tina Romero, Gaylen Ross, Josh Rothkopf, Stephanie Rothman, Ben Rubin, Richard P. Rubinstein, Dan Sacco, Denis Saltykov, Andy Sands, Kirk Savage, Steve Schlozman, Karl Schoonover, Meheli Sen, Adam Simon, Chris Stavrakis, Brad Stephenson, Aaron Sterns, Gary Streiner, Ramona Streiner, Russ Streiner, Gordon Sullivan, Kornelia Tancheva, Michael Temple, Johnny Twyning, Johnny Walker, Rick Warner, Jeff Whitehead, Tony Williams, Kris Woofter, and Jason Zinoman.

My editors at Columbia University Press, John Belton and Philip Leventhal, were remarkably generous with their time, energy, and expertise at each and every stage of this book's evolution. Corresponding with John and Philip during the especially isolating times of the COVID-19 pandemic kept the writing of this book going, and I will always be grateful for John's extraordinary commitment to watching and discussing with me every single film analyzed here. At the press, my thanks also go to editorial assistant Monique Briones, copy editor Annie Barva, production editor Michael Haskell, cover designer Milenda Lee, and the two anonymous readers of the manuscript. Genevieve HK provided invaluable assistance with the images.

Earlier versions of the material found in some of this book's chapters have appeared elsewhere, and I wish to thank the editors of those journals and anthologies for their support: Harry M. Benshoff, Jason Crouthamel, Will Dodson, Barry Keith Grant, Roy Grundmann, Kelly Hurley, Dawn Keetley, Julia Barbara Köhne, Peter Leese, Cynthia Lucia, Art Simon, Kyle Stevens, Rob White, and Kristopher Woofter. I am also grateful to the publishers for their permission to draw on that material here: University of California Press, Duke University Press, Ohio State University Press, Routledge, University of Texas Press, University of Toronto Press, and Wiley-Blackwell.

Thanks as well to the audiences of colleagues and students for the invaluable discussions at the many conferences and in the many classrooms where I developed the ideas that structure this book. Generous invitations from a number of institutions gave me important opportunities to share my research in progress: Birkbeck, University of London; Chautauqua Institution; University of Chicago; University of Copenhagen; Duke University; Emory University; New York University; North Carolina State University; Rutgers University; Tel Aviv University; University of Melbourne (which awarded me a Macgeorge Fellowship); and University of Southern California.

My closest collaborators were my family. My parents, Ed Lowenstein and Jane Lowenstein, along with my brother, Noah Lowenstein, have supported me since this book's very earliest childhood beginnings and continue to do so today. I am also grateful to their partners: Paula Friedman, Ron Wendt, and Bonnie Settlage. My wife's family, Gina Reyn, Mark Reyn, and Liza Reyn, are very much my family in every way as well; the life as well as the loss of Gina's father, Yakov Kreychman, left a deep imprint on this book.

I am extremely lucky to have a lifelong family of close friends: Glenn Alai, Emily Muschinske, Matt Rockman, and Gillian Waterman. They have inspired so many essential things in my life related to this book, and I wish there were a way to thank them adequately for the gift of so many years of remarkable friendship. I also wish there were a way to share this book with our "den mother," Lainie Rockman, who passed away before I could give her a copy. But Lainie's pride and belief in me and my work have always been there and always will be.

Finally, this book is dedicated to my wife, Irina Reyn, and our daughter, Simone Lowenstein. They brought this book to life by bringing so much life into this book. They make sure my diet of horror is mixed with generous helpings of love and laughter; this book and so much else would be unimaginable without them.

HORROR FILM
AND OTHERNESS

INTRODUCTION: SITUATING HORROR AND OTHERNESS

Tree of Life, *Night of the Living Dead*, Pittsburgh

What happens when horror comes home? When horror is no longer something out there, something alien, something other, but something intimate? When horror seeps into the everyday and ordinary rather than being bound solely to the fantastic and extraordinary?

For the past two decades, I have grappled with these questions as a film studies professor and horror studies scholar. But in October 2018, the shock of horror at home stunned me to the point where these questions took on a new urgency and importance. This book was born in that moment, in the time and place where I live: Pittsburgh, in the month of the fiftieth anniversary of George A. Romero's film *Night of the Living Dead* (1968) and the anti-Semitic killings at the Tree of Life synagogue.

Tree of Life. *Night of the Living Dead*. Pittsburgh. Let me explain why I am putting these things together. For me as a lifelong fan and then scholar of the horror film, one of the joys of teaching at the University of Pittsburgh has been sharing the city with George A. Romero. The legendary director established himself as a master of horror as well as one of America's most important independent filmmakers during the nearly fifty years he spent living and working in Pittsburgh. I was lucky enough to overlap with him during my early years in Pittsburgh and to meet him before personal and professional changes in his life took him to Toronto in 2005, where he lived happily until his death in 2017.

For me, Romero captured everything about Pittsburgh that has made me proud to call the city my adopted home. His intensely personal work ethic, paired with a deeply humane kindness and fierce commitment to social justice, embodied him and the city around him. It was easy to understand why Romero did not simply move to Los Angeles or New York after his first phenomenal success. Pittsburgh and Romero fit together perfectly, each providing crucial identities for the other. In my own small way, I felt that if Romero could call Pittsburgh home, then so could I.

It was natural for me to throw myself into the planning of a Pittsburgh tribute to Romero's landmark debut feature film, *Night of the Living Dead*, on the fiftieth anniversary of its release. I was thrilled that he was willing to return to Pittsburgh for the tribute and then devastated when his untimely death made that visit impossible. I felt renewed when the entire city pulled together to make sure that this tribute was not just about the anniversary of a pioneering film but a Pittsburgh-wide celebration of Romero's entire career. Helping to lead this tribute as well as working alongside Romero's widow, Suzanne Desrocher-Romero, and many others to establish the nonprofit George A. Romero Foundation have been high points in my life.

Then, just a few weeks later, this sense of civic pride and personal fulfillment came crashing down. On October 27, 2018, an anti-Semitic gunman invaded Pittsburgh's Tree of Life synagogue during Saturday morning Shabbat services. He killed eleven people and wounded six others before being apprehended. This happened in Squirrel Hill, a vibrant, diverse neighborhood that borders my own. It was a neighborhood where I would visit the Jewish Community Center and drop my daughter off at a synagogue where she attended Hebrew School. I wept with anger and fear and hurt, knowing that this senseless attack could have occurred in one of those places, where my daughter or my wife or I could have been among the murdered. This was an attack on us, on our community, on the Jewish people of Pittsburgh. It was the deadliest anti-Semitic attack in U.S. history. How could I live in a city where hatred like this exists? Shouldn't I get my family away from here? These were the questions I found myself asking as horror came home.

Unexpectedly, horror films came to comfort me. At first, it felt like a cruel irony that I had published a short article on *Night of the Living Dead*'s fiftieth anniversary in the *Pittsburgh Jewish Chronicle* just one day before the Tree of Life killings.[1] How could I continue to talk about horror films, especially as a Jew, in the face of such real-life horror? But the more I reflected on why I wrote the article in the first place and why Romero's films were so important to me and to Pittsburgh, the more I realized that the sort of socially conscious horror films that Romero created were a valuable way of understanding the horror of the killings at Tree of Life.

Romero's films were never really about zombies or vampires but about the horror that ensues when we refuse to recognize one another as fully human. After all, Ben (Duane Jones), the African American protagonist of *Night of the*

Living Dead, is not eaten by zombies but shot by his white human rescuers. The film suggests that Ben's otherness, his social difference as a Black man, kills him in a way that the zombie pandemic onslaught could not. Here and elsewhere in his films, Romero reminds us that we have no chance of triumphing over monsters if we cannot face our own capacity to be monstrous to one another, to treat fellow human beings as others. I concluded my article in the *Pittsburgh Jewish Chronicle* by noting how *Night of the Living Dead* is as much about today's intolerance as it is about yesterday's. And the events that have transpired since the Tree of Life killings, including the COVID-19 pandemic and the murder of George Floyd at the hands of the police in 2020, have underlined that truth again and again.

I felt lucky to be alive in the wake of the tragedy at Tree of Life and to experience the affirmation from the city where I lived that its Jewish community was not a community of others but at the very heart of Pittsburgh. The killings at Tree of Life were met with a stunning public outpouring of compassion and solidarity from every quarter of the city and beyond, in ways that made me feel as if the non-Jewish people around me were saying something closer to "this hurts us" rather than "this hurts them." I went from wondering whether I belonged in Pittsburgh to feeling as if I had never been prouder to live in Pittsburgh. In a moment of anguish, I was a part of the city, not apart from it—a human being, not an other.

Perhaps the image that spoke most eloquently to my sense of belonging in the city was the widely circulated logo that adapted the famous three-star insignia of the Pittsburgh Steelers football team to include a Star of David, accompanied by the message "Stronger Than Hate" (fig. 0.1). As anyone from Pittsburgh knows, the Steelers are the city's true secular religion. To assert that Steelers game days are sacred and that fans from every possible background worship the team is not an exaggeration. So for the city's religion to align itself with Judaism in this way moved me profoundly every time I saw it on a T-shirt, a banner, a lawn sign.

I even found myself imagining a variation on this logo that overlays the Steelers stars and the Star of David with another icon of Pittsburgh: the signature oversize eyeglasses worn by George A. Romero. And I understood anew what may have motivated Romero to adopt these glasses as part of his public persona: it was a means of reminding people that all of his films are about *seeing* otherwise—seeing the other as ourselves, seeing the other within ourselves, seeing ourselves as the other. Romero would always sign his autograph with the message "Stay Scared!"—an apparently simple but finally complex and hopeful message that now struck me as encompassing both "Stay Aware" and "Stay Alive." I realized that even after the devastation of the Tree of Life killings and the death of Romero, I was living in Romero's Pittsburgh after all. Scared, aware, alive. Alive to a new awareness of horror and otherness.

0.1 Pittsburgh, 2018, after the Tree of Life killings. (Photograph by the author, November 2018)

Of course, otherness is a vast and varied subject.[2] Even my much narrower focus here on the horror film's relation to otherness can take on "horror film" and "social difference" only as a matter of specific cases rather than as comprehensive categories. But my hope is that the exploration of otherness and the horror film in the following chapters sheds light on some of the larger issues at stake. If my book can provide enough clues about the nature of cinematic horror, otherness, and social difference to inspire kindred spirits to educate us about the cases and forms that go unmentioned in this book, then I will be deeply grateful. In fact, I will feel less alone, just as I hope this book will make some reader who feels othered in some way, whether through social difference or a passion for horror films or both, feel a little less alone as well.

This book believes that horror matters to questions of social difference. It is dedicated to the conviction that horror films and the study of horror films can teach us about otherness. Indeed, this book is built upon a foundation that places horror at the center rather than the margins of today's most pressing debates concerning the meaning of otherness. Its arguments are inspired by works such as Toni Morrison's *The Origin of Others* (2017), where the celebrated novelist reflects critically on a question that has animated her entire career:

"Race is the classification of a species, and we are the human race, period. Then what is this other thing—the hostility, the social racism, the Othering?"[3]

Morrison turns to horror when addressing this question. She explains how when she wrote her masterpiece *Beloved* (1987), she "inserted a speaking, thinking dead child whose impact—and appearance and disappearance—could operate as slavery's gothic damage."[4] This undead child, Beloved, killed by her own mother in order to spare her from a hellish life as a slave, is by Morrison's own admission a "gothic" construction. Since the gothic tradition forms some of the strongest bedrock underlying the horror genre, it is appropriate to speak of Beloved as a ghostly figure of horror. But Morrison's deployment of horror applies not only to the imaginary, fictional creation of a "speaking, thinking dead child" but also to the very real historical institution of slavery and its living legacies of racism.

Indeed, Morrison senses in the gothic a power needed to convey the actual horror of slavery in ways that a nonfiction study of Margaret Garner, the slave whose real-life history was the seed of *Beloved*, cannot. Morrison insists that her transformation of Garner's history in *Beloved* does not evade reality but embraces it on the deepest level of slavery's lived horror —a level where the act of child murder becomes "understandable" instead of simply "savage," where we have "an opportunity to be and to become the Other." Morrison admits that "for me the author, Beloved the girl, the haunter, is the ultimate Other." It is clear in *The Origin of Others* that Morrison remains haunted by Beloved, that she still hears the Other "clamoring, forever clamoring for a kiss." In this "clamoring," we can detect what Morrison calls "the risk of self-examination" delivered by the Other, an often frightening invitation to transform the self.[5] For me, the horror film's relation to otherness can be imagined similarly as confrontational, insistent, transformative.

Horror's Transformative Otherness

To discuss the horror film and otherness requires an engagement with the work of the pioneering critic Robin Wood (1931–2009), in particular his vastly influential essay that helped set the terms for contemporary horror studies and even today anchors much discussion of the genre: "An Introduction to the American Horror Film" (1979). My book's first chapter is dedicated to a close reading of this essay, and chapters 3–5 focus on directors who were central to the critical apparatus that Wood built around horror (Tobe Hooper, George A. Romero, and David Cronenberg). My own readings of these directors differ significantly from Wood's, and chapters 6–7 encompass more recent films outside Wood's purview, such as *The Babadook* (Jennifer Kent, 2014) and *Get Out* (Jordan Peele,

2017). This book's attention to Wood acknowledges his remarkable success; his courageous attempt to take the often reviled or dismissed horror genre seriously by pointing out its relevance for social difference continues to reverberate in current scholarship and film practice. But Wood's influence has been so profound that many of his foundational formulations have gone relatively unchallenged.

Horror Film and Otherness begins as a critical conversation with Wood but ultimately moves beyond his theoretical model to establish a new understanding of the horror genre's relation to social difference. I call this relation "transformative otherness": horror's ability to cast social difference as a matter of ongoing metamorphoses across "normal" self and "monstrous" other, where the struggle to acknowledge other and self as fundamentally intertwined is never resolved and always renewed. Horror never settles into comforting solutions or certainties about "progressive" or "reactionary" approaches to otherness but instead offers vexed yet invaluable opportunities to hear the social other speak, to have the other's experience recognized rather than demonized. Horror's transformative otherness is not simply a return of the self's repressed other but also the metamorphosis of monolithically imagined repression into constantly shifting expression. The act of repression cannot be safely isolated within the bounds of "normality," nor can the expression of "monstrosity" be clearly adjudicated as either a sympathetic otherness or an unsympathetic otherness. Transformative otherness instead resists ideologically rigid solutions that legislate horror's relations to otherness in favor of contingent, ongoing struggle surrounding those relations.

The distinctions between my own concept of horror's transformative otherness and Wood's account of the horror film will become clearer in each chapter, but for now a brief summary of those distinctions may prove useful.

- Normality and monstrosity. Wood's well-known "basic formula" for the horror film is "normality is threatened by the Monster," with normality standing in for dominant social norms and the monster embodying a threat to those norms.[6] The monster is society's other, the minority force that threatens to upset the norms that structure the majority's sense of selfhood. Wood claims that the films imagine normality in "boringly constant" ways: "the heterosexual monogamous couple, the family, and the social institutions (police, church, armed forces) that support and defend them" ("An Introduction," 84). The monster, in contrast, is "much more protean, changing from period to period as society's basic fears clothe themselves in fashionable or immediately accessible garments" (84).

Transformative otherness refuses this dichotomy between "constant" normality and "protean" monstrosity on the grounds that such a distinction can produce only further dichotomies. For Wood, not only is the conception of normality static, but that of monstrosity is as well—the monster may change its garments, but underneath it is always the same. According to this view, normality and monstrosity, in terms of their opposing roles, are equally fixed in an ahistorical stasis. In transformative otherness, however, normality and monstrosity are variations on self and other that cannot be fixed but are instead always shifting, always metamorphosing. There is no originary normality that monstrosity threatens, just as there is no originary self that the other threatens. They are mutually constitutive, always imbricated, and must be thought together dynamically rather than separated ideologically.

- Progressive and reactionary. Wood insists that the "relationship" between normality and monstrosity is actually the heart of his basic formula, with "ambivalence" denoting a horror film that critiques the status quo in "progressive" ways and the absence of "ambivalence" denoting a horror film that reaffirms the status quo in "reactionary" ways ("An Introduction," 84–85, 94, 102). Wood claims that his theorization of "ambivalence" encompasses the doubleness of normality and monstrosity: how the best horror films present normality and monstrosity as contaminating each other, with "the monster as normality's shadow" (85). But when Wood puts his theory into critical practice, true ambivalence disappears, and a legislative morality takes its place. This moral certainty regarding the distinction between a progressive horror film and a reactionary horror film accentuates the same stark binaries that structure Wood's logic of normality and monstrosity as fundamentally opposed. A progressive horror film is valuable and good because it challenges the status quo, whereas a reactionary horror film is regrettable and bad because it accepts the status quo. Transformative otherness, in contrast, refuses to categorize horror films as progressive or reactionary in terms of good or bad, valuable or regrettable. Some politically progressive horror films are bad art, and some politically reactionary horror films are good art, but more often than not "progressive" and "reactionary" are categories that fail to capture the unruly power both of the films and of the spectators' complicated experience of those films. Transformative otherness insists on this unruliness and complexity rather than simplifying and legislating clear-cut categories that may indeed feel comforting from a moral standpoint but just as often betray the films' heterogeneous texture and their viewers' equally varied experience.

- Narrative and spectacle. The evidence Wood values particularly highly when judging whether a horror film is progressive or reactionary stems from the film's narrative content. For Wood, the narrative's resolution in a "happy ending" typically indicates a reactionary triumph of normality over monstrosity, and the narrative's conclusion in a bleak ending can indicate a progressive critique of the normal through normality's inability to extinguish the challenge of monstrosity ("An Introduction," 79). Leaving aside how the bleak ending often functions as an expected rather than subversive generic feature of horror films, I want to focus on Wood's admission that both progressive and reactionary horror films contain negative, even nihilistic elements. These shared elements can potentially blur the line between progressive films and reactionary films, so Wood separates the "negativity" of progressive horror films from the "negation" of reactionary horror films. For Wood, progressive negativity is "apocalyptic" and sociopolitical, whereas reactionary negativity expresses "*total negation*" in a metaphysical register incompatible with the sociopolitical (102, 104).[7] Even though *The Texas Chain Saw Massacre* (Tobe Hooper, 1974) is deemed progressive and *The Omen* (Richard Donner, 1976) is ruled reactionary, both feature bleak endings. For Wood, however, *The Texas Chain Saw Massacre* is productively negative as it channels its apocalyptic negativity toward the destruction of a particular, sociopolitical world: "the end of the highly specific world of patriarchal capitalism" (102). *The Omen* is reactionary in its gravitation toward "negation," made plain in its portrayal of its monster as "purely evil" and thus unproductively negative because the film can imagine "the end of the world" only in metaphysical terms, not in sociopolitical ones (95, 102).

As chapter 1 explains in more detail, transformative otherness refuses this distinction between progressive "negativity" and reactionary "negation." One major problem with such a distinction is that it is wedded too closely to the narrative content of the films alone, ignoring or minimizing the sights, sounds, and spectacle that deliver the film's meaning at least as much if not more so than narrative logic. For example, Wood is stymied when watching *The Texas Chain Saw Massacre* with a "large, half-stoned youth audience who cheered and applauded every one of Leatherface's outrages against their representatives on the screen" ("An Introduction," 101). For Wood, this reaction was a "terrifying experience" explainable only in terms of the audience participating in the film via the "sense of a civilization condemning itself, through its popular culture, to ultimate disintegration, and ambivalently (with the simultaneous horror/wish-fulfillment of nightmare) celebrating the fact" (101).

But Wood reaches this conclusion primarily through narrative logic, where the audience is assumed to identify with the characters who resemble them on the screen rather than moving between experiences of self and other and into the sensory thrills of the spectacle as well as the knowing sharing of those thrills with fellow viewers. Transformative otherness posits "spectacle horror" as an alternative way of understanding such a moment: the staging of spectacularly explicit violence or gore for purposes of audience admiration and giddy delight as much as of shock or terror, but without necessarily breaking ties with narrative development or historical allegory.[8] Wood acknowledges the possibility of delight in the horror-viewing experience through his theorization of how horror films serve as a form of wish fulfillment: "their fulfillment of our nightmare wish to smash the norms that oppress us and that our moral conditioning teaches us to revere" ("An Introduction," 85). But, again, when this theory is put into practice, as in Wood's interpretation of *The Texas Chain Saw Massacre*'s audience, narrative logic constrains the imagination of spectatorship to the point where delight is not delight at all but self-condemnation and false consciousness. Even Wood's perceptive observation that the phenomenal commercial success of *The Omen* "cannot possibly be explained in terms of simple, unequivocal *horror* at the devil's progress" (85) ultimately gets buried when he passes summary judgment on the film as reactionary. But to see *The Omen* and *The Texas Chain Saw Massacre* through the lens of spectacle horror, in the register of transformative otherness, is instead to take spectacle as seriously as narrative, a seriousness that acknowledges what the labels *progressive negativity* and *reactionary negation* tend to deny.

• Solution and struggle. Two of the directors that Wood sees as disappointing according to his critical apparatus are equally and oppositely valuable for understanding horror through transformative otherness: David Cronenberg (chapter 5) and Stephanie Rothman (chapter 6). Wood's qualified admiration for Rothman's films is much more positive than his self-professed "hatred" of Cronenberg's work, but Wood characterizes the limitations of both directors in similarly political terms.[9] On the conclusion of Rothman's *The Velvet Vampire* (1971), Wood writes, "But the kind of liberation Diane embodies—if indeed she can be said to embody any at all (but if she doesn't, then what is the film about?)—is by this time so unclear that the spectator scarcely knows how to react."[10] On the conclusion of Cronenberg's *Shivers* (1975), Wood writes, "And what, in any case, could we possibly make of a film that dramatized liberation like *that*?"[11] Again, Wood's emphasis on the endings of these films signals his reliance on narrative structures to determine whether their potentially progressive concern with liberation can transcend a potentially reactionary confusion around what liberation might mean. His final verdict on *The Velvet Vampire* is split: "imaginative and audacious," on the one hand, but "riven by contradictory impulses and confusions," on the other.[12] *Shivers* is utterly reactionary: "With its unremitting ugliness and crudity, it is very rare in its achievement of *total* negation" ("An Introduction," 104).[13]

My own readings of Rothman and Cronenberg seek to see in their films what Wood does not: horror as transformative otherness, where the notion of liberation moves from idealized solution to ongoing struggle. The liberation offered by transformative otherness is not Wood's total, absolutist liberation of social revolution, where the present social order is simply and completely overturned. It is a more contingent, painful, nuanced, and piecemeal liberation that comes about through changes in thinking and feeling around self and other—the kind that leads to acknowledging the fraught complexities of social change, not just reifying an "us versus them," "with us or against us," "progressive versus reactionary" logic that collapses under the weight of its ideological oppositions.

For a concrete example of horror's transformative otherness, let us return to *Night of the Living Dead*. The "others" of this film are not only its monsters, the zombies or "ghouls" that have risen from the dead to eat the living, but also its humans, its agents of normality. Sometimes the zombies are more threatening than the humans; sometimes the humans are more threatening than the zombies; but finally there is no easy way to distinguish between the two. The heroine, Barbara (Judith O'Dea), has her heroism complicated when she becomes traumatized, catatonic, zombielike, yet within her zombieness she registers grief and loss in a more "human" way than any of her human compatriots. The hero, Ben, survives after all of his compatriots have succumbed to the zombies but only after having his heroism complicated by failing disastrously in his escape plans and resorting to a strategy he has repudiated throughout the film (barricading himself in the basement). And, of course, Ben is finally perceived as a zombie, not a human being, by the very humans designated as his saviors— they execute him automatically, unthinkingly, as if driven by zombie instinct. When Ben's body burns in a bonfire alongside zombie corpses (fig. 0.2), it is yet one more transformation of human into zombie (Ben's killers dispose of him as if he were a zombie) and of zombie into human (we feel Ben's humanity confirmed in our outrage at his unjust fate, his relegation to zombie status enabling

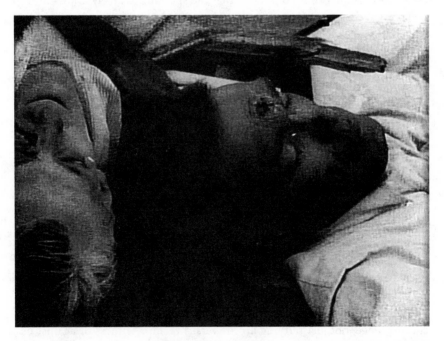

0.2 The African American hero Ben (Duane Jones) ends up as just another corpse indistinguishable from the zombies that surround him in *Night of the Living Dead*.

us to recognize him not only as human but also as a lynched Black man). The bottom line is that Romero insists on a constantly transforming otherness rather than on a neatly delineated "self versus other," "us versus them," "normality versus monstrosity" structure.

So what then counts as horror in *Night of the Living Dead*? What are the zombies really? Romero's answer is more telling and more complicated than it might seem initially: "They are us."[14] Not "they are our others" or "they are ourselves," but "they are us." They are us becoming them becoming us in an endless series of unfolding transformations. That is the source of the film's horror as well as of its power. The zombies do not just represent; they do not just metaphorize; above all else, they simply *are*. And they are because they always exist in a state of transformation, of becoming in relation to an other. They cannot be defined as truly other because they are also ourselves, just as we cannot be solely ourselves because we are also they. It is important to note that *Night of the Living Dead* is Romero's lone zombie film to offer even a whisper of scientific explanation for what brings the dead to life, and this "explanation" proves to be a half-hearted, unconfirmed reference to an irradiated space probe returning from Venus. In short, there can be no convincing explanation or cause for the zombies because the logic of transformative otherness insists that they are us, that they have been us all along, that their relationship to us is a matter of ongoing transformation, other–self, rather than of self/other dichotomies.

This other–self embodied by the zombie–human relationship exemplifies the transformative otherness of horror that this book argues is the genre's rule, not its exception. Wood argues the opposite: that the zombies of Romero's films are the exception in horror, not the rule. For Wood, Romero's zombie films are "somewhat to the side of the main development of the horror film" and cannot be considered "fully representative specimens of the genre."[15] Romero's zombie films, however admirable in Wood's account, fail to function along the lines of those normality/monstrosity and progressive/reactionary binaries that Wood finds fundamental to understanding the horror genre. But to consider Romero's films through the notion of transformative otherness is to see his work as representative of rather than an exception to horror's relation to social difference.

Even if I ultimately disagree with Wood's adoption of what I find to be an overly dichotomized approach to the horror film, I am nonetheless indebted to his model's strengths and sympathetic to its motivations. It is important to remember that shortly before the publication of "An Introduction to the American Horror Film," Wood wrote his seminal essay "Responsibilities of a Gay Film Critic" (1978).[16] That essay's dedication to weaving together the critical and the autobiographical not only elucidates the ideological commitments that inform Wood's work on the horror film but also helps me to articulate how my own theorization of horror's transformative otherness is connected to my experience as a Jew and a horror studies scholar in the wake of the Tree of Life killings. Our approaches to the politics of horror may differ, but the need to recognize horror's political significance as a matter of acknowledging social otherness is something that I believe Wood and I share.

That being said, reckoning with horror as transformative otherness opens up new vistas for understanding the horror genre. This book offers fresh conceptualizations of horror's aesthetics and politics as well as new vantage points on horror's relation to otherness. The goal of the chapters, individually and collectively, is to assess the past and forge a vision for the future of horror studies. The emergence of horror studies as a scholarly field can be seen in recent developments such as the creation of the journals *Horror Studies* and *Monstrum*, the founding of the horror studies scholarly interest group within the Society for Cinema and Media Studies, and the establishment of the world's first Horror Studies Archive at the University of Pittsburgh, with the George A. Romero Collection as its founding acquisition. Horror studies is still an emergent field, existing thus far without the benefit of organized programs, majors, or degrees at the university level. But the roots of horror studies in film studies and literary studies reach back to the very beginnings of those disciplines, and its branches now extend to everything from philosophy, psychology, sociology, history, art and architecture, and medical humanities to media studies, gender and sexuality studies, critical race studies, Indigenous studies, disability studies, trauma studies, global studies, cultural studies, religious studies, childhood studies, age studies, posthumanism, and ecocriticism.[17]

Transforming our understanding of horror studies requires wrestling with its foundational critical assumptions, including its engagement with social otherness. Returning to Wood in order to move beyond him emanates from a desire to illuminate the "prehistory" of horror studies while pointing the way toward its future, its history to come. That is the mission of *Horror Film and Otherness*.

The Chapters

This book's mission is reflected in its three-part structure. Part I (chapters 1 and 2) focuses on reading Wood to come to terms with the strengths and weaknesses of his critical model and to offer pathways outside his model's limitations. Chapter 1 returns to "An Introduction to the American Horror Film," in particular the dichotomy it erects between *The Texas Chain Saw Massacre* and *The Omen* as well as its critique of *Halloween* (John Carpenter, 1978), in order to refigure our baseline assumptions concerning horror and otherness by positing acts of transformation as the heart of the genre. Chapter 2 examines the ambitious, underappreciated horror film *The Shout* (Jerzy Skolimowski, 1978) as a means of opening Wood's general claim that horror and surrealism, and by extension horror and art, share a connection. *The Shout*'s investments in ethnographic surrealism specify, correct, and exceed Wood's general notion that horror and surrealism are similarly interpretable through psychoanalysis. In addition, *The Shout*'s merging of elements from genre cinema and art cinema highlights and challenges the ways in which Wood's account of the American horror film was always linked to the European art cinema.

Part II (chapters 3–5) revisits three directors essential to Wood's critical model but approaches them in different ways: Tobe Hooper, George A. Romero, and David Cronenberg. When Wood wrote about these directors in "An Introduction to the American Horror Film" and in a subsequent series of related articles, they were at relatively early stages of their careers. Today, all three have become legendary masters of horror with much longer filmographies to their names. Hooper, like Romero, passed away in 2017. Cronenberg continues to direct impressive and important work, but he has not made films easily identified as horror in many years.

Wood, who passed away in 2009, stopped writing about Hooper shortly after "An Introduction to the American Horror Film" and returned to Cronenberg for a short time afterward but never changed his critical opinion of him as a reactionary filmmaker.[18] Romero is the exception: Wood found his later films *Day of the Dead* (1985) and *Diary of the Dead* (2008) to be as distinguished in their progressive politics as his earlier work, even if Romero's nonzombie films never impressed him to the same degree.[19] It is telling that Wood's ability to keep faith with Romero runs opposite to his increasingly disappointed and dismissive attitude toward the horror genre after the rise of the slasher film in the 1980s. By 2004, Wood asks, "Aside from *Day of the Dead*, is there *any* American horror movie made since 1980 that could be championed as any sort of radical statement about our impossible (so-called) civilization?"[20] The nature and tone of this question, along with its corresponding negative answer in Wood's judgment, are a powerful invitation to return to these directors and see what Wood may have missed.

Chapter 3 studies Hooper's work in relation to a form of social otherness left unexplored by Wood: aging. Looking beyond *The Texas Chain Saw Massacre* to *Salem's Lot* (1979), *The Funhouse* (1981), *Poltergeist* (1982), *Lifeforce* (1985), and *The Texas Chainsaw Massacre 2* (1986) enables us to see how nightmare images of aging constitute Hooper's special contribution to horror as transformative otherness. Chapter 4 focuses on *Martin* (1978), a Romero project that is not a zombie film and never garnered the same kind of critical or popular attention afforded to those films by Wood or mass audiences. But I argue that Romero's treatment of economic otherness in *Martin* as a slow, subtle "individual" trauma rather than as the sudden, event-based "collective" trauma characteristic of, say, *Night of the Living Dead*'s engagement with the Vietnam War provides a new framework to understand Romero's achievements in horror. Chapter 5 juxtaposes the early Cronenberg of *The Brood* (1979) and *Scanners* (1981) with the later Cronenberg of *A Dangerous Method* (2011) and *Maps to the Stars* (2014) to argue that it is not adequate to divide his early and later career into "horror" and "non-horror" components. We must instead see the strands of transformative otherness that unite his work from its beginnings to its present: a fascination with the theory and practice of therapy that intersects with a form of social otherness exceeding the scope of Wood's and most other Cronenberg critics' analyses of his films—Jewishness. In this light, Cronenberg's proximity not only to horror but also to a tradition of Jewish-inflected philosophical and cultural thought that includes Emmanuel Levinas, Siegfried Kracauer, and Sigmund Freud begins to take shape.

Part III (chapters 6 and 7) asks what happens when those minority voices othered by the dominant culture speak in the language of horror. Chapter 6 turns to three women directors who have made invaluable contributions to horror as transformative otherness: Stephanie Rothman, Marina de Van, and Jennifer Kent. What Rothman's *The Velvet Vampire*, de Van's *In My Skin* (2002), and Kent's *The Babadook* (2014) share is a commitment to refiguring how we imagine the relation between women and horror (or "feminine horror"), especially around the subjects of gender, sexuality, embodiment, surrealism, and motherhood. Chapter 7 turns to race and horror, focusing on Jordan Peele's *Get Out* (2017) as a watershed event in portraying African American experience through horror as transformative otherness. By tracing some of Peele's inspiration to the work of the Jewish American author Ira Levin, the writer of *Rosemary's Baby* (1967) and *The Stepford Wives* (1972), this chapter posits a shared Black/Jewish genealogy for horror's minority vocabulary of transformative otherness. This genealogy reaches back to Curt Siodmak, the German Jewish exile who fled Nazism and channeled his harrowing experience as an othered Jew into his writing, including his thrice-filmed novel *Donovan's Brain* (1942) and his remarkably influential screenplay for *The Wolf Man* (George Waggner, 1941).

A brief conclusion looks to the potential futures of horror as transformative otherness by reflecting on the Black/Jewish alliances constructed in one of Peele's post–*Get Out* projects as a producer, the television series *Hunters* (David Weil and Nikki Toscano, 2020–). The conclusion also reflects on what horror means in the age of the COVID-19 pandemic and the racist killing of George Floyd, a Black man, by the Minneapolis police in 2020. These traumatic events are not the first to cry out for horror as a mode of expression capable of engaging the searing pain they encompass, nor will they be the last. But they are a vivid reminder that horror matters, that approaching horror as transformative otherness offers us a means to change our understanding not only of horror studies but also of ourselves and our society.

There is no denying that the Tree of Life killings remind us of how anti-Semitism, with its echoes of murderous hatred before and after the Holocaust, is very much with us today, just as the murder of George Floyd reminds us of how systemic anti-Black racism kills and how those deaths are very much with us today. But our art, even and especially in our horror films, gives us a means of answering back to these facts: not erasing them, not transcending them, not compensating for them, but seeing them, confronting them, learning from them. Learning about otherness, that is, from horror films.

PART I

TRANSFORMING HORROR AND OTHERNESS

CHAPTER 1

A REINTRODUCTION TO THE AMERICAN HORROR FILM

Revisiting Robin Wood and 1970s Horror

I n 1979, the critic Robin Wood (collaborating with Richard Lippe) organized "The American Nightmare," a special retrospective at the Toronto International Film Festival (then the Festival of Festivals) highlighting what he saw as evidence that "the true subject of the horror genre is the struggle for recognition of all that our civilization *re*presses or *op*presses."[1] By arranging screenings of films by and dialogues with directors such as John Carpenter, Wes Craven, Brian De Palma, Tobe Hooper, George A. Romero, Stephanie Rothman (the lone woman), and David Cronenberg (the lone Canadian), Wood set out to locate the contemporary American horror film at the center of American culture. "The American Nightmare" bravely sought to move beyond the conventional associations attached to the horror genre: heartless exploitation, slipshod filmmaking, gratuitous violence, unrelieved misogyny, and an inherent silliness that precludes any substantial aesthetic or political ambitions. Against all odds, Wood wanted to take the horror film seriously.[2] In fact, he titled his wide-ranging essay that opens the program notes "An Introduction to the American Horror Film," with its unmistakable connotations of wiping the slate clean, of showing us anew something we thought we understood perfectly well (or never deigned to understand at all).

By almost any measure, Wood's mission was remarkably successful. "An Introduction to the American Horror Film" quickly became the single most influential critical essay on the horror film ever published; it is frequently cited and reprinted even today. Before Wood, it was relatively rare for critics and scholars to ascribe much psychological or cultural significance to the horror film. After Wood, studies of the horror film emerged that argued the genre could teach us valuable things about female sexuality, queer sexuality, racial difference, disability, family dynamics, philosophy, critical theory, historical trauma, cultural history, and the nature of cinematic spectatorship. Nearly all of these studies, whether explicitly or implicitly, owed much to Wood's trailblazing convictions about why the horror film deserves serious critical consideration. Indeed, the recent efforts toward establishing horror studies as a distinctive scholarly field in its own right would be unthinkable without Wood.

Yet today, more than forty years after "The American Nightmare," we need a reintroduction to the American horror film—not because Wood's claims are necessarily incorrect or outdated but because they have been so foundational to critical discussion of the horror film that a number of their premises have simply been accepted as conventional wisdom. By returning to the historical moment of Wood's essay in the 1970s, we can discover an opportunity to review his findings alongside the films that shaped them. The fame and influence of films that were central for Wood, such as *The Texas Chain Saw Massacre* (Tobe Hooper, 1974), *The Omen* (Richard Donner, 1976), and *Halloween* (John Carpenter, 1978), have grown only more pronounced during the intervening years. In fact, the entire slasher subgenre galvanized by *Halloween* remains very much a part of the cinematic present tense, even generating its own now-classic study informed by Wood: Carol J. Clover's *Men, Women, and Chain Saws: Gender in the Modern Horror Film* (1992). As my chapter title suggests, returning to Wood constitutes both a tribute to his work and a desire to reframe it. My attempt to reintroduce the American horror film seeks not to leave Wood and his critical legacy behind but rather to see his arguments in a new light that will illuminate this book's explorations of the horror film and otherness. At stake in these explorations are our fundamental understanding of the horror film's relation to social difference, the centrality of transformation for the horror genre, and therefore the need to transform horror studies.

"An Introduction to the American Horror Film"

When Wood argues that "the true subject of the horror genre is the struggle for recognition of all that our civilization *represses* or *oppresses*," what exactly does he mean? For Wood, outlining the similarities and differences between repression and oppression forms a primary critical task. Repression, following the political economist Gad Horowitz, comes in two varieties: basic repression, which "makes possible our development from an uncoordinated animal capable of little beyond screaming and convulsions into a human being," and surplus repression, which makes us into "monogamous heterosexual bourgeois patriarchal capitalists" ("An Introduction," 74). Wood focuses on surplus repression, which he subdivides into psychological and cultural components. He refers to the psychological aspects of surplus repression as simply "repression," defined along Freudian lines as an internal, unconscious process of disavowing all that threatens the individual from within. The cultural aspects of surplus repression become "oppression," defined along Marxist lines of social alienation, where the threat emanates from social sources outside the individual. For Wood, oppression is socially expressed repression. For example, "our social structure demands the *re*pression of the bisexuality that psychoanalysis shows to be the natural heritage of every human individual, and the *op*pression of homosexuals." Wood concludes that "the two phenomena are not identical" but "closely connected": "what escapes *re*pression has to be dealt with by *op*pression" (75).[3] So when the horror film seeks to recognize what we have repressed psychologically and oppressed socially, it confronts us with a combination of internal and external otherness.

The concept of "the Other" occupies the center of Wood's argument. "The Other" is what "bourgeois ideology cannot recognize or accept but must deal with" through rejection, annihilation, or assimilation ("An Introduction," 77).[4] Examples include women, the proletariat, foreign cultures, racial or ethnic minorities, homosexuals, alternative political ideologies, and children (78–79). For Wood, these others enter the American horror film as monsters that threaten American society's investments in monogamous, heterosexual, bourgeois, patriarchal capitalism ("bourgeois ideology" or "normality," for short). Here Wood arrives at his influential "basic formula" for the horror film: "normality is threatened by the Monster" (83).[5] The flexibility and utility of this formula offset its obviousness and simplicity, according to Wood. The formula's three variables (normality, monstrosity, and the relationship between them) offer the means to categorize horror films as politically "progressive" or "reactionary" (102). Progressive horror films challenge conventional distinctions between normality and monstrosity by generating ambivalence between the two—through a sympathetic monster, for instance, or a doubling between the forces of normality and the forces of monstrosity. Reactionary horror films consolidate the status quo divisions between normality and monstrosity by squelching any possible ambivalence—most often through aligning the monster with such complete negativity that normality's oppressions are rationalized and reinforced. The two films Wood compares and contrasts in his initial presentation of the horror film's progressive and reactionary tendencies are *The Texas Chain Saw Massacre* and *The Omen*. Examining how Wood draws distinctions between the progressive *Massacre* and the reactionary *Omen* will allow me to conclude my summary of "An Introduction to the American Horror Film" and begin the work of reintroduction.

The Texas Chain Saw Massacre and The Omen

The Texas Chain Saw Massacre depicts the encounter between a group of young friends traveling in rural Texas and the terrifying, murderous family they meet there. The friends set out in a van to visit the empty house that belongs to relatives of Sally (Marilyn Burns) and her brother, Franklin (Paul A. Partain), who is confined to a wheelchair. Accompanying Sally and Franklin are Sally's boyfriend, Jerry (Allen Danziger), and the couple Kirk (William Vail) and Pam (Teri McMinn). The family of unemployed slaughterhouse workers who live nearby now survives through a meager service station business that sells barbecue made from the unlucky human victims who cross their path. This family includes the brothers Hitchhiker (Edwin Neal) and Leatherface (Gunnar Hansen), the latter named for his habit of wearing masks made of human skin, as well as their older relative the cook (Jim Siedow) and their ancient grandfather (John Dugan). The slaughterhouse family kills the young people one by one, until only Sally remains. After a harrowing, pro-tracted series of captures and escapes, Sally, now nearly unrecognizable through the blood that soaks her and apparently driven mad, manages to ride off with a passing driver. The Hitchhiker is crushed on the highway while pur-suing her, and a wounded Leatherface swings his chain saw wildly in the air in the film's final shot.

In The Omen, the prominent American diplomat Robert Thorn (Gregory Peck) and his wife, Katherine (Lee Remick), stationed in Rome, exchange their stillborn child for an infant born at the same time. Only this child, Damien (Harvey Stephens), will grow up surrounded by a series of violent "accidents" that result in the spectacular deaths of those who get too close to him. These "accidents" point more and more definitively to his concealed identity as the prophesied Antichrist, the spawn of Satan who will lay waste to the world. Rob-ert slowly comes to realize that he must destroy his son, but he ultimately fails and dies in the attempt. The film ends with the revelation that Damien has now been adopted by the president and First Lady of the United States, making his rise to power all the more inevitable.

Wood begins his comparison of the two films with a "chart of oppositions." These oppositions include the status of The Omen as "bourgeois entertainment" versus the "nonbourgeois 'exploitation'" of Massacre as well as the sense that in The Omen "traditional values" are "reaffirmed," whereas in Massacre they are "negated" ("An Introduction," 94). Another major difference Wood observes between the two films does not appear on the chart but crystallizes its organi-zation: The Omen does not qualify as a "work of art," whereas Massacre "achieves the force of authentic art" (95, 101). These key contrasts illustrate how Wood distinguishes between progressive horror films and reactionary horror films, but I argue that they also indicate how such distinctions are ultimately insupportable.

In many ways, Wood's sense of the basic differences between *The Omen* and *Massacre* rings true. *The Omen*'s lavish production values and use of major stars such as Gregory Peck and Lee Remick diverge sharply from *Massacre*'s obviously low budget and unknown cast. But Wood's decision to label this difference as one between bourgeois entertainment and nonbourgeois exploitation equates mode of production with ideological stance in problematic ways. *The Omen*, a major Hollywood studio film produced by Twentieth Century-Fox, therefore becomes aligned with "good taste" and the reaffirmation of traditional social values, but the independently produced *Massacre* is filed under "bad taste" and the obliteration of traditional social values ("An Introduction," 94). *Massacre*'s distance from Hollywood and proximity to bad taste help to prove its progressiveness, just as *The Omen*'s studio mode of production points toward its reactionary tendencies. Wood's desire to rescue *Massacre* from the category "exploitation," a label he sees as the enemy of serious critical consideration, forces a hasty equation of the independent mode of production with the progressive (nonbourgeois) and the studio mode of production with the reactionary (bourgeois). But can mode of production really provide such a clear-cut guide to a film's political meaning? Are the connections between Hollywood and bourgeois good taste as well as those between independent film and nonbourgeois bad taste really as distinct as Wood's chart of oppositions suggests?

Despite these films' titles, *The Omen* is anchored by a time-honored hallmark of bad taste and exploitive gratuitousness, graphic gore, at least as powerfully as *Massacre* is. In fact, *The Omen* depends on a visual logic of escalating graphic violence for its dramatic impact in a way that *Massacre* does not. The "accidents" of *The Omen* must convey an increasingly vivid sense of Damien's evil essence because the appearance and actions of the child over the course of the film change only in very limited ways. So the accidents progress accordingly. First, a nanny's suicidal hanging captured mostly in extreme long shot, with very little warning granted beforehand. Second, the impaling of a priest in much more detail, complete with an extended build-up where he is chased by wind and lightning and stares screaming at the falling rod that kills him. Third, the shocking fall of Katherine caused physically by Damien, which includes a slow-motion descent as well as a close-up of Katherine with blood trickling from her mouth once she hits the floor. Fourth, the attack on Robert and the photographer Jennings (David Warner) by a pack of dogs in which no one dies but where the visual ante is upped through a more graphic presentation of imagery used in the previous two accidents: Robert's arm is impaled on the cemetery gates while he tries to escape, the blood now more plentiful than Katherine's after her fall. Fifth, Katherine's death, which is relatively brief but functions visually in a manner similar to the dog attack, embellishing previous imagery in more spectacular detail: she falls again, only this time breaking through an upper-story window and crashing through the roof of an ambulance below. The sequence ends by zooming in to a close-up of Katherine's face, but this time blood streams from her nose *and* mouth. The final accident is the most spectacular of all: Jennings decapitated by a sheet of glass, filmed in slow motion and complemented by two graphic aftermath shots displaying the severed head (fig. 1.1).

By comparison, *Massacre* resists graphic escalation as its dominant visual logic. The film *begins* with some of its most explicit and disturbing images: a series of close-ups of decaying body parts. But the presentation of these close-ups foreshadows the unconventional approach to graphic spectacle characteristic of the film as a whole. The close-ups are shot in the brilliant but instantly fading light of Polaroid flash photography at night, resulting in images often more puzzling than identifiable. The sounds of digging alert us to the possibility that the images may represent unearthed corpses, but not until the flash photographs are replaced with a sunlit close-up of a corpse's decomposing face do we gain confidence about that assessment. This close-up, without a cut, becomes a slow tracking shot away from the corpse that reveals the full extent of the labor caught only in fragments by the flash photographs: the corpse's entire body has been attached to the top of a tall gravestone, with the phallic monument protruding obscenely from the corpse's groin. The corpse's hands cradle above its groin the severed head of a second corpse, suggesting a bizarre simulation of fellatio or intercourse. A radio broadcast voice-over accompanies this tableau, explaining that grave-robbing incidents have been reported in rural Texas. The announcer's voice describes the construction made by the grave robbers, which we now realize we are viewing, as "a grisly work of art" (fig. 1.2).

1.1 Jennings (David Warner) decapitated in *The Omen*.

1.2 The "grisly work of art" at the opening of *The Texas Chain Saw Massacre.*

And so it is. A work of art in bad taste, perhaps, at least in terms of its repellent use of corpses for material and crude sexual metaphor for meaning. But in terms of cinematic presentation, it is good taste epitomized. The complex interplay between sound and image, the alternation of showing and telling, the balance between a static and moving camera, the transition from briefly glimpsed, nearly abstract images at night to a long take that unveils those images in the illuminating detail of daylight—all of these techniques pertain to good taste in cinematic form, not to bad taste. Indeed, *Massacre* in its entirety functions along lines indicated by this opening sequence: "good taste" in cinematic form collides with "bad taste" in content.

One major way in which good taste ultimately overshadows bad taste in *Massacre*, contrary to Wood's assertions, is its avoidance of precisely the kind of one-dimensional visual logic of graphic escalation characteristic of *The Omen*. The film's opening corpse tableau is followed by scenes of violence that emphasize not mechanical increases in graphic spectacle but the process of revealing more and more about who the slaughterhouse family is and how they live. This process climaxes with Sally's captive participation in a macabre family dinner at the home of the slaughterhouse clan, where she sees the entire family in more detail than ever before. The dinner concludes with Grandpa's attempt to kill Sally, but he is so feeble that Sally escapes with only a minor head wound. This wound barely registers as graphic spectacle when compared with the corpse tableau that begins the film, and the family's refusal to acknowledge Sally's sexual offer in exchange for her life during the dinner ("I'll do anything you want," she whimpers) eliminates the possibility of enacting the sort of sexually explicit spectacle suggested by the obscene arrangement of dead bodies in the opening sequence. So the promises of bad taste intimated by the film's beginning go unfulfilled at the film's end, while what transpires in between varies widely between graphic display and implicit suggestion. Even the film's most nightmarish conceit, that the family robs graves and kills people in order to support a barbecue business, is established more by connotation than by denotation.

Although Wood acknowledges that *Massacre*'s "*mise-en-scène* is, without question, everywhere more intelligent, more inventive, more cinematically educated and sophisticated, than that of *The Omen*" ("An Introduction," 95), he still aligns *Massacre* with bad taste and *The Omen* with good taste based on mode of production.[6] For Wood, *Massacre* is "raw" and "unpolished" in terms of "the overall effect of the film as it seems to be generally experienced"—only after multiple viewings, as one "gets over the initial traumatizing impact" (bad taste), can one "respect the pervasive felicities of camera placement and movement" (good taste) (95). What Wood misses here is how the *coexistence* of good and bad taste in *both* films cannot be resolved through differences in mode of production. *Massacre*'s good taste in cinematic form and tasteless mode of production (where "unpolished" and "traumatizing" become linked), as opposed to *The Omen*'s bad taste in cinematic form and tasteful mode of production, cannot be reduced to the dichotomy between *Massacre*'s bad taste and *The Omen*'s good taste that Wood insists upon. Isn't *Massacre*'s commitment to tasteful cinematic form, even art (no matter how grisly), just as "bourgeois" as *The Omen*'s investment in Hollywood-studio production values? Isn't *The Omen* challenging conventional bourgeois taste when it wallows in an "unrespectable" visual economy of graphic escalation?

Wood's unwillingness to address such questions stems from the equivalences he draws between *Massacre*'s progressive politics and its status as an authentic work of art, on the one hand, and *The Omen*'s reactionary politics and its failure to be a work of art, on the other. Wood claims *Massacre* for art by describing the film as "profoundly disturbing, intensely personal, yet at the same time far more than personal[;] . . . as a 'collective nightmare' it brings to focus a spirit of negativity, an undifferentiated lust for destruction, that seems to lie not far below the surface of the modern collective consciousness" ("An Introduction," 101). *The Omen*, meanwhile, falls beneath the requirements for art: "the most one could say is that it achieves a sufficient level of impersonal professional efficiency to ensure that the 'kicks' inherent in its scenario are not dulled" (95).

Aligning *Massacre* with personal art and *The Omen* with impersonal professionalism highlights how much Wood's argument depends on the critical paradigm of auteurism. Shaped by a complicated exchange of currents in film criticism among France, Britain, and the United States from the 1950s through the 1970s, auteurism argued for the recognition of directors as the true "authors" of their films, with an important index to the artistic value of a director's film or body of films based on the amount of personal expression stamped on it.[7] Auteurism provided an essential critical apparatus for lionizing the European art cinema of the day, but it also legitimated the past and present efforts of such mainstream Hollywood directors as John Ford and Alfred Hitchcock. Indeed, Wood's own pioneering auteurist study of Hitchcock, *Hitchcock's Films* (1965), begins by resolving to take Hitchcock as "seriously" as we take Ingmar Bergman or Michelangelo Antonioni.[8] So Wood's willingness to elevate *Massacre* but not *The Omen* to the level of art cannot be interpreted as an inherent preference for independent film over Hollywood film. In fact, "An Introduction to the American Horror Film" tends to equate "Hollywood cinema" with American cinema in general, therefore understanding a film like *Massacre* as produced in a low-budget, "exploitation" mode but still within "Hollywood" rather than outside it—it is still an American film ("An Introduction," 94). I return to Wood's blanket use of the term *American* later, but for now the issue of art demands further attention.

If *Massacre* achieves the status of art for Wood, it is not solely by means of recognizing director Tobe Hooper as an auteur.[9] It is also through the film's definition as a "collective nightmare." This critical move toward social and psychological concerns rather than pure auteurism reflects the seismic changes in film studies that began in the mid-1970s and collected around the British academic film journal *Screen*.[10] Innovations in film theory at *Screen* included applying particular strands of Marxist and psychoanalytic thought to analyses of cinema as an ideological instrument. The politicizing of film studies in *Screen* involved the belief that criticism could and should unmask the ideological messages embedded in cinema, particularly in the dominant, mainstream style of narrative film associated with Hollywood. "An Introduction to the American Horror Film" participates in this politicization, but with a difference. Wood mentions *Screen* by name as a reference point in his essay, but he qualifies his debt to the journal by wondering whether its "new academicism" may prove "more sterile than the old[,] . . . driving its students into monastic cells rather than the streets" ("An Introduction," 73–74). As a result, Wood distances himself from the preferred theorists of *Screen*, Louis Althusser on Marxism and Jacques Lacan on psychoanalysis, by turning to Gad Horowitz's synthesis of Freud, Wilhelm Reich, and Herbert Marcuse.[11] Wood's distrust of academic approaches to film criticism dovetails with his sense that those who study film should be working toward a particular form of social revolution, one that he summarizes as "the overthrow of patriarchal-capitalist ideology and the structures and institutions that sustain it and are sustained by it" (73). Wood's convictions that such a revolution is the only way to imagine desirable social change, that it must come from action rather than thought, and that its realization may be imminent undergird all of the claims in "An Introduction to the American

Horror Film," including the distinctions between *Massacre* as nonbourgeois, progressive, authentic art and *The Omen* as bourgeois, reactionary, inauthentic entertainment.

But when it comes to film, can critical judgments lodged in auteurism (art versus entertainment) map themselves so neatly onto political judgments (progressive versus reactionary)? I think not, as I hope my account of Wood on *Massacre* and *The Omen* has begun to demonstrate; furthermore, even Wood himself appears to strain under the weight of this method. He tempers his dismissal of *The Omen* as reactionary by maintaining that "the film remains of great interest" because "'normality' [bourgeois patriarchal capitalism] is not merely threatened by the monster, but totally annihilated: the state, the church, the family" ("An Introduction," 95). Here Wood gestures toward a problem that eventually undermines his critical apparatus: If a typical progressive horror film introduces ambivalence into the relationship between the "normality" of bourgeois patriarchal capitalism and the "monstrosity" of those elements that threaten it, then what could be more progressive than a film that attacks in explicit, systematic fashion the state, the church, and the family? *The Omen* depicts a state so blind that it happily embraces forces of evil bent on destroying it (the president adopts the Antichrist), a church infiltrated by priests who have sold their souls to the devil (representatives of the church scheme and murder to make Damien's birth and adoption possible), and a family so dishonest with each other that they seal their own doom (Robert never tells his wife what he knows from the beginning: that Damien is not their biological child).

Massacre, by comparison, remains relatively silent on church and state. Even its assault on "normal" conceptions of family seems less obvious than the assault in *The Omen*. Wood claims that *Massacre* presents its slaughterhouse family as sympathetic despite their monstrousness: "We cannot cleanly dissociate ourselves from them . . . *they* are victims, too—of the slaughterhouse environment, of capitalism—*our* victims, in fact" ("An Introduction," 100).[12] But is sympathy of this kind very likely in relation to a family so clearly intended, first and foremost, to terrify and disgust with their acts of murder, torture, grave robbing, and cannibalism? Wood is right that *Massacre* channels much more creative energy toward the monstrous family than toward the young friends whom they kill, but does the film's management of creative energy translate into viewers' sympathy for its monsters?

For Wood, the slaughterhouse family does "not lack that characteristically human quality, an aesthetic sense, however perverted its form," due to the fact that some "artworks among which the family live . . . achieve a kind of hideous aesthetic beauty" ("An Introduction," 100). The "artworks" Wood refers to appear most prominently when Pam enters the slaughterhouse family's home. She stumbles into a room furnished with an array of decorations, including a couch whose arms and legs are adorned with the literal arms and legs of human

1.3 The couch with "arms" and "legs" in *The Texas Chain Saw Massacre*.

skeletons as well as a human skull hanging upside down with an animal horn protruding through its gaping mouth (fig. 1.3). Without doubt, these decorations are constructed and shot in such a manner that viewers are invited to admire the filmmakers' skillful craft in imagining them, right down to the witty play with the notion of "arms" and "legs." But admiration for cinematic craft outside the film is not the same as sympathy for the slaughterhouse family within it. Indeed, Hooper frames these decorations as an extended series of point-of-view shots from Pam's perspective, whose wariness about the house transforms into terror and disgust as she soaks in the surroundings of the room. Through Pam's distressed perspective, the effect of the sequence is not appreciation for the slaughterhouse family's taste in interior design but an alarming sense of disorder, danger, and death.

This sequence's soundtrack combines eerie, nondiegetic washes of metallic echoes (emphasizing Pam's subjective response) with the diegetic clucking of a chicken trapped in a cage hanging from the ceiling. The sound and image of the chicken, coupled with the floor strewn with feathers and other human and animal remains tossed together indiscriminately, point not to the presence of Wood's proclaimed sense of "characteristically human" qualities for the slaughterhouse family but to their absence. This family does not comprehend the boundaries between human and animal, a far more basic human trait than an aesthetic sense. When Pam retches and flees the room, her disgust solidifies rather than challenges the viewer's sense of the slaughterhouse family as closer to animals than to humans. Viewers, unlike the unknowing Pam, will add to this impression by incorporating the recent horrifying images of Kirk's death. Leatherface slaughters Kirk just like an animal, with sledgehammer blows to the skull accompanied by the spastic convulsions of Kirk's dying body. Leatherface's guttural squeals, closer to the grunts of a pig than to the voice of a human being, only enhance the overall atmosphere of animality within the house, a place where meaningful distinctions between the human and the animal have disintegrated.

Again, Hooper establishes this atmosphere of animality with masterful cinematic skill, but the evidence for a sophisticated aesthetic sensibility on the film's part should not be equated with a sympathetic, "human" aesthetic sensibility displayed by the slaughterhouse family. *Massacre*'s art primarily involves conveying the animality of the family, not generating sympathy for its humanity. By the same token, admiration for *Massacre*'s art need not lead necessarily to admiration of its "progressive" politics, nor should distaste for *The Omen*'s art lead necessarily to disapproval of its "reactionary" politics. Wood's critical methodology simplifies the relations between art and politics, leaving little room for those polyvalent negotiations that might result in artful reactionary films, artless progressive films, or films that careen between such categories or resist integration into the categories at all. For example, a horror film where sympathy for the monster is beside the point need not automatically condemn that film to reactionary oblivion the way Wood often suggests. *The Omen* does not devote much effort to making Damien sympathetic, but that does not detract from (and may even enhance) its power to mount an institutional critique of bourgeois patriarchal capitalism.

Wood attempts to resolve the contradictions that arise when trying to demarcate between progressive and reactionary horror films by distinguishing between politically productive, "apocalyptic" negativity ("An Introduction," 102) and politically counterproductive "*total* negation" (104).[13] The latter phrase emerges when Wood attacks David Cronenberg's *Shivers* (1975), *Rabid* (1977), and *The Brood* (1979) as reactionary. I have explained elsewhere how this distinction between apocalyptic negativity and total negation fails to account for the aesthetic and political complexity of Cronenberg's films,[14] so I will not rehearse that here; chapter 5 returns to Cronenberg in greater depth. However, I do want to pause to note how Wood's desire to assimilate Cronenberg, a Canadian director, into the catch-all category of the "American" horror film points toward his tendency to overlook questions of national identity as well as the differences between studio and independent versions of American cinema (as I mentioned earlier). Another film that Wood champions in "An Introduction to the American Horror Film" is *Death Line* (Gary Sherman, 1972; also known as *Raw Meat*), a British horror film that Wood describes as "American derived" and not truly British because its director is American (89). In these ways, important contexts for understanding a film disappear as "horror film" and "American horror film" become synonymous. I return to this point in more detail in chapter 2.

A related problem surfaces in Wood's analysis of *The Omen* when he remarks that one of the film's most "obvious" reactionary traits involves how " 'horror' is disowned by having the devil-child a product of the Old World, unwittingly *adopted* into the American family" ("An Introduction," 95).[15] Actually, *The Omen*'s detailed attention to multiple national locales (moving between action in Italy, Britain, Israel, and the United States) constitutes more than just a touristic display of glossy production values—it simultaneously embeds the film's events in a wide geopolitical context that hardly resembles a simple "Old World versus New World" dichotomy. There are even glimmers of recognition in *The Omen* that imagining radical evil historically in the old-fashioned terms of Old World and New World no longer works after Auschwitz: Robert first mistakes the sign of the devil on a priest's body for a concentration camp tattoo, intimating that the sins of the fathers have historical as well as supernatural implications. This important suggestion, however tentative and fleeting in the film, goes unnoticed in Wood's schema, where horror "owned" is American and horror "disowned" is non-American.

Wood concludes "An Introduction to the American Horror Film" by lamenting how the genre's most recent commercial successes, most notably *Alien* (Ridley Scott, 1979) and *Halloween*, fail to realize the progressive potential of the horror films of the late 1960s and 1970s, such as *Massacre*, *Night of the Living Dead* (George A. Romero, 1968), *Sisters* (Brian De Palma, 1973), and *God Told Me To* (Larry Cohen, 1976; also known as *Demon*). Wood perceptively observes how *Alien*, at least "at first glance," appears to be "little more than *Halloween* in outer space" (107). What he could not have known then was just how influential the barebones narrative structure of *Halloween* would prove over time: the story of a masked male killer hunting down and butchering a series of mostly young, mostly sexually active women (along with their male partners), only to be defeated in the end by a resourceful young female who converts her virginal sexual state into effective combat and survival tactics. This is the narrative blueprint for the slasher film, a subgenre birthed by *Halloween*'s phenomenal success that would dominate the American horror film during the 1980s and then reformulate itself in the 1990s and beyond as the ambitious serial-killer film (*The Silence of the Lambs* [Jonathan Demme, 1991], *Zodiac* [David Fincher, 2007]), the self-knowing slasher film (*Wes Craven's New Nightmare* [Wes Craven, 1994], *Scream* [Wes Craven, 1996]), and the retro slasher film (*It Follows* [David Robert Mitchell, 2015], *Halloween* [David Gordon Green, 2018]). *Halloween* did not, of course, invent the slasher film, as its debts to *Psycho* (Alfred Hitchcock, 1960), *Massacre*, and the Canadian film *Black Christmas* (Bob Clark, 1974), among others, are considerable, but it certainly ushered in a flood of imitators in a way that made the slasher film visible as never before. Studying the slasher film means picking up where Wood leaves off.

The Slasher Film

If Wood gave critical shape to the American horror film before the rise of the slasher film, then Carol J. Clover did so afterward. Clover's essay "Her Body, Himself: Gender in the Slasher Film" (1987) and her subsequent book *Men, Women, and Chain Saws: Gender in the Modern Horror Film* have been just as important as "An Introduction to the American Horror Film" for defining the genre in groundbreaking ways.[16] Clover, a scholar of Scandinavian and comparative literature, draws on Wood's work but approaches the horror film quite differently. Where Wood emphasizes questions of art and politics, Clover turns to matters of cinematic spectatorship.

For Wood, the ultimate goal is to classify individual horror films as progressive or reactionary. For Clover, the horror film's primary interest lies not with any one particular film but with the cumulative effect of so many similar films telling versions of the same story over and over again. Wood wishes to raise *Massacre* to the level of art by virtue of the politics expressed within the film; Clover is drawn to films such as *Massacre* and its slasher imitators for their artlessness, for their "crudity and compulsive repetitiveness," because these qualities convey "a clearer picture of current sexual attitudes, at least among the segment of the population that forms its erstwhile audience, than do the legitimate products of the better studios" (*Men, Women*, 22–23).

In the transition between Wood and Clover, then, we can detect a shift from film to spectator as the center of critical gravity. Clover avoids the conflation of art and politics that weakens Wood's model by turning to the audience for meaning in a way that Wood resists. Not surprisingly, Clover embraces precisely the sort of film theory Wood remains wary of: psychoanalytic constructions of spectatorship as pioneered in *Screen*. By placing her research in conversation with this rich, ambitious body of scholarship, Clover can theorize how these films are seen, not just what the films show. Not least among Clover's many impressive achievements in this regard is her ability to integrate the horror film into a discussion of film theory, where it was not hitherto central, thus changing the nature of that discussion in the process. In fact, Clover's engagement with the single most influential document of the *Screen* moment in film theory, Laura Mulvey's "Visual Pleasure and Narrative Cinema" (1975), makes it difficult to read Mulvey in the same way afterward.

Mulvey's essay is a compellingly formulated, still-forceful feminist manifesto on cinematic spectatorship (to which I return more fully in chapter 6). She argues that classical Hollywood film delivers pleasure to the spectator by presenting male characters on-screen as active agents of looking but female characters in the passive role of "to-be-looked-at-ness."[17] By implication, then, all film spectators are positioned as "male" and "heterosexual" by the films themselves, and the spectacle of women is drained of their potentially threatening psychoanalytic substance (castration anxiety) through the visual and narrative strategies of voyeurism (the sadistic investigation and punishment of the female) and fetishistic scopophilia (the masochistic overvaluation and fragmentation of the female).[18] In the years since Mulvey published "Visual Pleasure and Narrative Cinema," many scholars (including Mulvey herself) have come to question a number of the essay's assumptions, including its lack of room for spectators who may not identify as male and heterosexual or whose race, class, national, or other identities may affect their experiences as viewers. Clover intervenes not so much to posit a specific, concrete spectator in place of Mulvey's hypothetical, universalized spectator—Clover's determination of "the younger male" as the primary audience for the horror films she studies is, by her own admission, largely anecdotal and hardly exhaustive (*Men, Women,* 7)—but to challenge Mulvey's division of spectator experience into sadistic voyeurism and masochistic fetishism.

In *Men, Women, and Chain Saws,* Clover describes the possibilities of sadomasochistic spectatorship, where the younger male spectator of a slasher film can switch "back and forth with ease" between the sadistic position of terrorizer and the masochistic position of terrorized (62). To call the former position "male" and the latter position "female" is not really accurate because Clover demonstrates how the killer in a slasher film tends to be an anatomical male in "gender distress" and the hero an anatomical female, a "Final Girl," who becomes masculinized in her climactic victory over the killer (27, 35). In short, the slasher film's sadomasochistic spectatorship, where viewer identifications shift among killer, victim, and victim/killer (the Final Girl), illustrates how "gender is less a wall than a permeable membrane" (46). Clover's most striking departure from Mulvey is her suggestion that it is the masochistic side of spectatorship that functions most powerfully for audiences of the horror film, so that Mulvey's sadistic male spectator is replaced by Clover's masochistic male spectator—even within a subgenre such as the slasher film, regarding which most critics would assume Mulvey's sadistic male gaze must be overwhelmingly dominant.

For all the differences between Wood and Clover, they resemble each other when they encounter certain seemingly puzzling aspects of horror film spectatorship. As mentioned in this book's introduction, Wood reports his "terrifying experience" while watching *Massacre* "with a large, half-stoned youth audience who cheered and applauded every one of Leatherface's outrages against their representatives on the screen." He cannot really fathom this reaction except as a sign of "a civilization condemning itself, through its popular culture, to ultimate disintegration, and ambivalently . . . celebrating the fact" ("An Introduction," 101). Similarly, Clover comes up short when she observes that slasher film audiences respond to the extremely graphic gore routinely offered by these films through "uproarious disgust" as well as "fear," suggesting a "rapid alternation between registers—between something like 'real' horror on one hand and a camp, self-parodying horror on the other." Like Wood, Clover appears stumped by the audience's behavior: "Just what this self-ironizing relation to taboo signifies, beyond a remarkably competent audience, is unclear" (*Men, Women*, 41). These moments of puzzlement in both Wood and Clover point toward certain uncharted aspects of spectatorship in their models. In my own discussion here, I use the period's most influential slasher film, *Halloween*, to map some of this uncharted territory in terms of what I call "spectacle horror": the staging of spectacularly explicit gore for purposes of audience admiration and giddy delight as much as of shock or terror, but without necessarily breaking ties with narrative development or historical allegory.

Halloween and Spectacle Horror

Halloween tracks the murderous deeds of Michael Myers (Nick Castle), an unstoppable masked killer who commits his first crime as a young child on Halloween night: after spying on his older sister, Judith (Sandy Johnson), before and after she has sex with a boyfriend, he dons a mask and stabs her to death. After spending the next fifteen years in a mental institution under the supervision of the psychiatrist Dr. Sam Loomis (Donald Pleasence), he escapes and returns to his hometown, Haddonfield, Illinois, on Halloween to murder others who seem to remind him of his sister—young, attractive, sexually active women (and their boyfriends if they happen to get in the way). But Michael expresses a special fascination with Laurie Strode (Jamie Lee Curtis), a virginal, bookish student who spends more time on her homework and babysitting than on dates with boys. In the climax of *Halloween*, Michael turns from killing Laurie's friends Annie (Nancy Loomis) and Lynda (P. J. Soles) to stalking Laurie. Laurie fights back tenaciously, first outrunning and then wounding Michael. By the time Loomis finally arrives on the scene to shoot Michael repeatedly, Laurie seems to anticipate what Loomis then witnesses: the disappearance of Michael's corpse. Laurie may have won her safety for now, but the relentless Michael will not die.

In many ways, *Halloween* lacks the sort of explicit carnage characteristic of spectacle horror. The common perception of Alfred Hitchcock as the master of cinematic suggestion, of horror implied rather than horror shown, is more reductive fantasy than consistent reality.[19] But director John Carpenter, clearly under Hitchcock's spell while making *Halloween* (Laurie is played by Jamie Lee Curtis, the daughter of *Psycho*'s star Janet Leigh; Dr. Loomis is named after a character in *Psycho*), often strives to mimic the fantasy of Hitchcockian restraint. This quality in *Halloween* becomes apparent when it is compared to the gorier horror films that preceded it, such as *Night of the Living Dead* and *The Last House on the Left* (Wes Craven, 1972), and to those that followed it, such as *Friday the 13th* (Sean Cunningham, 1980).[20] But the staging of over-the-top set pieces as occasions for audience admiration of cinematic technique and the sheer enjoyment of outrageous explicitness can still be found in *Halloween*.

The film's opening sequence unfolds as a thrilling exercise in fluid camera movement. In long takes composed to evoke a single, restless tracking shot, a roving point of view (POV) travels outside and inside a middle-class suburban home. From outside the house, this POV spies Judith Myers making out with her boyfriend on a downstairs couch, then the couple heading upstairs together. The POV enters the house and acquires a large knife from a kitchen drawer. While heading toward the staircase, the POV pauses to remain unseen, allowing the boyfriend, still putting his shirt back on, to descend the stairs and leave the house. Then the POV climbs the stairs and, upon reaching the landing, picks up a clown's mask discarded by the boyfriend. Now the POV is filtered through the eyes of the mask. The POV moves to the bedroom, where a topless Judith brushes her hair while seated in front of a mirror. She does not notice that she is being watched until the POV is nearly upon her. "Michael!," she calls out, identifying the bearer of the POV. Still within the POV of the mask, Michael stabs Judith multiple times in the chest while she screams; then he leaves her bloody corpse crumpled on the floor. He exits the room quickly, heads down the stairs and out the front door. At just that moment, a car pulls up in front of the house, and a middle-aged couple steps out. "Michael?" the man asks, removing the mask. With the mask off and the source of the POV now finally revealed, we see that Michael is a young boy in a clown suit, still holding the bloodied knife. As the sequence ends, Michael's parents stare at him in uneasy disbelief.

Halloween's opening articulates the structure of spectacle horror without providing the full dose of explicit spectacle. The presentation of Judith's nudity, the plunging of the knife into her body, and the image of her bloody corpse are certainly graphic, but they are tempered through the POV of the mask, which necessarily obscures portions of the frame. Many of *Halloween*'s slasher successors will dispense with this kind of restraint, but they will retain the formula for graphic spectacle as a pairing of explicit female nudity with explicit violence. A good number of them will also imitate the POV technique, or I-camera, putting the viewer behind the eyes of the killer. Although this technique may seem to literalize the sadistic male gaze, I believe Clover is closer to the mark when she refers to it as a "visual identity game," one where the spectator can "view the action in the first person long before [the film reveals] who or what the first person *is*" (*Men, Women*, 56, italics in original). Clover also notes that in the slasher film such I-camera sequences privileging the killer's POV are "usually few and brief" compared to the extended climaxes where the POV shifts to the Final Girl (45). *Halloween*, at least at first glance, appears to offer no exception in this regard.

The I-camera sequence that begins *Halloween* has its complement near the end of the film, when Laurie battles Michael. Laurie's subjectivity motivates most of the action in the last part of the film, after her friends Annie and Lynda have died at Michael's hands. Indeed, the film's final section commences when Laurie temporarily leaves the house where she is babysitting to enter the house across the street, where Annie has been babysitting and where Lynda and her boyfriend, Bob (John Michael Graham), have come to have sex. Carpenter films the spatial transition between the two houses, one of safety and sleeping children, the other (as Laurie will discover, but as the audience already knows) of danger and dead bodies, in a manner that recalls *Halloween*'s opening. Laurie's POV generates tracking shots that take us closer and closer to the house of death, just as Michael's POV inspired similar camera movements toward the similar-looking Myers house (right down to a nearly identically placed jack o' lantern on the front porch) when the film began. The difference now is that we know who Laurie is (in contrast to not knowing who the earlier mysterious POV belongs to) and that Carpenter cuts back and forth between shots from Laurie's POV to shots of Laurie looking at the house (rather than long takes that forsake cutting in order to preserve the mystery of the POV's source).

But the resemblance between the two sequences in terms of mise-en-scène and camera movement highlights a motif that runs throughout *Halloween* and that ultimately challenges Clover's treatment of Michael's I-camera POV as a relatively isolated exception: the mirrored relations between Michael and Laurie (note that the jack o' lantern occupies the right side of the porch at the Myers house but sits on the left side of the house that Laurie approaches—mirror images). Both characters motivate tracking shots that take us toward houses of nondescript normalcy on the outside but sex and death on the inside. Clover points out how the somewhat feminized male killer (proficient in murder but not in regular sexual functioning) and the somewhat masculinized female Final Girl (physically active once the killer attacks but sexually inactive beforehand) ease the sadomasochistic, back-and-forth movement between spectator positions in the slasher film, with its reliance on "cross-gender identification" (*Men, Women*, 46). But for Clover, who is rightly dedicated to interrogating "the astonishingly insistent claim that horror's satisfactions begin and end with sadism," the analytic weight rests with how the young male audience of the slasher film must identify with the Final Girl across gender boundaries (19).

Although I agree with Clover that the interstitial gender status of the Final Girl and young male viewers searching for a stable sexual identity help enable cross-gender identification, I want to suggest instead that this exchange involves a much more intimate incorporation of the killer's POV—not as a "sadistic" identification opposite from "masochistic" identification with the Final Girl but as a mirroring between the killer's POV and the Final Girl's POV that resists concepts of "identification" altogether. If identification does not tell the whole story or even the primary story of spectatorship in the slasher film, then neither do the attendant assumptions of sadism, masochism, and the exclusivity of a young male audience. Let me explain these claims by returning to *Halloween*.

Yes, when Laurie's POV rushes to the forefront most flamboyantly, we seem to have a perfect visual complement to *Halloween*'s opening sequence—we see through her eyes as she squirms inside a locked closet, following her gaze upward in low-angle shots from the closet floor as Michael attempts to break in. But just as identification with Michael's gaze in the opening sequence is complicated by the fact that we do not yet know to whom this gaze belongs, so our identification with Laurie's gaze here is complicated by our knowing too much about the context within which this gaze is situated. Identifying solely with Laurie as the determined Final Girl scrambling to survive collides with a fascination linked to the growing relationship between Laurie and Michael. Perhaps theirs is no ordinary romantic relationship, but it does unfold visually as a sort of dance—by the time Laurie hides in the closet, she and Michael have already gone through enough choreographed moves together (surprise, flight, pursuit, confrontation, wounding, resurrection) for their interaction to feel like an alternate version of the prom date Laurie never manages to secure in her everyday life. And *choreographed* is the key term here, for identification with Laurie's POV must compete not only with the mirroring between herself and Michael that has become a shared cinematic relationship by this juncture but also with the mechanics of spectacle horror.

Spectacle horror does not rely primarily on spectator identification with characters. It instead more closely resembles the mode of viewer address that the film historian Tom Gunning describes when characterizing early cinema (1895–1906) as a "cinema of attractions." Gunning's well-known definition of the cinema of attractions, first published in 1986, is still worth quoting at some length because I will use it to extend my own discussion of spectacle horror:

The cinema of attractions directly solicits spectator attention, inciting visual curiosity, and supplying pleasure through an exciting spectacle—a unique event, whether fictional or documentary, that is of interest in itself. . . . It is the direct address of the audience, in which an attraction is offered to the spectator by a cinema showman, that defines this approach to filmmaking. Theatrical display dominates over narrative absorption, emphasizing the direct stimulation of shock or surprise at the expense of unfolding a story or creating a diegetic universe. The cinema of attractions expends little energy creating characters with psychological motivations or individual personality[;] . . . its energy moves outward towards an acknowledged spectator rather than inward towards the character-based situations essential to classical narrative.[21]

In *Halloween*, one striking moment of "attraction" occurs while Laurie searches the house of death. Viewers know that Laurie's calls for Annie, Lynda, and Bob will go unanswered because we have already seen them brutally murdered by Michael. Therefore, when Laurie enters an upstairs bedroom to find Annie's dead body on the bed beneath Judith Myers's gravestone, we do not share fully in her revelation at the level of narrative information. By that point, we know Annie is dead; we know Michael has stolen Judith's gravestone. With narrative concerns stripped away, we focus instead on the shock and pleasure of display, on the attraction itself. The sense of a "cinema showman" addressing us directly—"Look at this!"—is heightened by a musical sting (a synthesizer screech) that coincides with the attraction's presentation and that is paired with a slow tracking shot that moves in to magnify the spectacle's details. The presence of a "cinema showman" becomes even more palpable as the sequence continues. Laurie, horrified by the sight of Annie, backs away from the bed only to have Bob's swinging, upside-down corpse almost knock her over when it emerges without warning from a nearby closet. Again Laurie backs away; only this time the cabinet she stands alongside opens of its own accord to reveal Lynda's strangled body (fig. 1.4). Carpenter's direct address of the audience comes through loud and clear—he is quite literally pulling the strings on this series of attractions, right down to opening cabinet doors without any on-screen agency.

Common audience responses to this sequence that I have observed fit squarely within Clover and Wood's puzzled accounts of the behavior of horror

1.4 A corpse in the cabinet reveals itself in *Halloween*.

film viewers: squeals of surprise or fright followed by giddy laughter and appre-ciative hoots and hollers. Such behavior is more easily explained as responses to an aesthetic of attractions rather than as the forms of narrative-based iden-tification Clover and Wood favor. The mixed viewer affect of fear, excitement, humor, and admiration must be understood, then, as responses to the direct address of the "cinema showman," not as viewer identification with on-screen characters or situations. When it comes to spectator engagement with attrac-tions, sadistic identification with the killer or masochistic identification with the Final Girl is often beside the point. In fact, "identification" itself, at least in the conventional, psychologized sense, does not always apply. Attractions do not require an audience, whatever their gender may be, to identify with any par-ticular male or female character or to respond to how these characters embody relative degrees of masculinity or femininity. Viewer involvement occurs else-where, no longer chained to the realm of identification.

So is *Halloween* really a textbook case of spectacle horror as equivalent to attractions? It's important to remember that it is not just Carpenter outside the film but also Michael within the film who orchestrates these attractions. In this way, the spectacle represented by these three corpses does indeed function as an attraction, but it also develops the film's narrative and thematic content. The choreographed corpses are yet another maneuver in Michael's "dance" with Laurie, another bid to "impress" her in his own twisted way. And Laurie's discovery of the corpses emphasizes once again her mirroring of Michael—she retraces the steps he walked in *Halloween*'s opening sequence, first outside the house, then through the ground floor, then up the stairs to the bedroom. The line between Michael making the corpses and Laurie discovering them grows blurrier as the film proceeds to its conclusion, with Laurie twice creating a fallen body of her own (at least temporarily) as she attacks Michael with a knitting needle, a hanger, and finally his own knife.

When Laurie takes possession of Michael's knife and uses it against him, their mirrored relations have all but converged to establish one shared being. This is why Laurie's subsequent unmasking of Michael—a brief, quickly cor-rected event—carries no dramatic charge whatsoever. What is the point of unmasking the killer when the Final Girl and the killer are no longer dueling entities, but two halves of a whole? By this juncture in *Halloween*, we sense that seeing Michael means not removing his mask but observing Laurie's interactions with him. In short, the killer–Final Girl relationship as estab-lished in *Halloween* is ultimately yet another example of what I refer to in this book's introduction as horror's transformative otherness, where normality and monstrosity, self and other, shift endlessly in ongoing metamorphosis rather than settling into oppositional dichotomies.

To summarize, Clover's emphasis on identification between the spectator and the Final Girl minimizes the viewer's investment in the killer's POV, which I have demonstrated to be part of a constitutive mirroring of the Final Girl's

POV, not its opposite. Clover's account of spectator identification, even shifting, sadomasochistic, cross-gender identification, misses the thrill of the attraction and its resistance to psychologized processes such as identification. Gunning's attraction, at least when imported to the context of the slasher film, misses the ways in which attractions simultaneously lend themselves to certain forms of narrative and thematic knowing, such as the mirrored relations between Michael and Laurie. This is why my own theorization of spectacle horror aims to combine narrative and attractions as well as the possibility of historical allegory. I have described elsewhere how the horror film's interface with historical trauma might be imagined in particular cases as a series of "allegorical moments" that testify to "a shocking collision of film, spectator, and history where registers of bodily space and historical time are disrupted, confronted, and intertwined."[22] Spectacle horror may or may not generate the allegorical moments that utilize horror to illuminate historical trauma, depending on the specificities of the film, spectator, and history categories. What of *Halloween* in this regard?

For all of her illuminating work on spectatorship, Clover remains relatively silent on questions of history. In a rare moment of historical hypothesizing on the slasher film, she writes, "The fact that the typical patrons of these films are the sons of marriages contracted in the sixties or even early seventies leads me to speculate that the dire claims of that era—that the women's movement, the entry of women into the workplace, and the rise of divorce and woman-headed families would yield massive gender confusion in the next generation—were not entirely wrong" (*Men, Women*, 62). I think Clover is correct when she attributes the historical crises addressed by the slasher film to social developments connected to feminism, but I disagree with her decision to portray these crises as a list of unspecified and presumably equivalent phenomena that fall under the exceedingly general umbrella of "massive gender confusion." Instead, one of these social factors in particular preoccupies the slasher film and forms the basis for its historical allegories: an explosive increase in the divorce rate.

Between 1960 and 1980, the divorce rate in America "jumped ninety percent," meaning that during those years "the number of divorced men and women rose by almost two hundred percent."[23] These staggering statistics begin to inform Clover's work, at least implicitly, when she suggests that social gender confusion manifests itself in the slasher film via the feminine male killer standing in for a "parent" and the masculine female Final Girl standing in for "everyteen" (*Men, Women*, 63). What this account obscures is precisely what I have posited as central to my own analysis of *Halloween*: the mirroring between killer and Final Girl that makes them intimates, not opposites, bound together by horror's transformative otherness, and thus the failure of "identification" to explain adequately the interaction between spectator and film.

To describe Michael as a parental figure, for example, erases significant aspects of how the film visualizes him—not just his introduction as a young boy but also "childish" traits expressed later on, such as his curious, seemingly uncomprehending stare at Bob's lifeless body and his subsequent masquerade (complete with bedsheet and glasses) as Bob's "ghost." In these ways, Michael more closely resembles the children Laurie babysits than an adult. So the violence Michael wreaks need not be interpreted necessarily as "parental" punishment meted out to a misbehaving teen but rather the fantasies of domination and revenge directed toward parents by the child of divorce. Indeed, the teens Michael murders before stalking Laurie may be eager for sex and beer in ways that match conventional images of their age group, but their place within the mise-en-scène aligns them with parents more than with any other social group. Annie substitutes for absent parents as a babysitter, spending most of her time in the domestic spaces of the kitchen and laundry room, while Lynda and Bob occupy the parents' bedroom.

Annie, Lynda, and Bob, like Judith Myers and her boyfriend at the beginning of the film, fill spaces left vacant by their proper residents: parents. Absent or impotent parents in the slasher film are nearly as ubiquitous as masks, knives, and screaming. The image of Michael's parents in *Halloween*'s opening sequence crystallizes the typical parental presence in the slasher film: oblivious, away when they're needed, returning too late, saying nothing, paralyzed. Annie's father, Sheriff Brackett (Charles Cyphers), is kind and well intentioned but ultimately incapable of protecting his town or his daughter. Loomis, as Michael's "guardian," proves similarly ineffective in providing all but the most belated intervention to Michael's crimes. We glimpse Laurie's father only briefly (her mother is entirely absent) when he reminds her to deliver a key to the Myers house so some prospective buyers can get in. There is no warmth at all when Mr. Strode (Peter Griffith) hails Laurie, whom we are seeing for the first time. In fact, it's all business—Strode is a realtor attempting to sell the Myers place. The distance between Laurie and her father is underlined visually by preventing them from sharing the same frame. Carpenter cuts between medium shots of Mr. Strode and long shots of Laurie, who continues to walk away from her father when he speaks, even as she promises to do the work he has asked of her.

By comparison, Laurie's encounter with Tommy (Brian Andrews), the young boy she babysits, is a model of warm parental interaction—smiles, jokes, physical playfulness, patience, reassurance. Laurie runs across Tommy right after leaving her father, so the contrast between the two episodes is pronounced. In short, our first impression of Laurie codes her as an idealized parent yet also a child somewhat removed from her own parents. Our first impression of Michael codes him as a demonized child yet one capable of exacting the sort of recognition and revenge often craved emotionally by the child of divorce.[24] But, again, Michael as demonized child and Laurie as idealized parent are not opposing roles but mirror images. *Both* are children of absent parents; *both* are capable of improvising forms of parental power, whether that takes the shape of brute strength or kind understanding; *both* are suspended between child and adult roles by their lack of romantic partners.

What draws Michael and Laurie together as a "couple," then, are their commonalities and their shared needs—they not only see themselves in each other but also see the opportunity to fill the void left in their lives by their absent parents. The spectator, in turn, as a hypothetical teenage child of divorce, sees in Laurie and Michael's "union" the trauma of divorce (violence, danger, aggression) as well as a sort of fantastic resolution to that trauma—two parents who keep coming back together again, who seem destined for each other (if only to continue fighting as a result), and/or two children overcoming their divorce-induced fear of romantic relationships by reaching out to each other, however treacherous the odds (a "dance," a "prom date"). After all, Laurie delivers the "key" (literal and figurative) to Michael's house. Not surprisingly, Carpenter follows up the distant parent–child interaction between Laurie and her father and the intimate parent–child interaction between Laurie and Tommy in two ways: first, with a "scare" (Michael suddenly appears behind the door as Laurie drops off the key) and then with a "romantic" moment between Laurie and Michael. As Laurie walks away from the Myers house, Michael's left shoulder enters the frame—he stands behind her, unseen. Michael breathes heavily in the frame's foreground, while Laurie sings dreamily in the background: "I wish I had you all alone / Just the two of us . . ." (fig. 1.5).

In these four linked moments, *Halloween* conveys the divorce-related parent–child fantasies that govern the entire film: Laurie and Michael as traumatized "children" of absent parents *and* as potential "parents" with the power to take revenge for or even overcome together the trauma of that absence. Such fantasies do not depend on the spectator identifying with Laurie as "everyteen" or with Michael as a "parent"—the mirrored relations between Laurie and Michael instead allow for viewer investments that transcend character identification in favor of situations that evoke not only spectacle horror but also allegorical

1.5 Laurie (Jamie Lee Curtis) shares the frame with an unseen Michael in *Halloween*.

moments connected to the trauma of divorce. Taken together, these elements of viewer experience beyond character identification, shot through instead with spectacle and allegory, point toward horror's transformative otherness. Laurie and Michael are not two divided but one transforming, as is our experience of them. The horror they build for us is a dance of transformation: from child to parent to divorce victim to divorce avenger and back again, from narrative to spectacle to allegory and back again.

Halloween ends with a montage depicting the domestic spaces—a stairway, a living room, a front porch—where Laurie and Michael have "danced" together. These spaces are now empty, animated only by Michael's breathing and our memories of what took place there. The final shot presents the Myers house, where it all began—not just the spectacular murder that opens the film but also the first encounter between Laurie and Michael, the first time they share the frame. The Myers house *is* a haunted house. It is haunted by the audience's relief that the horror that began there is now over as well as by the audience's regret that the domestic spaces like it, once so full of thrilling cinematic spectacle and rich affective fantasy, are now empty. In this sense, Michael's breathing is not so much a threat as a reassurance—somehow, someday, these empty spaces will be filled again.

Horror and Transformation

Of course, the many sequels to and imitators of *Halloween* proved that spectators desired to revisit again and again the threat and reassurance offered by the slasher film. So the story of the slasher film's popularity in the wake of *Halloween*, from *Friday the 13th* to *A Nightmare on Elm Street* (Wes Craven, 1984) and everything in between, is in many ways the dominant story of the horror genre in the years following directly after Robin Wood's "An Introduction to the American Horror Film." In fact, the rise of the slasher film triggers Wood's overall disenchantment with the horror genre after 1980.

In a much later essay mentioned in this book's introduction, Wood reflects on developments in the horror genre since "The American Nightmare." He asks in 2004, "Aside from *Day of the Dead*, is there *any* American horror movie made since 1980 that could be championed as any sort of radical statement about our impossible (so-called) civilization?"[25] For Wood, the answer is a resounding no, and he places the blame squarely on the slasher film. He concludes:

> Given that all these films operate on a very low level of artistic or thematic interest, it is (I suppose) still possible to make certain distinctions. The original *Halloween*, which had the dubious distinction of initiating the entire cycle, and is therefore of historic interest, was a well-made and effective film; the entire *Friday the 13th* series fully deserves to go, with Jason, to hell; the *Nightmare on*

Elm Street films have a marginally more interesting monster and (especially in the first) a certain flair in invention and design. What more can one say?[26]

I hope that my reintroduction to the American horror film has suggested how there *is* much more to say about the theory and history of this genre. My account of horror's transformative otherness offers a means of understanding the genre beyond Wood's influential "progressive versus reactionary" dichotomies as well as beyond Carol J. Clover's important but identification-dependent interpretations of the slasher film. Even though Clover devotes serious and thoughtful attention to a form that Wood rejects almost entirely, she misses what my analysis of *Halloween* places front and center: horror as a spectacular and potentially allegorical experience that mixes the sensory with the historical and is transformational at its core.

Horror's investments in transformation, whether as spectacular act, historical allegory, viewer address, or the imagining of otherness, unite the genre's many threads. From *The Texas Chain Saw Massacre* to *The Omen* to *Halloween* and beyond, horror emphasizes actions that are essentially transformative in their ongoing metamorphoses between self and other, such as shape-shifting, possession, haunting, devouring, and sacrificing. Even slashing, as in the slasher film's encounter between killer and Final Girl, is revealed as a dance of transformation rather than a clash of oppositions. These transformative actions generate other–selves rather than monstrous others and an exchange between normality and monstrosity most accurately described as "transformative otherness." Indeed, horror's monsters are not usefully divided into sympathetic or unsympathetic categories but instead need to be recognized essentially as other–selves. Whether zombies, werewolves, vampires, demons, cannibals, Satanists, or serial killers, they are the other–selves that show us ourselves as others and our others as ourselves in constant transformation.

So *Halloween* and its slasher brethren, from *Friday the 13th* to *Zodiac*, belong to horror just as much as any of the genre's various subgenres. Slasher films are ultimately true to horror's transformative essence rather than, according to Wood's dismissal, simply betraying the genre's progressive potential. And there are indeed valuable, necessary distinctions to be made among individual slasher films, as Clover begins to do, in terms of aesthetic accomplishment and thematic ambition. But the most urgent work that remains to be done is the work that this book dedicates itself to: redefining horror as essentially transformational and identifying transformative otherness as the key that unlocks the genre's relation to social difference.

CHAPTER 2

THE SURREALISM OF HORROR'S OTHERNESS

Listening to *The Shout*

In the previous chapter, Robin Wood's landmark "An Introduction to the American Horror Film" (1979) was reframed with regard to its critical strengths and weaknesses as a model for studying horror. To summarize briefly, the strength of Wood's model is that it allows the horror film to be read in social terms, but its limitations involve the dichotomized manner in which the social realm and its cinematic representation are imagined.

In this chapter, I turn to a surprisingly neglected aspect of "An Introduction to the American Horror Film": the link it proposes between horror and surrealism. Where Wood tends to ascribe "realistic" rather than "surrealistic" meaning to horror, transformative otherness enables us to imagine the horror film alongside surrealism's challenge to self/other distinctions. Through a close analysis of Jerzy Skolimowski's *The Shout* (1978), this chapter refigures our understanding not only of horror and otherness but also of horror and surrealism.

Surrealism, Horror, and *The Shout*

Surrealism and the horror film share a long history of mutual admiration and reciprocal influence, but thus far connections between the two have been relegated to specialized and rather minor mentions in the scholarly literature. Neither are most critical accounts of surrealism particularly interested in the horror film, nor are most critical accounts of the horror film very concerned with surrealism. "An Introduction to the American Horror Film" devotes a short paragraph to the topic as a way of legitimating horror's intellectual value, particularly regarding the psychoanalytic theory Wood applies to the genre:

> It is worth noting here that one group of intellectuals *did* take American horror movies very seriously indeed: the writers, painters, and filmmakers of the Surrealist movement. Luis Buñuel numbers *The Beast with Five Fingers* (1946) among his favorite films and paid homage to it in *The Exterminating Angel* (1962); and Georges Franju, an heir of the Surrealists, numbers *The Fly* (1958) among *his*. The association is highly significant, given the commitment of the Surrealists to Freud, the unconscious, dreams, and the overthrow of repression.[1]

Wood deserves praise for noting the horror/surrealism relationship at all, but he also neglects to mention or misconstrues enough details to make the relationship seem less significant than it actually is. For example, the surrealist affection for horror did not limit itself to American films, even though Jean Ferry's appreciation of *King Kong* (Merian C. Cooper and Ernest B. Schoedsack, 1933) is one of the great enactments of surrealist film criticism; think also of André Breton's and Georges Bataille's shared admiration for *Nosferatu* (F. W. Murnau, 1922) and the widespread surrealist fascination with Louis Feuillade's horror-inflected crime serials *Fantômas* (1913), *Les vampires* (1915), and *Judex* (1917).[2] Luis Buñuel may or may not have enjoyed *The Beast with Five Fingers* (Robert Florey, 1946), but more pertinent is the fact that he made an important uncredited contribution to its production during his sojourn in Hollywood—he wrote a sequence in which the disembodied hand of the film's title becomes alive, an image he had already begun to explore in his surrealist masterwork *Un chien andalou* (1929).[3] Buñuel's collaborator on *Un chien andalou*, Salvador Dalí, went on to work with no less a horror innovator than Alfred Hitchcock on *Spellbound* (1945). Hitchcock's own brand of horror owes something to surrealism, as he himself admitted and as *Psycho* (1960) in particular makes plain.[4] Georges Franju may have liked *The Fly* (Kurt Neumann, 1958), but his own syntheses of horror and surrealism in *Blood of the Beasts* (1949) and *Eyes Without a Face* (1960) remain unparalleled cinematic achievements that Wood was certainly aware of but chose not to cite.[5] Finally, although it is true that Freud exercised a powerful influence on the surrealists (and that his essay "The Uncanny" from 1919 also functions as an incisive piece of literary criticism on horror), Freudian and surrealist conceptions of the unconscious, dreams, and repression are often so at odds that it is no wonder the famous meeting between Freud and Breton in 1921 resulted in nothing more than mutual disappointment.[6]

I have gone on at some length concerning Wood's account of the horror/surrealism relationship for several reasons. First, the influence of "An Introduction to the American Horror Film" on the scholarly study of horror cannot be overstated, so it is noteworthy how few critics have followed up on the connection it makes between surrealism and horror. Second, Wood's formulations of horror and otherness encompass horror traditions that reach back at least as far as German expressionism, therefore linking the European art film and the American horror film. *The Shout*, a British horror film directed by a celebrated Polish auteur that demonstrates strong affinities with art cinema, fits squarely within this nexus and is contemporaneous with "An Introduction to the American Horror Film" but does not appear in it. Third, the crossroads of surrealism and horror were already more crowded and complex than Wood recognized at the time, but it has become even more so in the years since the publication of his essay. Horror-associated directors as varied as Dario Argento, David Cronenberg, Marina de Van, Michael Haneke, David Lynch, Takashi Miike, Gaspar Noé, Roman Polanski, Arturo Ripstein, Stephanie Rothman, and Jan Svankmajer (to name a prominent few) have made major contributions to the horror/surrealism imaginary, no matter what their stated loyalty toward or distance from the original surrealists may be. I believe Skolimowski belongs on this list as well. Fourth, Wood's statement, however brief and incomplete, ranks as elaborate when compared with the notice taken by most scholarship on surrealism, which tends to marginalize surrealist cinema in general by favoring surrealist painting or literature and to ignore surrealist cinematic investments in horror.[7]

In this chapter, I argue that surrealism and the horror film deserve more detailed consideration as intersecting discourses, particularly around what the anthropologist and historian James Clifford calls "ethnographic surrealism." For Clifford, ethnographic surrealism is born of the historical moment in interwar France when surrealism and ethnography developed in close proximity, often overlapping in surprising ways that remain productive for us today because they illuminate "a crucial modern orientation toward cultural order."[8] Rather than enforce clear boundaries between self and other, familiar and strange, domestic and exotic, ethnographic surrealism endeavors to locate the other in the self, the strange in the familiar, the exotic in the domestic. In this way, it challenges our basic assumptions about the nature of cultural order and the politics of its representation.

How does the horror film's transformative otherness contradict, support, or alter surrealism's desire to change our very habits of perception? How does surrealism oppose, embrace, or complicate the horror film's desire to terrify, to project fear onto otherness, as well as to transform that fear into self-recognition and acknowledgment of the other–self? By pursuing these questions, I want to show how the horror film can advance our knowledge of cinematic surrealism in general and of ethnographic surrealism in particular. At the same time, I maintain that we can learn important things about the nature of horror's transformative otherness through the notion of ethnographic surrealism. Although I focus on a single, remarkably ambitious horror film that exists in the borderlands between art cinema and genre cinema, my analysis provides a guide for alternative interpretations of more canonical examples of the horror film. Furthermore, recent works of criticism and scholarship suggest that the line often used to separate conventional, genre-based horror from unconventional, art-based horror is thin, porous, or entirely illusory.[9] The other is a constant presence in horror, and my larger argument is that we have often simplified or misunderstood how otherness functions in the genre. By turning to the conjuncture between horror and ethnographic surrealism, I hope to enrich our understanding of horror's transformative otherness.

The Shout, based on a short story by Robert Graves from 1924 and adapted by Jerzy Skolimowski and Michael Austin, tells a horror story embedded within an ethnographic framework. Charles Crossley (Alan Bates), a white British man who claims to have spent the past two decades living among Aboriginal people in the Australian outback, enters the world of the troubled English couple Anthony Fielding (John Hurt) and Rachel Fielding (Susannah York). Crossley seduces and terrorizes the Fieldings with his Aboriginal-derived otherness, which includes a "terror shout" that kills all living things within its radius. Many scholarly accounts of the horror film, including Wood's, critique the genre for its tendency to code its threatening monsters as inseparable from the social or political other. But in *The Shout* Crossley's relation to Aboriginal people is constructed as unreliable—the product of fantasy and desire on the part of the Fieldings or of Crossley or perhaps even of the audience as they struggle to make meaning from a deliberately fragmented narrative. Skolimowski, a onetime student of ethnography and a longtime veteran of transnational filmmaking, turns to the methods of ethnographic surrealism in ways that refigure our understanding of the horror film, surrealism, and how the two imagine the ethnographic others haunting the shadowy terrain that traverses them.[10]

The Otherness of Horror

As I explained in chapter 1, Robin Wood's "An Introduction to the American Horror Film" defines the other as "that which bourgeois ideology cannot recognize or accept but must deal with" through rejection, annihilation, or assimilation (77). Examples include women, the proletariat, foreign cultures, racial or ethnic minorities, homosexuals, alternative political ideologies, and children (78–79). For Wood, these others enter the American horror film as monsters that threaten American society's investments in monogamous, heterosexual, bourgeois, patriarchal capitalism ("bourgeois ideology" or "normality," for short). Here Wood arrives at his "basic formula" for the horror film: "normality is threatened by the Monster" (83).[11] Progressive horror films challenge conventional distinctions between normality and monstrosity by generating ambivalence between the two—through a sympathetic monster, for instance, or a mirroring between the forces of normality and monstrosity. Reactionary horror films consolidate the status quo divisions between normality and monstrosity by squelching any possible ambivalence—most often by aligning the monster with such complete negativity that normality's oppressions are rationalized and reinforced.

In order to recognize how *The Shout* ultimately resists Wood's understanding of otherness in the horror film, I would first like to apply his terms to the film. To do so, we need to align the Fieldings with normality and Crossley with monstrosity as well as to define the relationship between them as a reactionary one; by the end of the film, Crossley is dead, and the Aboriginal magic with which he bewitched Anthony and Rachel dispelled. When *The Shout* concludes, nothing would seem to remain of Crossley's otherness, his challenge to the bourgeois, heterosexual, patriarchal, capitalist world represented by the Fieldings having ultimately failed. Added fuel for a Wood-style analysis of *The Shout* would include its trafficking in precisely the sort of psychoanalytic theory that Wood considers essential for describing the horror film's "true subject" as "the struggle for recognition of all that our civilization *represses* or *oppresses*, its reemergence dramatized, as in our nightmares, as an object of horror, a matter for terror" ("An Introduction," 79).[12] Crossley is monstrous not just as an ethnographic other, through his connection to Aboriginal people, but also as a psychoanalytic other—he is diagnosed as mad, imprisoned in an asylum, and haunts Anthony and Rachel's dreams. What's more, his apparently heterosexual masculinity carries enough queer connotations, perhaps in an allusion to the author Robert Graves's own bisexuality, to qualify Crossley as other for his sexuality as well. For example, Crossley showcases his nude body for Anthony and flirtatiously nudges the foot of a character named Robert Graves and portrayed by Tim Curry, fresh from his transsexual turn in *The Rocky Horror Picture Show* (Jim Sharman, 1975).

At the levels of narrative and realism, all of these claims seem true, and *The Shout* fits quite comfortably within Wood's critical apparatus. But at the levels of image, sound, and surrealism, *The Shout* refuses to conform to these interpretations. Crossley's status as monstrous other in the ethnographic, psychoanalytic, and sexual sense depends on our belief in him as a character whose psychology, history, and actions are, however bizarre, recognizable as realistic within the diegetic universe of the film. They are not. In fact, Skolimowski takes great pains to remind us that they are not.

One might argue that the ambiguity surrounding Crossley is not about the horror genre at all but rather about *The Shout*'s proximity to art cinema and the art film's suggestions that viewers should "read for maximum ambiguity."[13] Yet Wood traces the otherness he finds fundamental to the American horror film back to German expressionism and thus insists on a powerful connection between the European art film and the American horror film: "I think my analysis of what is repressed, combined with my account of the other as it functions within our culture, will be found to offer a comprehensive survey of horror-film monsters from German Expressionism onwards" ("An Introduction," 79). Even Wood's initial case study in "An Introduction to the American Horror Film," *Murders in the Rue Morgue* (Robert Florey, 1932), is selected because its images "suggest Surrealism as much as Expressionism," and it offers links to both the German expressionist film *The Cabinet of Dr. Caligari* (Robert Wiene, 1920) and the American horror film *King Kong* (86). In other words, *The Shout* as a horror film and Crossley as a monstrous other are interpretable within the bounds of Wood's model because Wood strives to connect the American horror film and the European art film through shared investments in surrealism and expressionism. In fact, *The Shout*'s use of a frame-story device as well as an asylum setting suggests the influence of *The Cabinet of Dr. Caligari* specifically, perhaps with additional echoes of *King of Hearts* (Philippe de Broca, 1966), the asylum-centered cult art film that also stars Alan Bates.

There are at least two Crossleys in *The Shout*. One appears in the film's opening and closing frame story, set during a cricket match held at an asylum in North Devon where the inmates and villagers mix in ways that make them difficult to distinguish. Here, Crossley is a mild-mannered inmate who offers to tell Graves, the visiting friend of the asylum's chief medical officer (Robert Stephens), a story while he and Graves score the match. The second Crossley appears within this story, which constitutes the majority of the film. Here, Crossley is an imposing, powerful stranger who upends the lives of the Fieldings through his mastery of Aboriginal magic and is vanquished only when Anthony discovers the stone that houses Crossley's soul and smashes it to pieces. The first, weaker Crossley of the frame story thus comes into being when the second, stronger Crossley is made impotent—he is arrested and taken from the Fieldings' house to the asylum. But as Crossley insists (at least according to the chief medical officer), his soul is split into four fragments, not two, presumably corresponding to the four pieces of the broken stone (although we do not see a clear image of these four stone fragments at any point). In addition, Crossley prefaces his story by telling Graves that his tale is very much true but does not correspond to typical notions of veracity (he changes the "sequence of events" and varies "the climaxes a little" in each telling in order to "keep it alive"). He also admits that he deliberately lards his stories with flamboyantly symbolic imagery (fathers, snakes, apple pies) to please the chief medical officer.

So to think of Crossley as a single, realistically psychologized character who fulfills the role of the monstrous other is simply not adequate to the way he is presented in the film. Rather than calling him a person or even a monster, it is far more accurate to say that Crossley attracts a number of forces, desires, and dreams that may at times belong to him but at other times belong to those surrounding him. His is not the single, rational subjectivity of psychologized realism but the dispersed, irrational subject-as-object common to surrealism. "I believe in the future resolution of these two states, dream and reality, which are seemingly so contradictory, into a kind of absolute reality, a *surreality*, if one may so speak," writes Breton in "Manifesto of Surrealism" (1924).[14] Crossley materializes at precisely this intersection of dream and reality, so he cannot be said to be any more or less "real" than the objects through which he manifests his power (a bone, a stone, a shoe buckle, an English tailcoat). Even his most fearsome quality, the shout that kills, is ultimately immaterial. It cannot be seen or measured or proven or reproduced but is only heard, felt, sensed. The effects of his shout are real (the corpses of animals and humans attest to this), but its essence is surreal—pulsating between dream and reality. The same can be said for Crossley, as his introduction in the film testifies.

The first time we see Crossley, we can recognize him only as a presence, not a character with a name, a history, or even an identifiable face. *The Shout* begins with a flash-forward to its ending as Rachel races to the asylum in search of someone she speaks of only as "he." She is directed to a well-appointed dining room, where three of the long tables have been partially cleared of their plates and silverware to make room for corpses covered by the fresh white tablecloths. She uncovers two of the faces without pausing—she clearly has not found what she is looking for, although we will be able to identify the bodies later as those of the chief medical officer and one of the other inmates playing in the cricket match—but when she moves to reveal the third, a whipping wind overwhelms the soundtrack. When Crossley's face is uncovered, the image immediately dissolves, and we are transported, via the sound bridge of the wind, to a desert landscape with a single, hazy human figure wandering among the sand dunes. As this figure draws closer to the foreground of the frame, we can see him more clearly: an Aboriginal man wearing a dark-blue English tailcoat and pointing a bone he has unearthed from the sand menacingly at the camera—at us (fig. 2.1). The atmosphere of threat is enhanced by the ominous electronic score composed by Tony Banks and Mike Rutherford (of the British rock band Genesis) that mixes with the sound of the wind in this scene.

But before we can learn anything more about this man, we are overcome by sound once more. Only this time, the wind of the desert gives way to the mechanical drone of an engine as another sound bridge overlays the cut from the Aboriginal man to reveal the source of the noise: a white man on a motorcycle speeds down a country road and soon overtakes a car with two occupants. The motorcycle driver's face is obscured by goggles, but the woman who is driving the car and who exchanges a look of recognition with him when he passes is Rachel, and the man we will come to know as Anthony is seated beside her. (Does she wish she could jump into the motorcycle's empty sidecar? Or is she relieved not to be there?) We, too, have a nagging sense that we know this man

2.1 The vision of an Aboriginal man carrying a bone menacingly in *The Shout*.

on the motorcycle, for he wears a sport jacket of the same dark-blue color as the Aboriginal man's tailcoat and beneath it a cricket uniform as white as the tablecloths covering the corpses in the film's first scene. This man, we will soon learn but already sense, is Crossley.

Skolimowski's introduction of Crossley makes meticulous use of sound and image to implant questions that compete with answers about who or what he is. On the one hand, he seems familiar: the colors he wears match him visually with the mysterious figures we have seen in the film's first two scenes, while Rachel's look toward him (which he seems to return, although the goggles and the encounter's brevity make this moment of recognition rather uncertain) indicates that he is known. On the other hand, he is unfamiliar: he has no name, no face we can easily see, no way of connecting him explicitly with the Aboriginal man or the corpse. But we do have the film's title to direct us toward sound as a form of identification, and this force called "Crossley" registers in these opening scenes as an aural presence at least as much as a visual one. The sound-bridge transition from the dining room to the sand dunes and then from the sand dunes to the roadway is prominent and unusual enough to draw attention to itself. Perhaps we are not sure of what Crossley looks like, but we do have a notion of what he sounds like: loud, sudden, unexpected, jarring. Yet even these sound signatures are split and ambiguous. The first sound bridge (wind) arises from the natural world; the second (engine) comes from the world of modern, human-made technology. To which world does Crossley belong?

Even with plenty of additional information about Crossley at our disposal by the time the film concludes, that question is no easier to answer at the end of *The Shout* than at the beginning. What Skolimowski has done so masterfully in the film's opening scenes he deepens as the film continues, generating a cumulative experience for the spectator that instructs us how relying on our eyes and ears in the conventional, rational sense will not allow us to unlock this film's meaning. Skolimowski instead encourages us to follow our sensory impressions rather than our need to make sense of what we see and hear. In other words, he encourages us to inhabit that shadowland between dream and reality where surrealism lives. The very contradictions that Crossley embodies—familiar/unfamiliar, natural/artificial, ancient/modern, Aboriginal/English, sane/insane, even alive/dead—are surrealist signposts insofar as they blur distinctions between subject and object, dream and reality. Crossley's initial incarnation, as a corpse on a dining-room table, evokes one of surrealism's favorite phrases, Lautréamont's definition of beauty: "the fortuitous encounter on a dissecting table of a sewing machine and an umbrella." Crossley's body appears ready for dissection in its shrouded, medicalized presentation, but the incongruous setting of the dining room also suggests that this body is a meal awaiting consumption (fig. 2.2). The doubleness creates a disorienting, vertiginous

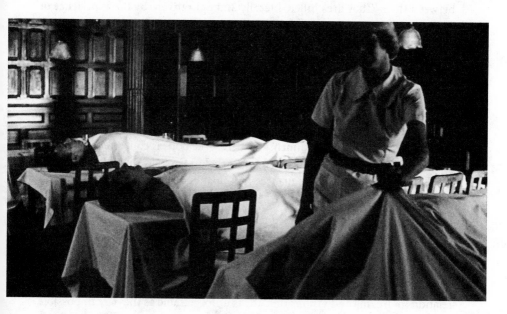

2.2 Shrouded bodies on dining room tables in *The Shout*.

sensation, in which we know where we are yet cannot feel the ground beneath our feet, and is symptomatic of the surrealist "spark," that surprising, often shocking connection between two disparate images or levels of reality. Crossley belongs nowhere—his place of origin is neither the asylum nor the desert—but he simultaneously matters everywhere in that Rachel looks for him or toward him at the asylum, on the roadway, and, as the film's next section shows, in the desert as well.

The Shout returns to the desert once Crossley begins narrating his tale to Graves. As Crossley asks Graves, "Have you ever wandered the sand dunes?," his words fade away and are replaced, in a superimposition enabled by a slow dissolve, with an image of the Aboriginal man from the earlier sequence, again wandering in the desert. The Aboriginal man, due to the dissolve, appears to spring quite literally from Crossley's forehead—a figment of his imagination, perhaps? No, as it turns out. Or at least this figment does not belong to his imagination alone. The Aboriginal man is soon shown to emerge also from a dream shared by Anthony and Rachel. They are sleeping on the very sand dunes we have seen the Aboriginal man traversing (so have we always been in North Devon rather than in the Australian outback?), but when they awake, the Aboriginal man is nowhere to be found. Each of them describes him in terms that match the images we have seen and cause him to rematerialize briefly as a visual flashback to the dream, but they do not pause to comment on the strangeness of the dream or the even more unusual fact that the dream was shared between them. They are chilled, literally and figuratively, by the experience of the dream and seem eager to shake its influence. When Rachel finds buried in the sand in North Devon the bone that she and Anthony saw the Aboriginal man carrying in their dream, she reburies it hastily.

This bone is familiar to us not only as the bone carried by the Aboriginal man but also as the same bone that falls out of Crossley's jacket as he begins to narrate his tale to Graves. Crossley, like Rachel, attempts to hide it, but Graves has seen it, and so have we. The bone is the object that cues us to how dream and reality are not separate dimensions here—the bone is concrete for Crossley and Graves in the film's frame story, for Rachel in Crossley's narrated tale, and for the Aboriginal man in sequences that float between dream, memory, and imagination. But the only way the bone can exist on all of these planes at once is through a distribution of dream and reality that makes standard demarcations of what is real and what is unreal fall away. In the same spirit, Crossley is not only objectively real in terms of being a man spoken about and with by Graves and the chief medical officer (men of science) but also subjectively unreal—his presence as the Aboriginal man that doubles for him appears only in relation to dreams and visions that are as unforgettable as they are impossible to verify. Indeed, we never see the Aboriginal man again during the remainder of *The Shout*, causing us to wonder by the film's end whether we ever really "saw" him at all.

In all of these ways, Crossley fails to function as a monstrous other in Wood's sense. Crossley's surreal presence in the film, his location between dream and reality as well as between Aboriginal and English, immunizes him against the entire normality/monstrosity dichotomy and its conflations of fear with social otherness according to the delineated progressive and reactionary categories. His indeterminacy is not about a monster lying in wait for the sake of suspense or a monster whose actuality or artificiality remains unclear for the sake of narrative structure or even a monster whose patently fantastic or "primitive" nature encourages an allegorical social interpretation. Crossley's transformative otherness is instead inseparable from our own modes of perception, our own habits of ordering our sensory impressions according to dream/reality and Western self/non-Western other classifications. Ultimately, he is the embodiment of those tensions that constitute ethnographic surrealism.

The Otherness of Ethnographic Surrealism

Clifford's account of ethnographic surrealism emphasizes its ability to forge a path between science and art, to denaturalize both ethnography's drive toward empirical, classificatory science and surrealism's drive toward a romantic cult of the artist as transgressive genius ("Ethnographic Surrealism," 147). At the height of ethnographic surrealism's influence, in France during the interwar years, ethnography and surrealism informed each other in profound ways that would be much more difficult to maintain once surrealism's identity as "art" and ethnography's identity as "science" became more fully entrenched (134). The promise of ethnographic surrealism is its insistence on questioning what counts as cultural value and cultural order once the anchoring notions of self and other are unmoored, so that the self, often hidden or obscured in ethnographic analysis, becomes at least as much an object of research as are the ethnographic others under anthropological examination. The risks of ethnographic surrealism are its sometimes queasily close proximity to Orientalism and racism as well as the danger of dispensing too quickly with crucial specifics of historical and cultural difference when unleashing the decentering heat of juxtaposition and collage. Clifford admits that his conception of ethnographic surrealism is a "utopian construct" in that it productively merges forms of science and art that much more often than not remain separate or come together in more troubling, unproductive ways, but I agree with his conviction that excavating ethnographic surrealism is not merely an archival project—it matters enormously as "a statement at once about past and future possibilities for cultural analysis" (119).

Although Clifford explores a host of guises for ethnographic surrealism—literature, museum collections, academic research, avant-garde journals, ad hoc intellectual collectives, organized expeditions to foreign countries—film surfaces only at the vanishing point of his study. The film he mentions as an example of ethnographic surrealism is the celebrated documentary *Trobriand Cricket: An Ingenious Response to Colonialism* (Gary Kildea and Jerry Leach, 1975). This anthropological film, which chronicles how Trobriand Islanders in Papua New Guinea adapt and transform traditional English cricket for their own purposes (fig. 2.3), shares striking affinities with *The Shout*. These affinities suggest that connecting cinema and ethnographic surrealism is a project that has really only just begun despite pioneering efforts by a number of film scholars and the flowering of visual anthropology as a field in its own right.[15]

The Shout, like *Trobriand Cricket*, presents a game associated with Englishness, whiteness, and colonialism in a manner that makes that game strange, that recasts our assumptions of known and unknown, self and other. Not only does the cricket match in *The Shout* take place at an asylum with inmates as players (fig. 2.4), but it also transpires in a meadow where cows have already laid their claim (the immaculately attired players and bystanders must slip and slide through shit), the scoring is entrusted to a man who seems to practice

2.3 Trobriand Islanders create their own version of English cricket in *Trobriand Cricket*.

2.4 Asylum inmates create their own version of English cricket in *The Shout*.

Aboriginal magic, and the match ends in destruction and death most likely wrought by that magic (a violent thunderstorm masks Crossley's shout so that the ensuing deaths are probably attributed to a lightning strike). Clearly, we are far from the traditional decorum of English cricket. Yet those traditions remain strong as an organizing visual presence, from the whiteness of the uniforms to the equipment and procedures of the game. Skolimowski's goal is not to make cricket unrecognizable but to defamiliarize it enough so that "we" who "know" the game meld with "they" who "do not" (the insane, the Aboriginal, the other).

The cricket match is already a central conceit in Graves's short story, but it is not outlandish to imagine the ethnographic surrealist impulses behind *Trobriand Cricket* influencing *The Shout*, whether directly or indirectly. Skolimowski studied ethnography earlier in his life while at school in Poland, but when he made *The Shout*, he was living and working as a Polish exile in an England whose alienness provides crucial inspiration for some of his most important films, including *Deep End* (1971) and *Moonlighting* (1982).[16] In addition, Jeremy Thomas, the producer of *The Shout*, had just completed the Australian film *Mad Dog Morgan* (Philippe Mora, 1976), so Australia (the country of origin for *Trobriand Cricket* as well) was likely not just an abstract idea on set. Skolimowski was also doubtlessly aware of his fellow Pole Bronislaw Malinowski, the famed anthropologist who conducted groundbreaking fieldwork on the Trobriand Islands as well as in Australia (among other locales).

The eyes and ears of an outsider are fundamental to *The Shout*'s structure, so that even those situations, settings, and activities associated with normality or even banality—work, couplehood, meals, the countryside, cricket—return to us as uncanny. I have already described how the film's opening scenes use sound to unsettle our sense of how much we can trust or even understand what we see, and the cricket match is treated similarly. Voices are subtly detached from the bodies of those speaking; sound perspective is inconsistent (sometimes we hear as if we are almost inside the head of a player who mutters to himself, at other times the sounds of the match are conveyed more evenly); noises that are electronic and nondiegetic abruptly override those that are diegetic but disappear just as suddenly. The result: when the Aboriginal bone drops from Crossley's jacket, it is not so much an entirely disruptive moment as a consistently incongruous one. The sights and sounds of the "familiar" cricket match have become at least as unfamiliar to us as this image of the "other," especially since this is not the first time we have glimpsed the bone. The appearance of an Aboriginal ritual object alongside the ritual objects of English cricket has the effect, in Skolimowski's hands, of ethnographic surrealism's doubled disorientation—we see the strange in the familiar, the familiar in the strange ("Ethnographic Surrealism," 121). "The surrealist moment in ethnography," Clifford writes, "is that moment in which the possibility of comparison exists in unmediated tension with sheer incongruity" (146). In such a moment, there is no attempt to "explain away those elements in the foreign culture that render the investigator's culture newly incomprehensible" (147). This moment in *The Shout*, like so many others in the film, captures this provocative power of ethnographic surrealism as a mode of transformative otherness: familiar culture and foreign culture are no longer discrete but endlessly metamorphosing.

Another important example of ethnographic surrealism in the film occurs when Anthony's and Crossley's methods of creating extraordinary sound are juxtaposed. Anthony is a musician who spends much of his time generating and recording otherworldly sounds in his home studio by amplifying and distorting "natural" noises through modern technological means. Marbles colliding in a metal pan, a violin bow drawn across a ruptured sardine tin, a drag on a cigarette—Anthony warps all of these sounds and others electronically to exaggerate their most discordant aspects. So by the time we hear Crossley's shout, we are accustomed to experiencing sound as a force subject to unsettling manipulation. But what Anthony toys with through machines, Crossley accomplishes with his own body to much more dire effect (fig. 2.5). Still, the obvious equation of Anthony with the technologically modern (the Western, scientific "us") and Crossley with the physically primitive (the non-Western, magical "other") proves as impossible to maintain here as it did in the film's opening scenes. Crossley's shout is the film's technical centerpiece, a spectacular showcase for state-of-the-art Dolby sound experimentation achievable only through

2.5 Crossley (Alan Bates) releasing his deadly shout in *The Shout.*

precisely those sorts of devices that populate Anthony's studio. As Skolimowski describes the production of this shout, "The human voice is fortified on forty or more tracks by all the things that came into my mind that might be helpful, the Niagara Falls, the launching of a Moon rocket, everything. But over the top is the real human voice of a man shouting like hell."[17] In the tenor of ethnographic surrealism and transformative otherness, Anthony and Crossley sound more like inseparable halves of a single whole than stark opposites; they are other–selves in constant metamorphosis.

But we do not simply hear the similarity between Anthony and Crossley—we also feel it. Anthony's studio-produced sounds grate on our ears almost as dramatically as Crossley's gut-wrenching shout overpowers us; in both cases, the impact is visceral. Anthony and Crossley may look like opposites, almost to the point of parody (Skolimowski makes brilliant use of the wildly contrasting physiques of John Hurt and Alan Bates), but the effect their sounds make on us cause them to feel like one being, not two. This is quite different from the "doppelgänger motif" that Wood privileges as an indicator of progressive horror, from Robert Louis Stevenson and F. W. Murnau to James Whale and Larry Cohen, where doubled figures reveal the monster as "normality's shadow" ("An Introduction," 84–85). For Wood, the doppelgänger signals an ambivalent "contaminating" of normality by monstrosity, but this ambivalence functions in the end as a rational, categorical means of sorting progressive horror from reactionary horror (88). Wood relies on realist thinking, not on surrealist feeling, to describe the narrative and thematic effects of the doppelgänger.

By contrast, *The Shout* presents other-selves whose constant transformations we must feel our way through. This feeling is a form of viewer participation in the film irreducible to narrative or theme alone. According to Clifford, a dominant mode of ethnographic surrealism is "a prevailing attitude of ironic participant observation among the hierarchies and meanings of collective life" ("Ethnographic Surrealism," 130). There is plenty of irony on hand in *The Shout*, most notably with regard to Christianity, a belief system ridiculed by Crossley philosophically and by Anthony through his blasphemous actions (he uses his post as guest organist at the local church to conduct an extramarital affair). Christianity clearly holds no moral or practical superiority to Aboriginal beliefs in *The Shout*, so we are invited to reflect on religious faith as a matter of ironic relativism. But what I want to focus on now in Clifford's formulation is participant observation. By transforming self/other distinctions along the axis of sensory impressions rather than strictly narrative meaning, the film encourages us to feel our way through those distinctions when our habit is to think. *The Shout* asks us to participate in its constructions of transformative otherness, to feel those constructions the way we feel Crossley's shout in the pit of our stomach.

Skolimowski invites viewer participation at the level of feeling in a variety of ways, but one important strategy I have touched on already but wish to elaborate is training spectators to process image and sound unconventionally. For example, Anthony's studio decorations include reproductions on paper of disturbing paintings by Francis Bacon (1909–1992), the well-known Irish British artist often referred to as a modern surrealist. The first one we see, *Paralytic Child Walking on All Fours (from Muybridge)* (1961; fig. 2.6), is not simply presented to us as a symbol of Anthony's alienated, conflicted soul but as an image we must look *through* as much as look *at*. The painting appears to breathe as it flutters against the speaker it is posted on in time to the vibrations produced by Anthony's sound experiments. A lesson for the viewer along the lines of "This image is not static, it is alive, available for transformation and incorporation" begins to emerge through this simultaneously visual, aural, and tactile treatment. This lesson develops further when Anthony's dog appears in the studio soon after, as if the painting's haunting humanoid figure that appears doglike by walking on hands and feet were taking on material form. This impression is heightened when Anthony announces the dog's name: Buzz. Is Buzz an extension of the painting as image, with his visual resemblance to Bacon's half-human, half-dog figure? Or is he a manifestation of the painting as sound, with his name mimicking the noise that causes the painting to tremble (literalized further when Anthony rubs his microphone directly on Buzz's fur, making buzz out of Buzz)?

2.6 A reproduction of Francis Bacon's *Paralytic Child Walking on All Fours (from Muybridge)* in *The Shout.*

Rather than answer these questions, Skolimowski expands their range by modulating the connotations of Bacon's painting throughout the film. One side of *Paralytic Child* depicts a window with two panes of glass, an image foreshadowed earlier in the film when Anthony and Rachel encounter their own reflections in a large mirror that two men carry across their path as they walk through town. This image of their doubleness is doubled by the shots Skolimowski places on either side of it: Anthony's lover looking down from an open window split into multiple panes of glass, the lover's husband peering out from behind a window similarly divided. So the visual associations with splitting so central to Bacon's painting (human/dog; upper windowpane/lower windowpane) have been anticipated earlier in the film and continue to radiate outward later. When Crossley enters the Fieldings' house, he rests in a spare room that contains a tall, narrow window much like the one in *Paralytic Child*, but this particular window has been removed from its mounting and set aside for repair because one of its panes is shattered.

The shattered pane reminds us of a feat Crossley just performed at the dinner table: breaking a wine glass through sound vibrations made using a separate glass. Yet another instance of glass breaking occurs soon after, when a frustrated Anthony sends a piece of firewood sailing through a nearby windowpane; the accident creates a damaged window similar to the one we have already seen in Crossley's room. Again, these chains of related images and sounds (shots of windows and broken glass are legion in this film) trouble routine attempts to set them in temporal, narrative, or even allusive order. What is more primary: the painting or the mirror and the windows that resemble it? Are all of the examples of broken glass separate or one and the same, variations on a single event unstuck in time and place? Is the film imitating the painting or recovering the painting's cinematic origins? After all, as Bacon's subtitle points out, this painting began as a form of film—the proto-cinematic pioneer Eadweard Muybridge's *Infantile Paralysis, Child Walking on Hands and Feet* (1887), a series of photographic plates that record the locomotion of a disabled child.

The painting continues to metamorphose later in the film, when Rachel, under the spell of Crossley's magic, traipses nude through the spare room and crouches beside the broken window pane. The image switches momentarily from color to black-and-white, completing a striking materialization of the chief visual elements in Bacon's painting (which is in color in its original form but reproduced in black-and-white in Anthony's studio) as well as in Muybridge's photographic plates. Is painting possessing film here, or vice versa? Is this scene an image of Rachel's actions or of Anthony's imagination of her actions? Is Rachel under the influence of Crossley's magic, or is she responding to Anthony's split loyalties, captured so hauntingly in Bacon's painting through divided visual structures? Or is she somewhere outside and above the two men, as it seems in the film's beginning and end when she appears to hold more knowledge about her relationship with each of them than either do on their own? Again, Skolimowski does not want us to answer these questions as much as he wishes for us to hold them in tension and forces us to challenge our habits of making meaning. In the face of such a challenge, our instinct to pin down Crossley's identity as monstrous other crumbles, and the invitation to inhabit the stance of ethnographic surrealism's participant observer coalesces.

In fact, Crossley is both participant and observer when it comes to the other. He seems to be the other when he employs Aboriginal magic to dark purposes as if it were his own, but he also reveals that this expertise is the result of many years spent observing Aboriginal people in the Australian outback. So Crossley is at least as much an ethnographer as a monster. This point is underlined when he relates an anecdote from his outback experience to Anthony. Crossley describes witnessing an Aboriginal chief magician, a "genuinely terrifying figure" dressed in an English tailcoat, slice open his own skin with a stone and shed it "like a snake" in order to bring rain during a long drought. Anthony is aghast and not just due to the horror of what Crossley describes. It seems Crossley's ethnography matches Anthony and Rachel's shared dream of the Aboriginal man in the dunes. The vision is both dream and ethnography—it is ethnographic surrealism.

Crossley also tells the Fieldings that he took an Aboriginal wife while living in the outback but killed all of the children he fathered with her. He explains that this is the lawful right of every parent in Aboriginal society and that he chose to exercise this right because he knew he would eventually leave and the children would have nothing in his absence. Rachel is more visibly upset by this story than Anthony, but not for the reasons we might assume. She mentions that she and Anthony have been unable to have children, a topic that Anthony is eager to avoid. The conflict between Anthony and Rachel over their child-lessness surfaces again later, but this time in images rather than in words. When Crossley temporarily leaves Rachel after he has bewitched her, Anthony scoops up in a white towel the bone Crossley has left behind like a toothbrush in the bathroom and throws it out the window. Later, when he rises to cover himself after he and Rachel caress each other in the bath (the closest thing the Field-ings have to a love scene), the bloodstain left by the bone on the towel is appar-ent to both of them. "It's probably Crossley's," Anthony says. "I don't know why you let him bother you so much," Rachel replies.

The arresting image of the white linen stained with blood spins both of their statements back toward the earlier discussion of infanticide and childlessness. Crossley has brought them together again, metaphorically encouraging the reconsummation of a relationship that has languished in infidelity and child-lessness, but he has also left the taint of death on them. The Fieldings' lovemaking is interrupted by news from the vicar that Harry the shepherd (Peter Benson) has died. We know that Harry's death was caused by Crossley's shout and that his shout was in turn caused by Anthony's insistence that Crossley demonstrate it for him—an insistence rooted in Rachel's flirtation with Crossley, which pushes Anthony toward an attempt to diminish him by proving his stories false. So Harry, a mentally disabled innocent whom Anthony addressed earlier in the film in the tone one uses with a child (emphasizing Harry's kinship with Bacon's and Muybridge's paralytic child), is dead through the collaboration of Anthony, Crossley, and Rachel.

Crossley has made the Fieldings killers as well as lovers; in the surrealist logic of associated images, their relationship partakes of the lifeblood of Crossley's energy as an exotic other as well as of the spilled blood connected with Cross-ley's most heinous, othering crimes. Perhaps this is why the film ends with Rachel's ambiguous expression of relief as well as loss when uncovering Cross-ley's corpse. She finds a string tied around his neck that holds her shoe buckle, the personal possession he has used to exert his magic on her. She takes back the buckle, indicating the end of Crossley's power over her and the resumption of her own individual agency (which is further underlined by Anthony's com-plete absence). But then she stays beside Crossley's body and looks at him with a mixture of puzzlement and affection, suggesting that their relationship is still unfolding and that we are returning with her, as if in a loop, to the film's beginning. She will then have another opportunity to integrate—as will we along with her—the surreal, transformative otherness of Charles Crossley in all of its allure and horror.

This chapter has posited ethnographic surrealism alongside the previous chapter's descriptions of transformative otherness as concepts that move beyond Robin Wood's formulations for understanding the formal and social significance of the horror film. Through this analysis of *The Shout* via the lens of ethnographic surrealism, the limitations of Wood's investments in narrative meaning and realist form to determine horror's relation to otherness emerge. Just as transformative otherness troubles Wood's categories of "progressive" and "reactionary" horror, so too does ethnographic surrealism disturb his preference for narrative over nonnarrative signification, realist representation over surrealist suggestion, and story structure over sensory modes of spectator participation. Through transformative otherness and ethnographic surrealism, we can see, hear, and feel horror's relation to otherness rather than just think it.

The stakes of this shift from thinking horrific otherness to sensing horrific otherness are not just about understanding the horror film in ways that Wood misses. The shift entails a new reckoning with horror's risky but invaluable potential to recast cinema's relation to forms of otherness that escape our conventional, too easily deployed distinctions between "progressive" and "reactionary." For example, one can imagine an extraordinary horror film such as *The Shout* being relegated to the dustbin of history with a swift verdict that runs along the lines of "that's nothing more than an exploitive, racist fantasy of Aboriginal otherness." This verdict is not without relevance or power. In fact, this verdict would be compelling if the film were reduced to its narrative dimensions alone in the sort of analysis encouraged by Wood's model.

But such a verdict cannot produce an adequate account of *The Shout* with regard to horror and otherness. Indeed, my hope is that *The Shout* can eventually join the ranks of kindred cinematic experiments that use horror to express Aboriginal otherness in ways where the rewards (not always easy to discern) outweigh the risks (easier to identify). Weighing such risks and rewards is never anything less than excruciatingly difficult, especially in light of how much damage even well-intentioned cinematic representations of otherness can wreak on real communities that have been socially and historically othered.[18] But to dispose of *The Shout* along with Australian horror (or horror-adjacent) films such as *The Last Wave* (Peter Weir, 1977), *Cargo* (Ben Howling and Yolanda Ramke, 2018), and *The Nightingale* (Jennifer Kent, 2019) as "reactionary" uses of horror to exploit Aboriginal otherness misses more than it captures, even if it captures something true. All of these remarkable films use horror to activate otherness as a sensory experience, not just as a narrative trope. In short, these films have much more to teach us about the complex interchanges between horror and otherness than labels such as *reactionary* and *progressive* can provide.

Perhaps there is no more persuasive testament to the lessons offered by these films than the existence of *Cleverman* (Ryan Griffen, 2016–2017), a pioneering television series created and produced largely by Aboriginal Australians. *Cleverman*, like Tracey Moffatt's underappreciated *beDevil* (1993) before it, shares something in common with *The Shout* and its cinematic cousins because of the registers in which it chooses to speak about Aboriginal experience: the fantastic, science fiction, horror. This chapter has suggested ways to listen in those registers, to hear those voices. The next three chapters extend our ability to listen differently to horror and otherness by returning to three directors who were essential to Robin Wood's critical model but whose careers now demand new interpretations: Tobe Hooper, George A. Romero, and David Cronenberg.

PART II

TRANSFORMING THE MASTERS OF HORROR

CHAPTER 3

NIGHTMARE ZONE

Aging as Otherness in the Cinema of Tobe Hooper

Tobe Hooper knows what scares us. In fact, the language most often used to describe Hooper's films, whether by critics or by the director himself, is the language of the nightmare. A particularly vivid account of Hooper's cinema as nightmarish comes from Robin Wood's "An Introduction to the American Horror Film." For Wood, Hooper's breakthrough horror landmark *The Texas Chain Saw Massacre* (1974) is the one film that captures "the authentic quality of nightmare" more than any other he has ever seen:

> I have had since childhood a recurring nightmare whose pattern seems to be shared by a very large number of people within our culture: I am running away from some vaguely terrible oppressors who are going to do dreadful things to me; I run to a house or a car, etc., for help; I discover its occupants to be precisely the people I am fleeing. This pattern is repeated twice in *Massacre*, where Sally "escapes" from Leatherface first to his own home, then to the service station run by his father.[1]

Massacre, as we also saw in chapter 1, is nothing less than foundational for Wood's critical account of the horror film. In his description of the film as nightmarish, a key ingredient is the omnipresence of the "oppressors," those monsters or others that pursue the victimized self. Even if these others may at first seem to offer the illusion of refuge from horror, their true natures are revealed in very short order. So an essential element of Wood's characterization of *Massacre* as nightmarish is its clear demarcation between victimized self and monstrous other. The threat to the self from the other is unidirectional; the self is never in danger of becoming the other, nor is the other ever capable of becoming the self. What my own accounts of horror as transformative otherness, whether through spectacle horror (chapter 1) or ethnographic surrealism (chapter 2), have emphasized, however, is precisely the opposite: how horror encompasses the confrontational possibilities of ongoing transformation, where self and other do not simply oppose or double one another but exist in an endless state of becoming one another. As I demonstrated in chapter 2, horror's transformative otherness is something quite different from Wood's "progressive" ambivalence between normality and monstrosity. For Wood, any such ambivalence does not alter the fact that "normal" self and "monstrous" other are ultimately distinguishable because this ambivalence is lodged in the narrative meaning of the film as either progressive or reactionary; for me, self and other are always transforming into one another, often on the plane of spectatorship's nonnarrative dimensions and beyond the designation of progressive or reactionary.

Seeing horror through the lens of transformative otherness opens up new territory for understanding how the horror film works. When we look beyond Wood's categories of normality and monstrosity, toward transformative otherness, our ability to see the otherness within horror expands. For example, Wood's inventory of social others that he claims horror relies upon does not include the aged. Yet I argue here that the otherness of aging is essential for reckoning with horror in the cinema of Tobe Hooper. Indeed, it is striking that in a career brimming with nightmare images of many kinds, a particularly haunting and persistent subset of these images involves themes of aging: life's perceived decay, dissolution, and decrepitude. In other words, Hooper knows that we are especially afraid of old age, to the point that we struggle mightily to render it invisible. But how and why does Hooper work so hard to achieve just the opposite: the conjuring into visibility of old age as a preoccupation of our nightmares?

In an overview of the humanistic field of age studies, the psychology and gender studies scholar Lynne Segal writes, "In western societies especially, we find ourselves early on directed to become, and above all to remain, autonomous, independent, future-oriented individuals. Such teaching, with its disavowal of so much about our human vulnerabilities, passivity, interdependence, and mortality, can only shore up trouble for the future. It ensures that all too soon, our registering of aging is likely to prove a perplexing, even frightening, affair."[2] What Segal observes about our difficulty in registering aging can extend to forms of social blindness toward older people. Kathleen Woodward, in her introduction to a seminal anthology in age studies (drawing on research by the anthropologist Barbara Meyerhoff), describes Western society's sometimes quite literal inability to see older people, and older women in particular, as "death by invisibility."[3]

Hooper's films suggest that he would not be surprised by these formulations from age studies. He knows that old age scares us, but he also knows that we have built powerful defenses to deny it and neutralize it, to counteract its visibility. So he shows old age to us in a funhouse mirror: the image distorted just enough for us to look on rather than to look away, enabling us to catch a terrifying glimpse of who we really are that burrows straight into what Hooper calls our "nightmare zone," where horrific images arranged by the director for "harmonic" impact force into visibility "the stuff that we don't open the door on."[4] This nightmare zone functions as a sort of primal nerve center, where visceral horror and psychological horror cross paths as mutually informing experiences of sensation and understanding. We know the horror because we feel it, and we feel the horror because we know it. In Hooper's films, what we come to feel and know and therefore to *see* are precisely those nightmare images of aging that we usually wish to relegate to invisibility. In short, Hooper shows us horrific encounters with aging as a matter of transformative otherness: youthful "self" and aged "other" cease to be easily distinguishable, existing instead simultaneously through ongoing states of transformation.

This chapter does not offer a comprehensive survey covering all nightmare images of aging in Hooper's films but rather meditations on a few important examples that illustrate how and why Hooper disrupts the "death by invisibility" pattern that concerns age studies. The examples proceed thematically rather than chronologically so that readers can gain a sense of how Hooper constructs these images across his oeuvre. *The Funhouse* (1981), *Salem's Lot* (1979), and *Lifeforce* (1985) constitute the chapter's main focus, but it concludes with considerations of Hooper's two *Texas Chain Saw Massacre* films (1974 and 1986) and *Poltergeist* (1982).

The Funhouse

Since I have already evoked the metaphor of the funhouse mirror, I begin with *The Funhouse*. In this film, the teenaged Amy (Elizabeth Berridge) and three friends visit a traveling carnival and decide to sneak into the funhouse after hours so they can spend the night there illicitly. They stumble upon a host of secrets hidden by the carnival folk, including the true identity of the funhouse barker's mysterious son: an abused, murderous, and deformed man who works at the carnival but shields his face from the world by wearing a Frankenstein's monster mask. Once the barker and his son learn of the intruders and their knowledge of the carnival's secrets, they set about killing them, one by one.

Amy and her friends fight for their lives, but only Amy survives; both the barker and his son perish as well. Amy leaves the funhouse alone the following morning.

Curiously, Hooper does not show us a funhouse mirror despite setting most of his film at a carnival and offering us a fairly encyclopedic tour of various rides and amusements. Perhaps this absence can cue us to how the entire film itself can be usefully construed as a funhouse mirror. Hooper shows ourselves to ourselves in a manner that combines monstrous distortion and honest recognition. Just as Amy and her friends discover a nightmare reflection of their own lives and desires in the twilight world of the funhouse (sex, parents, siblings, family), so too does the film's central nightmare image of the barker's son (listed in the credits as "The Monster" and played by Wayne Doba) reflect back an image of aging that strikes us as both shocking and familiar. The Monster's embodiment of aging is the source of his shocking familiarity and ultimately makes him something quite different than the freakish creatures who surround him as carnival attractions.

The Monster is a familiar image of aging in terms of his elderly appearance: unkempt, thinning white hair, clawlike wrinkled hands. But the Monster is also a shocking image of aging with regard to his simultaneous youthfulness: pre-verbal, sexually inexperienced, bullied by his father, prone to fly into tantrum-like rages directed at himself and others. In addition, he is imposingly strong, demonstrating how his twisted, arthritic-looking hands are actually lethal tools for slashing and strangulation. Hooper drives home the Monster's transformative otherness, his deeply disturbing amalgam of young and old, by giving him an unforgettably horrifying "multiplied" face. The Monster's face features a deep, almost ax-wound-like indentation running from his forehead down through his nostrils that gives him the appearance of splitting in two (fig. 3.1);

3.1 The face of the Monster (Wayne Doba) in *The Funhouse*.

he also dies when cut in half by the mechanical gears beneath the funhouse. It may be that the Monster's transformative otherness functions as an internalized funhouse mirror, where he is always both himself and his distorted reflection, simultaneously young and old, through ongoing metamorphosis.

An additional dimension of the Monster's transformative otherness concerns his parallels to Amy's young brother Joey (Shawn Carson). Like the Monster, Joey owns a Frankenstein's monster mask, and early in the film he "stalks" Amy in the style of *Psycho* (Alfred Hitchcock, 1960) and *Halloween* (John Carpenter, 1978). Joey's "stalking" of his sister as she showers is ultimately revealed as playful mischief, even if Amy's enraged reaction to his "game" and Joey's internalization of her reaction suggest there is more at stake here for both of them than mere sibling teasing. Indeed, Joey's fear of entering the funhouse later in the film (where he could potentially help his sister) is conditioned in part by his fear of once again violating Amy's sexual privacy (as he did in the shower). The Monster's pursuit of Amy is of course more terrifyingly murderous than Joey's stalking, but, like Joey, the Monster is capable of adolescent confusions about where to draw the line between childlike and adult behavior (as we saw with his precursor, *Halloween*'s masked Michael Myers, in chapter 1). Figuratively, then, the Monster is both as threatening as an older psychotic killer and as innocent as a younger brother.

The Monster is emblematic of Hooper's approach to aging through horror: transform signs of youthfulness (what we can usually bear to see) and those of old age (what we usually do not want to see or cannot see) to defamiliarize both, allowing unorthodox images of aging to penetrate our defenses. Like Frankenstein's monster, whose visage becomes his disguise, and the closely related Leatherface in the *Texas Chain Saw Massacre* films, the Monster possesses disconcertingly human qualities alongside his deadly monstrosity: clumsily craving female romantic contact, vulnerable to his father's abuse, unable to contain his frustration with himself. This human/monster mixture certainly informs *The Funhouse*'s debt to classic horror traditions, but it is even more striking how Hooper employs human/monster as one more layer of transformative otherness that deepens the young/old metamorphosis. Indeed, Hooper's films help to highlight how aging figures in classic horror's cinematic imagination, whether in the shape of Frankenstein's monster as the childlike mind within an old, lumbering body assembled from corpse parts; of Dracula as the ancient being with the voracious appetite of a newborn; of the Mummy as an age-old monster frozen in time, yearning for the reincarnation of his young love from long ago; or of the Wolf Man as the victim of an olden curse that not only robs him of his memory during transformations in a sort of lunar-induced dementia but also turns back the evolutionary clock (see chapter 7).

In fact, we might say that Hooper makes modern horror images out of classic horror themes precisely through his nightmarish visualization of aging. The

Monster of *The Funhouse* revises Frankenstein's monster by discarding the reassuringly familiar mask to reveal the shocking horror beneath: a face splitting in half through the colliding signs of youth and old age. Turning from Hooper's take on Frankenstein's monster in *The Funhouse* to his interpretations of the vampire in *Salem's Lot* and *Lifeforce* will enhance our understanding of how Hooper uses aging to make modern horror from classic horror as well as how his merging of youth and old age participates in horror's transformative otherness.

Salem's Lot and Lifeforce

Salem's Lot, Hooper's made-for-television adaptation of Stephen King's novel (1975) about vampires terrorizing a small town in Maine, is instructive in its capacity to produce nightmare images of aging even within the restricted visual vocabulary of network television. Hooper withholds the image of his main vampire, Kurt Barlow (Reggie Nalder), until late in the film. When Barlow does appear, he resembles Max Schreck in *Nosferatu* (F. W. Murnau, 1922) much more closely than Bela Lugosi in *Dracula* (Tod Browning, 1931). Barlow is an aged, ratlike vampire, not the ageless, seductive Dracula. Like a very old man or an animal or a hairless newborn infant, he does not speak; he allows his human assistant Richard Straker (James Mason) to speak for him. The fact that Straker is played by an aging James Mason, once a dashing leading man in his own right but now locked into battle with the much younger David Soul as the charismatic writer Ben Mears out to expose the vampire epidemic, adds weight to the film's investment in aging imagery. In a sequence near the film's conclusion, Straker demonstrates a disturbingly youthful, even superhuman strength as he protects his master Barlow's home from intruding investigators. He even impales a man on a set of decorative trophy antlers with his bare hands. By the time Straker succumbs to a hail of bullets from Mears, we can no longer equate old age with weakness or aging star with fading star—Mason's presence handily overpowers Soul's in each of their shared scenes.

But neither Barlow nor Straker embodies the most intense nightmare image of aging in *Salem's Lot*. Instead, it is the young boy Ralphie Glick (Ronnie Scribner). As a victim of vampirism early in the film, Ralphie visits his brother Danny (Brad Savage) during the night, tapping insistently on Danny's window to let him in. Hooper's vision of Ralphie, floating in an otherworldly mist outside the window and displaying equally the characteristics of a young, innocent boy (small, vulnerable body dressed in pajamas) and an old, evil vampire (menacing fangs, glowing eyes), reaches its apex in Ralphie's obscene smile. His smile is a truly chilling expression of young playfulness and old murderousness that lays waste to conventional young/old distinctions. We know who Ellen

(Greta Schröder) is letting in when she opens her window to the vampire in *Nosferatu*, but who exactly is Danny letting in? Is it his beloved little brother? A monstrous vampire? Or some terrifying combination of the two that defies our categorizations of young and old by situating them as a matter of transformative otherness?

Horror studies scholarship has often drawn attention to how category violations that cross boundaries such as alive/dead and subject/object tend to structure definitions of monstrosity presented in the genre's texts.[5] But young/old differs from these sorts of category violations by finally not really being a violation at all. As the cultural studies scholar Jodi Brooks observes in her analysis of aging female film characters such as Baby Jane Hudson (Bette Davis) in *Whatever Happened to Baby Jane?* (Robert Aldrich, 1962), "What these characters and their performances offer is a form of crisis in which time is loaded to the breaking point[;] . . . their refusal to leave the stage and the ways in which they negotiate their status as image take the form of *stretching time*, of re-pacing the temporality of spectacle, display, and performance."[6] In other words, the act of stretching time in this way undoes our ability to neatly parse time into young and old categories. Baby Jane Hudson is both child star and aging star at once, her performance (especially as realized by Davis) slyly refusing to respect young/old boundaries by stretching our perception of time's passing. Aren't we all simultaneously young and old in our relative awareness or unawareness of ourselves in relation to our age? When exactly do we become "old"? Most of us fear becoming old, perhaps even more than we fear death, because old age seems to represent the end of life in full and the beginning of life in diminishment. But this whole notion of youth as more and old age as less is just one very particular approach to perceiving time—an approach with limitations that become clear when time is stretched beyond the conventional markers of old and young. Hooper's image of Ralphie achieves this stretching of time, just as the performance of Baby Jane Hudson does. Of course, Ralphie is a young boy merged with a supernatural vampire, while Baby Jane Hudson is an older woman without any explicit connection to the supernatural (no matter how grotesque her appearance).[7] Given the close relation between age studies and feminist theory, this difference in gender is worth dwelling on for a moment. A number of age studies scholars have pointed out how women in Western societies experience aging quite differently from men. As Kathleen Woodward puts it, women around fifty experience aging in a way "that does not have the same counterpart in men" with regard to "psychological, social, and economic consequences." Woodward continues, "By experiencing aging, I am referring primarily to the internalization of our culture's denial of and distaste for aging, which is understood in terms of decline, not in terms of growth and change."[8] E. Ann Kaplan presses harder on such a formulation, arguing that for women aging can be a traumatic experience.[9] So if women bear the social brunt of our fear of aging, then why does Hooper tend to prefer males for his nightmare images of aging?

One way to begin answering this question is by noting that Hooper is certainly not above misogynist codings of aging in his work. Consider, for example, how the aging fortune-teller Madame Zena (Sylvia Miles) in *The Funhouse* must absorb the horrific punishment for the Monster's failed sexual encounter with her by paying with her life. It is hard to miss how an older woman engaging in sex is portrayed as somehow inherently monstrous (compounded with the moral condemnation of prostitution), while the younger Amy's "natural" experience of sex in the funhouse with her boyfriend is survivable. But Hooper, in his dedicated quest to breach our nightmare zone, to get to the root of what really scares us, also seems to know that women often provide a convenient deflection for what truly scares his male viewers: male aging, with its attendant perceived losses of virility and perhaps even masculinity itself. So Hooper shows us not only the aging we would rather not see but also the male aging that is even more unthinkable than female aging. When Ben's lover turned vampire, Susan (Bonnie Bedelia), attempts to seduce him at the conclusion of *Salem's Lot*, he kills her in a manner that suggests he is guarding himself selfishly more than he is selflessly releasing her from a curse. She, after all, has now transcended the conventional human understanding of young and old as opposed states of being to become vampiric in the register of transformative otherness. Susan, like Barlow, Straker, and Ralphie, is no longer interpretable according to the young/old dichotomy on which so much patriarchal privilege rests. On some level, Ben seems to sense this and perceives Susan's promise that they can "love each other forever" as a threat; he eliminates Susan not just because she has become a vampire but also because she has exposed nonvampiric eternal youth as an empty fantasy to which men cling most ferociously and eternal couplehood as an affront to male power. As Ben drives the stake through Susan's heart, he closes his eyes and turns away; he refuses to look at her. But Hooper graces the dying Susan with a startling close-up that captures everything Ben cannot face: her strength, her beauty, her love, her vampiric refusal to conform to classifications of young or old (fig. 3.2). At his most ambitious and adventurous, Hooper suggests that even female aging can really be imagined by men only as a defense against their own fears of aging. In *Lifeforce*, Hooper enacts this thesis in a remarkably flamboyant way.

Lifeforce, like *Salem's Lot*, is a vampire film. But where *Salem's Lot* prefers the microcosm of its isolated small-town setting, *Lifeforce* embraces the macrocosm of outer space and the apocalyptic destruction of one of the world's largest cities (London). In this adaptation of Colin Wilson's novel *The Space Vampires* (1976), three humanoid alien life-forms are discovered in space, brought back to Earth for investigation, and then escape, triggering a mass vampirism outbreak that eventually reduces London to a fiery ruin. The nightmare images of aging in *Lifeforce* revolve around what the film's crew nicknamed "the

3.2 The dying vampire Susan (Bonnie Bedelia) in *Salem's Lot*.

walking shriveled,"[10] those victims of the space vampires whose living energy has been sucked dry but who become reanimated as frenzied husks of their former selves with a need to feed on others. The walking shriveled are, as their nickname implies, grotesquely aged. Their skeletal features barely covered by taut, grayish skin, they project old age as total desiccation, the evaporation of "lifeforce," utterly vampirized (fig. 3.3). But what makes these images of aging as decay most nightmarish are the crossed wires with desperately alive and embodied energy. They writhe, scream, grasp, and shake, eventually exploding into ash if they cannot feed. In short, the walking shriveled join the Monster of *The Funhouse* and Ralphie of *Salem's Lot* as nightmarish visions of aging as transformative otherness due to their wild mixing of signs associated with youth and old age.

What sets the walking shriveled of *Lifeforce* apart is how they are created through contact with their visual opposite: not only youth but also sexualized and feminine youth in particular. The key space vampire, referred to in the film's credits as the "Space Girl" (Mathilda May), takes the shape of a stunningly beautiful woman who appears entirely nude during most of the film. Even though she has two similarly striking male space vampire counterparts, Hooper focuses on her. Echoing the same visual logic, the two examples of the walking shriveled that Hooper emphasizes are male, although there is also a female

3.3 One of the vampirized "walking shriveled" in *Lifeforce*.

victim of the Space Girl who undergoes a memorably failed scientific inspection. *Lifeforce*'s sexual atmosphere is quite polymorphous overall, with the Space Girl's possession of a male doctor's mind leading to an on-screen suggestion of gay male sex that her "lesbian" encounter with her female victim also evokes but leaves off-screen. Still, Hooper assigns the majority of the film's visual weight to a female space vampire and male versions of the walking shriveled. By the time the Space Girl's true identity as a giant batlike alien is revealed, we have learned that her image as a beautiful woman was sourced from the lead male astronaut Carlsen's (Steve Railsback) imagination—perfect femininity as projected by male fantasy.

So it is, finally, the male imagination that is visualized and inspected in *Lifeforce*, with youthful, sexualized femininity only an illusion that distracts from man's ultimate destiny: to become the walking shriveled. Even when Carlsen copulates with the Space Girl, he must kill her and himself simultaneously by spearing their conjoined bodies with a long, phallic sword. Youth may live by the sexual sword but must also die by the same sword. With such images, *Lifeforce* becomes Hooper's most forceful presentation of old age as at heart a male nightmare. The denials and deflections provided by female aging and female youth may generate temporary relief, but behind the disguises the true fear of male aging can always be detected.

The *Texas Chain Saw Massacre* Films

The iconography of the mask is nearly as central to Hooper's work as the iconography of aging, and his most famous film stands at the crossroads between the two. In *The Texas Chain Saw Massacre*, we can find the original model for the walking shriveled in Grandpa (John Dugan), the eldest patriarch of the chain saw clan. He is almost impossibly wizened, so old that at times it is difficult to tell whether he is dead or alive. But, like the walking shriveled, when he comes to life, he expresses a disturbingly youthful energy. In Grandpa's case, this youthfulness is positively babyish. In an especially macabre moment, Grandpa sucks the blood from the slashed finger of Sally (Marilyn Burns), sending him into infantile ecstasies of kicking feet and twisting arms. In an instant, former slaughterhouse legend Grandpa transforms from an ancient invalid (who later has difficulty even grasping the hammer meant for Sally's head) to a vampiric baby thrilled by nursing. Again, we are shocked by this unexpected collision of youth and old age, with its nightmarish combination of horror, absurdity, and even black comedy. Hooper bursts through our conceptions of what aging means by scrambling visions of old age and youth on his way to our nightmare zone as part of a larger orchestration of what Christopher Sharrett calls the film's concern with "the collapse of time."[11] This is why Grandpa, who poses no real physical threat at all, can still occupy the foreground of our nightmares triggered by *The Texas Chain Saw Massacre*.

Grandpa shares the nightmare stage with several other unforgettable figures in the film, of whom the most well known is undoubtedly Leatherface (Gunnar Hansen). In his masks stitched together from human flesh, Leatherface extends the aging imagery in Hooper's work in significant ways. Unlike the masked Monster of *The Funhouse*, Leatherface is never unmasked. Even when alone at home, he does not remove his mask. He changes his appearance, most notably when dressing up as a maternal-like figure for dinner, complete with wig and kitchen apron (fig. 3.4), but Leatherface and his masks are one. In a strange way, his masks make him ageless. He has appropriated someone else's face and made it his own in such a horrifyingly literal manner that his own face melts away. The union of face and mask in Leatherface mocks all of our conventional notions about aging, with their obsessive focus on the face as the "truthful" index to age's visibility.

Indeed, Vivian Sobchack has argued that cinema and cosmetic surgery are aligned in their shared devotion to maintaining a seamlessly youthful body that does not speak of its aging. "The whole point is that, for the 'magic' to work, the 'seams'—both the lines traced by age and the scars traced by surgery—must not show."[12] Sobchack is thinking of aging women here and the sort of common plastic surgery that might at first seem entirely inapplicable to Leatherface's horrifying approach to "surgery" through human slaughter, but the point is that Leatherface wears a skin mask where the seams show, where aging and death are spoken. They are spoken by drawing attention to the mask itself as a face in its own right, not the illusorily youthful beautification of an aging face. Comparative scales of youthful "beauty" and aging "ugliness" are made

3.4 Leatherface (Gunnar Hansen) with his mask stitched together from human flesh in *The Texas Chain Saw Massacre*.

ridiculous by Leatherface's mask-as-face and face-as-mask. In Leatherface, Hooper crafts an image that overturns our instincts to "read" the face for traces of aging. Through the language of the nightmare, Leatherface offers a terrifying but potentially radical critique of how we perceive aging and the masks we employ (from surgery to self-deception) to keep aging invisible. Leatherface makes the mask visible to us and demands that we see through it, beyond it, without it.

The faceless vision of aging that Leatherface presents may be impossible to process. It appears to rob Sally of her sanity by the conclusion of *The Texas Chain Saw Massacre*, when her once angelically young face becomes nearly unrecognizable through layers of blood, tears, and maniacal laughter. But when Hooper revisits Leatherface in *The Texas Chainsaw Massacre 2*, he hints that even if the lessons Leatherface teaches us on aging cannot be *thought* (this may well be the road to madness), perhaps they can be *embodied*. In one of the film's most unsettling scenes, the intrepid female disc jockey Stretch (Caroline Williams), now stepping into Sally's shoes as the tortured prey of Leatherface and his family, receives a gift of sorts from Leatherface (Bill Johnson). He masks her face with the flesh he has ripped from her male coworker, puts a cowboy hat on her head, and then dances with her. It is as if Leatherface, who has clearly fallen for Stretch romantically by this point, wishes to teach her something about the nature of her face as well as of his own. "A face is a mask; you can change it and no longer feel beholden to it," Leatherface's strange gesture seems to say. He is temporarily concealing her from the rest of his homicidal family, but he is also likely reflecting on his earlier encounter with her, where Stretch "saved face" by simulating sexual arousal rather than screaming with fear at the sight of Leatherface's chain saw. "It's the dance that matters, not the face" might be the sentiment Leatherface is trying to communicate to Stretch in an attempt to get her to recognize something she knows instinctively on some level already.

Privileging the dance over the face turns out to be a lesson in aging as much as in slaughterhouse survival. Stretch, by the film's conclusion, not only out-lives her assailants but also inhabits Leatherface himself. She commandeers the chain saw from the lap of the clan's grandmother (a juxtaposed vision of decrepit age and buxom fertility that makes Grandpa seem tame) and disposes of Chop-Top (Bill Moseley). Stretch's final gesture is her version of Leatherface's dance that ended *The Texas Chain Saw Massacre*: chain saw buzzing aloft, now an ani-mating force in its own right because there is no one left to hunt or vanquish (fig. 3.5). Stretch's contorted face and frenzied yelling is not distant from Sally's madness, but Stretch's face–mask is decidedly her own. It is *her* chain saw, *her* dance, *her* face–mask. She wears no mask except the one that Leatherface willed to her: the mask-as-face and face-as-mask. Whatever the future may hold for Stretch, she will not fear the supposed emptiness of aging. She has activated

3.5 Stretch (Caroline Williams) lifts her chain saw aloft in *The Texas Chainsaw Massacre 2*.

the fullness of her name, stretching time beyond the breaking points of youth and old age. She even demolishes cinematic time as the conclusions of the two *Texas Chain Saw Massacre* films meld into one through her gestural becoming of Leatherface. This becoming can be understood in the senses of Vivian Sobchack's redefinition of "aging" as "always becoming" and of horror's transformative otherness as a process of ongoing metamorphosis between self and other.[13] Carol J. Clover deftly analyzes Stretch as an important iteration of what she calls the slasher film's "Final Girl" survivor–heroine.[14] But what my turn to aging imagery ultimately suggests is that Stretch is no Final Girl; she is a Final Woman.

Poltergeist

By way of conclusion, I turn briefly to the biggest commercial success of Hooper's career: *Poltergeist*. This film is often discussed as bearing a stronger authorial imprint from its producer, Steven Spielberg, than from its director.[15] But focusing on one of the film's indelible nightmare images demonstrates how much *Poltergeist* conforms to Hooper's signature deployment of aging as transformative otherness.

Poltergeist chronicles the struggles of the Freeling family as they are forced to admit that their everyday suburban home is haunted. The ghosts who terrorize them in increasingly menacing ways even manage to kidnap their youngest child, Carol Anne (Heather O'Rourke), and transport her to a ghostly plane of existence. The quest to rescue Carol Anne culminates in a spectacular breach between the everyday world and the ghostly one, where the corpses in the cemetery that the home has been illicitly built upon resurface along with a maelstrom of supernatural activity. Carol Anne is recovered, but the family's refusal of the ghostly has been lost; a hole has been punched into the fabric of their everyday world.

In the run-up to this climax, Hooper inserts one of his nightmare images of aging as transformative otherness. A young adult male parapsychologist, part of the team that visits the Freelings to aid them, looks into a mirror and watches himself savagely tear away the flesh of his face with his own hands to reveal the skull beneath (fig. 3.6). This harrowing image is quickly rationalized as a ghostly vision, but the damage has been done, and the echoes persist: the face of youth transforms into the face of death, suggesting that the notion of aging we depend on to divide youth from death is merely an illusion. The two faces are ultimately revealed as one, their illusory "halves" horrifically stitched together through a thin layer of skin prone to rending. The echoes of Hooper's other work, especially the face–masks of the *Texas Chain Saw Massacre* films, are unmistakable in this scene. Once again, Hooper overturns the separateness

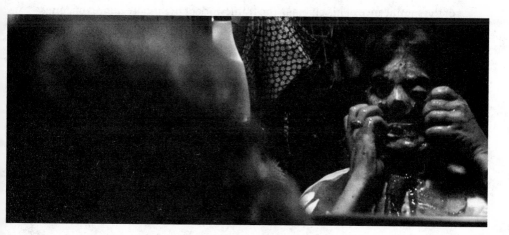

3.6 Flesh torn away from the face in *Poltergeist.*

of youth and aging with a horrific image that exposes aging's apparent otherness as a matter of becoming, of transformation always taking place.

In fact, this image in *Poltergeist* is so shocking that it invites spectators to reorganize related chains of imagery in the film through its logic. Carol Anne becomes not simply the angelic visage of innocent youth but an eerily intimate companion of death: she hears and joins the voices of the ghosts through the static of the television set, acknowledges the death of her pet bird in a way that her parents cannot, and even lovingly embraces her decapitated doll (matter-of-factly sticking its head back on its neck when it rolls off). Tangina (Zelda Rubinstein), the psychic medium committed to helping the Freelings rescue Carol Anne, becomes uncanny through a mixture of signifiers of childhood (high, squeaky voice and diminutive stature) and signifiers of the dead (she can see and speak with the ghosts). When Carol Anne's mother Diane (JoBeth Williams) returns from the ghostly "other side" after retrieving her daughter, she is "reborn" in a gooey plasma that recalls the afterbirth accompanying a newborn baby. But Diane is also marked by a prominent new gray streak in her hair that simultaneously characterizes her "rebirth" as a form of aging. The corpses who appear to pop out of their caskets in the film's climactic sequence recall the horrific combinations of aged desiccation and youthful energy throughout Hooper's work, from *The Texas Chain Saw Massacre*'s babyish Grandpa to the walking shriveled of *Lifeforce.*

All of these images in *Poltergeist* remind us how Tobe Hooper's career testifies to his expertise in knowing what scares us. The prevalence of aging imagery in his films, masterfully modulated to surmount our defensive reflexes toward old age and to erupt in our nightmare zone, offers an alternative account of the significance of his cinema. The framework of nightmare *images* of aging, rather than of perfectly wrought *films*, allows the power of these images to stand in their own right as one of Hooper's major cinematic achievements.[16] These images also stand as powerful emblems of horror's transformative otherness, crystallizing how much value Hooper's work offers for age studies, horror studies, and the nightmare territory shared between them.

CHAPTER 4

THE TRAUMA OF ECONOMIC OTHERNESS

Horror in George A. Romero's *Martin*

George A. Romero placed an indelible stamp on the horror genre's relation to historical trauma when he directed his debut feature, *Night of the Living Dead* (1968). Romero's pioneering horror film, as I mentioned in this book's introduction, is now widely considered not only one of the most important independent American films ever produced but also a savage commentary on the trauma of the Vietnam War and the civil rights struggle.[1] War, riots, assassinations—all are examples of what the trauma studies theorist Cathy Caruth calls "collective trauma," which is characterized by distinct and often sudden, violent, publicly recognized mass events. *Night of the Living Dead* certainly captures collective trauma through its images of horror that evoke warfare, urban unrest, and lynchings. But a broader look at Romero's career beyond *Night of the Living Dead* and its five sequels, with an emphasis on his underrated psychological vampire film *Martin* (1978) in particular, also reveals a remarkable talent for articulating what Caruth calls "individual trauma"—slower, quieter, more private, and less historically recognized forms of trauma, such as gradual economic and social disintegration or systemic, institutionalized injustice.[2] This chapter analyzes how Romero translates individual trauma (slow, process based, unrecognized) into collective trauma (sudden, event based, recognized) through a vocabulary of horror.

In *Martin*, the gradual economic and social decline of Braddock, Pennsylvania, in the wake of its collapsing steel industry is central to the film's horror. The young, mentally ill Martin (played with haunting sensitivity by John Amplas), who believes himself to be a vampire, arrives in Braddock to find a community already vampirized economically. This form of social catastrophe is closer to Caruth's definition of individual (process-oriented) trauma than to collective (event-oriented) trauma, so it fits less easily with previous studies of trauma and the horror film that have tended to focus on events rather than on processes.[3] Romero's approach in *Martin* demonstrates a counterintuitive relation between the horror film and trauma: one might suppose that a genre often perceived as being built on shock and spectacle would not be well suited to engage the subtleties of individual trauma. *Martin* teaches us just the opposite, though, and alerts us to the significant but underrecognized role that individual trauma plays in Romero's cinema. Next to *Martin*, the quiet humiliations of aging in his "lost" film *The Amusement Park* (1973), the struggle for agency when living with a physical disability in *Monkey Shines* (1988), and the desolation of a marriage that cannot acknowledge female subjectivity in *Season of the Witch* (1973) start to look more representative than anomalous. By remapping Romero's work in this way through a close analysis of *Martin*, this chapter recasts our assumptions about the horror film's relation to collective and individual trauma, a recasting that permits further exploration of horror's transformative otherness. If we recognize the trauma at the heart of Romero's film as a matter of economic otherness presented initially as individual trauma (the story of Martin the person) but then translated over time into collective trauma (the story of Braddock the community), then what appears at first as Martin's othering acts of horrific vampirism gradually become transformed as well. They become shocking encounters with an individual suspended between other and self that invite us to incorporate the collective, economically vampirized community of Braddock as our own.

Despite Robin Wood's admiration for many of Romero's films, Romero does not figure nearly as centrally in "An Introduction to the American Horror Film" (1979) as the positively portrayed Tobe Hooper (chapters 1 and 3) and the negatively portrayed David Cronenberg (chapter 5). But by 1980 Wood apologizes for his relative inattention to Romero as "an absence so glaring as to appear a major critical aberration." He corrects himself by proclaiming, "Romero has already produced a rich, coherent, and substantial oeuvre, an achievement matched, in the '70s horror genre, only by Larry Cohen." Wood is particularly impressed by the social dimensions of Romero's work in *Night of the Living Dead*, *Dawn of the Dead* (1979), and *The Crazies* (1973). He also notes the significant achievements of *Season of the Witch* and *Martin* but brackets them separately from Romero's social horror films due to their emphasis on "individual protagonists" rather than on socially based "events."[4] Wood's decision to divide Romero's "social" horror films from his "individual" horror films mirrors precisely those assumptions within trauma studies that draw sharp distinctions between individual trauma and collective trauma. By turning to economic otherness in *Martin*, this chapter illuminates how Romero unites rather than divides individual trauma and collective trauma alongside individual horror and social horror. Romero activates the transformative otherness of horror to speak a new language of trauma, between and across the individual and the collective.

The language of trauma spoken by *Martin* is not the one we might expect from the horror film, with its traditional investments in fantastic spectacle. It is instead a language that combines horror's fantastic vocabulary and documentary's realist vocabulary in ways that undermine our attempts to distinguish between the two modes. When Romero insists on interweaving the fantastic and the real along the axis of individual and collective trauma, he reveals how horror can speak about trauma in a manner that demands a new kind of vision from its viewers. This vision, rooted in a commitment to transformative otherness, urges us to see catastrophe where we are accustomed to seeing only the mundane and collective trauma where we routinely see only individual trauma. In *Martin*'s version of horror, the economic decline of Braddock is paired with trauma figuratively connected to the Vietnam War and immigration. The film moves between these coordinates to transform the distinctions that divide the fantastic from the real as well as the individual from the collective.

Documentary and Fantastic Impulses

Romero was fond of referring to *Martin* as his personal favorite among all of his films. I think one of the reasons for this is that *Martin*, with stunning power and precision, balances the two creative drives that characterize all of Romero's work: the documentary impulse and the fantastic impulse. These drives express themselves in all of his films to one degree or another, but it is in *Martin* that they harmonize most perfectly and are unmasked not as competing opponents but as interdependent partners.[5] When Romero's vision is at its sharpest, he shows us how documentary ways of seeing and fantastic ways of seeing can combine to reveal more truth about the world around us than either one on its own can.

So is *Martin* a vampire movie? Yes, but not just because Martin kills his victims and drinks their blood. After all, he has no fangs, no coffin, no fear of mirrors, garlic, or crucifixes. This is a vampire film in a deeper, more disturbing, and more social sense, where it is Martin's surroundings that have been bled dry of economic and emotional vitality. When he arrives from Indianapolis to live with his elderly cousin Cuda (Lincoln Maazel) in Braddock, a decaying Rust Belt town outside of Pittsburgh, he finds himself in a community that has already largely disintegrated. Something profoundly traumatic has transpired here, something that eludes words. The collapse of Braddock's steel industry is *Martin*'s implicit animating force rather than its explicit narrative engine, but the facts are that Romero places Braddock firmly at the center of his film and that by the 1970s Braddock had already begun a long, slow economic decline that would eventually result in the town losing 90 percent of its population.[6] In *Martin*, the collapse of the steel industry has wreaked havoc far beyond economic suffering alone—there is distrust between the older and younger generations, alienation between couples, and desperation among the poor echoed by listless depression among the rich.

Romero captures all of this with a documentarian's expert eye and ear, so much so that Braddock emerges as a character every bit as vivid as the unforgettable Martin. In fact, Martin, in his own strange and sick way, may be closer to representing the "new blood" Braddock needs to revive itself than the vampire out to drain life from the town. Although Cuda curses Martin as "Nosferatu" and maintains that Martin has inherited the "family shame" from "the old country" in an unnamed region of eastern Europe, Martin is decidedly modern in both his outlook and his methods. He dismisses vampire lore as superstitious "magic," substitutes hypodermic needles for fangs, masters the use of electronic technologies (the automatic garage-door opener, the telephone), and even dabbles quite successfully in mass-media exposure (his confessional calls to a late-night talk-radio show). What's more, Martin works hard—not just as a delivery boy for Cuda's butcher shop and a handyman for Mrs. Santini (Elyane Nadeau) but as the closest thing to an amateur therapist that Braddock can muster. Martin speaks very little, but he *listens* carefully and empathically: to his cousin Christina (Christine Forrest) about her struggles with her unreliable boyfriend, Arthur (Tom Savini), and undercutting grandfather, Cuda; to the lonely housewife Mrs. Santini, who becomes Martin's lover; even to Cuda, whom he hears out to the best of his ability (going so far as to sit through most of an exorcism ritual that Cuda subjects him to) and tries to educate by showing him how he, Martin, is not the Old World vampire Cuda imagines him to be.

Much of *Martin*'s most fantastic imagery is contained within a form then commonly associated with documentary realism and its connotations of reportage-oriented objectivity: black-and-white film.[7] *Martin* is a color film but switches to black-and-white for sequences that function as fantasy or memory flashpoints from Martin's subjective perspective. Much of this black-and-white imagery could sit comfortably with scenes from classic horror films—the torchbearing townsfolk, the fair maiden, the stern priest. So when Romero merges the black-and-white look of documentary with the images of fantastic horror, he alerts us to how *Martin* continually challenges the distinctions we tend to draw between these two registers. Part of the shock of Martin's death at the end of the film—Cuda hammers a stake through his heart as punishment for a murder Martin did not commit—is that what is supposed to be an image from a classic horror film has now erupted in the real world of Braddock. Romero presents this brutal killing in full color, with no recourse to black-and-white. The result is devastating on several levels: not only has Martin's subjectivity been snuffed out, but our ability to separate the "fantastic" from the "real" has also been destroyed as thoroughly as Martin's body.

The disintegration of distinctions between the fantastic and the real performed in *Martin* has important implications for our understanding of the relationship between individual and collective trauma. When Romero depicts the character of Martin through both horror genre imagery (in subjective yet documentary-coded black-and-white) and documentary realist iconography (in objective yet genre-coded color), he frustrates our desire to explain Martin as purely the product of either fantasy or reality. In this sense, Romero demonstrates an instinctive awareness of horror's connection to ethnographic surrealism (described in chapter 2). What Romero suggests is that we need the fantastic to fully comprehend the real, just as we need the real to fully grasp the fantastic. This blind spot in our ways of seeing corresponds to our difficulty in recognizing the presence and impact of individual trauma when our conventional yardstick is collective trauma. If Martin is not quite a fantastic vampire, then perhaps Braddock becomes much more of a real community for having been metaphorically vampirized of its economic vitality. In other words, the difficulty of imagining and visualizing the slow process of traumatic economic decline in Braddock is remedied through the addition of Martin with his potent mix of fantastic and real characteristics. Martin constantly reminds us how we are always missing something when we fall back on our habits of separating individual trauma from collective trauma. Images such as a dilapidated church left scarred by an unseen fire and the strained tone of an intergenerational conversation that questions whether Braddock has a livable future may not qualify as conventional markers of collective trauma, but they are certainly signs of individual trauma that matter. Romero wants us to see and feel that connection, to access the significance of individual trauma despite the absence of collective trauma's often authenticating imprint.

How *Martin* Begins

The opening sequence of *Martin* confronts us immediately with both the complexity and horror embedded in Romero's mission to make individual trauma recognizable for his audience. While boarding a train from Indianapolis bound for Pittsburgh, Martin glimpses his next victim: a beautiful woman dressed fashionably in an Annie Hall–style suit, separate from the rest of the passengers in both her look and her manner. She is standoffish, setting herself apart from the conductor and the passengers in their friendly greetings of each other. She makes it clear to the conductor that she is traveling alone in her private sleeper car and does not want to be disturbed when the train arrives in

Pittsburgh because she is destined for New York. She tips him as a way of cutting short his attempt at conversation with her about "the Big Apple." So this woman is marked from the outset by signs of things that Martin does not possess: wealth, upper-class sophistication, the demeanor of a kind of New Yorker who does not believe that Pittsburgh is worth waking up for.

Martin is marked in a completely different way. He is a young, awkward, quiet loner, carrying an army-style knapsack that contains what is revealed to be drug paraphernalia: needles, vials, razor blades. When he locks himself in the train's public bathroom and prepares a needle for injection (fig. 4.1), we are already beginning to form a profile of him: a drug addict, probably a damaged Vietnam veteran who never quite made it back from the war, likely dangerous.[8] This impression is solidified when Martin picks the lock to the woman's sleeper car and has a hallucinatory vision of what he will find behind the door that is akin to a post–traumatic stress disorder (PTSD) flashback in its sudden disjunctiveness (filmed in black-and-white): the woman dressed in sexy negligee, holding her arms out to him invitingly. What he discovers instead is that the woman is in her bathroom flushing the toilet, her face covered in an unappealing mud mask. He injects her with the needle and wrestles with her, trying to calm her when she fights back and calls him, quite appropriately, a "freak rapist asshole." He attempts to reassure her that he only wants her to sleep, that he is "always very careful with the needles." Once she becomes unresponsive, he

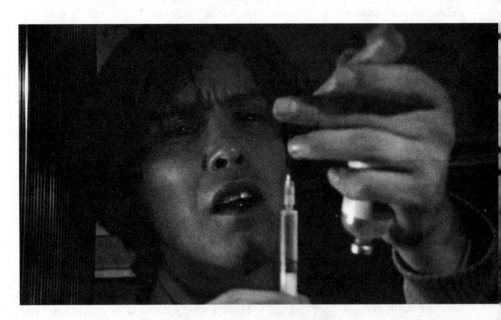

4.1 Martin (John Amplas) with syringe in *Martin*. © 1978 New Amsterdam Entertainment. All Rights Reserved. Image courtesy of Richard P. Rubinstein.

strips her and himself, arranges their bodies in an embrace, slits her wrist with a razor blade, and drinks the blood that spurts out.

So our initial impressions of Martin as a traumatized, drug-addicted Vietnam veteran, complete with hallucinatory visions and a propensity for sexual and murderous violence, shifts with this revelation of his vampiric nature. The drugs are not for him, they are for her; they replace the Hollywood vampire's seductive stare. The razor blade doubles for the Hollywood vampire's fangs and serves after the fact as evidence of the woman's apparent suicide (a scene that Martin carefully stages after the murder to cover his tracks). And Martin's hallucinatory vision, as we discover through later examples, is not a post-traumatic combat symptom but a subjective sense of history and/or fantasy regarding his life as a vampire.

When Romero mixes these signals surrounding our understanding of Martin—PTSD-suffering Vietnam veteran on the one hand, bloodsucking vampire on the other—he short-circuits our habits of perception on two levels. First, he activates but then refuses our desire to stereotype Martin in the registers of either realism (Vietnam veteran) or fantasy (vampire). Second, he visualizes the trauma of PTSD and rape in ways that are so vividly matter-of-fact, so viscerally horrifying that he creates a powerful cinematic argument for what was then a matter of controversy in the professional psychological community: the very existence of PTSD as a diagnosable disorder. The inclusion of PTSD in the American Psychological Association's *Diagnostic and Statistical Manual of Mental Disorders* in 1980 was due largely to a belated recognition of the painful experience of Vietnam veterans. In other words, the professional acceptance of PTSD as a diagnosis marks an important moment in the transformation of the Vietnam War from a buried, private, individual trauma to a recognized, public, collective trauma. Even today, rape still struggles to be understood as traumatic in ways beyond the personal and individual, as the recent #MeToo movement testifies. In the opening sequence of *Martin*, the Vietnam War and rape come together through shocking visuals that defy the viewer to dismiss these experiences as insufficiently traumatic. We are robbed of our habits of wishing away such disturbing images through dismissive rationalizations such as "that's just the actions of a crazy Vietnam vet" or "that's just the actions of an imaginary Count Dracula" or even "that's just the risk a woman runs when traveling alone." The real and the imaginary instead collide in ways that invite us to redraw the boundaries between individual trauma and collective trauma.

Romero extends this redrawing of boundaries in the sequence that follows the opening on the train. Once Martin arrives in Pittsburgh, he is picked up by a stern new guardian, his elderly cousin Cuda. Dressed in an imposingly formal all-white suit and issuing terse commands in thickly accented English that instantly conveys his distaste for and distrust of Martin, Cuda manages to make Martin seem more like a vulnerable child than a predatory threat. It is as if Martin shrinks in the presence of Cuda. But it is not just Cuda alone who enacts this shrinkage of Martin. It is also Martin's exposure to the wide outside world after being seen mostly in the confined quarters of the train. At first, this world is represented by Pittsburgh, with its tall, massive downtown buildings that turn Martin into a tiny figure by comparison, made smaller by Cuda distancing himself deliberately from him as he walks ahead of him, speaking to him only rarely, and even crossing himself at the sight of Martin (fig. 4.2). Cuda tells Martin they must board another train, this one headed to the town of Braddock just outside of Pittsburgh. This second short train ride effectively undoes the dread we experienced in the film's opening train sequence as Martin drags his luggage inelegantly, nearly misses the train after stopping in the public bathroom, and sits silently next to the cigar-smoking Cuda as if he were a child in need of supervision. Martin the predator who speaks confidently to his prey during his attack has become Martin the child who can only observe silently and helplessly.

What Martin observes when he arrives in Braddock is primarily emptiness, subtle but powerful signs of the town's depopulated decline. The streets lack people despite the sunny daytime weather, barking dogs run loose without owners, and the only functioning business seems to be a junkyard where the

4.2 Martin shrinks in the presence of Cuda (Lincoln Maazel) in *Martin*. © 1978 New Amsterdam Entertainment. All Rights Reserved. Image courtesy of Richard P. Rubinstein.

abandoned hulks of cars are compacted. Later, Christina's boyfriend, Arthur, complains to Cuda that he cannot find work as a mechanic in Braddock, underlining the initial impression that this is a town whose emptiness makes it more economically viable to dispose of cars as garbage rather than to repair them for active use. Even Cuda's neatly kept white Victorian house is empty. His granddaughter, Christina, who lives with him, is not at home. What fills the house instead is evidence of the superstitions that Cuda holds onto as weapons against Martin's vampirism: crucifixes, garlic, mirrors. When Cuda addresses Martin as "Nosferatu," it triggers Martin's second series of black-and-white visions. They depict a younger-looking Martin subject to the religious rites of priests meant to cast out the vampire, while Martin retorts, "There isn't any magic; it's just a sickness." Back in the color-film reality of Braddock, Martin repeats similar gestures with Cuda amid similar objects, including a Virgin Mary statue. Martin demonstrates to Cuda that he has no fear of crucifixes, no allergy to garlic, and no invisibility in the mirror. When Martin finally speaks to a somewhat shaken Cuda, he insists that he is not Nosferatu at all, just Cuda's cousin Martin.

One significant detail in Martin's black-and-white vision that appears to have no direct analogue in the color reality of Braddock consists of a hammer and a wooden stake with which one of the priests threatens Martin. Since Romero cross-cuts so skillfully between the black-and-white images and the color images, emphasizing graphic matching and matches on action between shots, the presence of the hammer and stake in black-and-white but absence in color becomes an important way of distinguishing between the two registers. The combination of the hammer and stake is synonymous with an ancient, perhaps even mythological Old World milieu more commonly associated with classic horror films, not with the contemporary American reality of the present. But by the end of the film, of course, the hammer and stake will indeed materialize in Braddock and facilitate Cuda's destruction of Martin. So Romero, from the very opening scenes of *Martin*, has already framed a relationship between the black-and-white footage and the color footage in his film that resists categorizations of subjective and objective, imaginary and real, even past and present. In short, Romero posits these categorizations in the register of transformative otherness, where the distinctions between these apparently opposed terms shift as constantly as those between self and other.

A Vampire Documentarian

One result of Romero's framing of his film in this way is that he asks his audience to occupy a vampire documentarian's point of view on Braddock. Martin, after all, is like us: he is the stranger in the strange land of Braddock, trying to comprehend an alien environment where he must observe carefully to make sense of his new surroundings. The oxymoronic concept of a vampire documentarian becomes less puzzling when we see how carefully Romero positions us to experience Braddock in ways that are not simply the defamiliarizing perceptions of a vampire alone or of a documentarian alone but of the two together simultaneously. The film's opening scenes have established our horror of Martin and our fear of his actions, but they have also aligned us with Martin's illness, vulnerability, and oppression. We know him better than Cuda or any of the other characters we will encounter in Braddock, and we will ultimately trust his perceptions more than theirs because he, like us, is a stranger here.

Just as Romero evokes Martin as a figurative Vietnam veteran (but not a literal one), so too does Martin's status as a stranger in Braddock present him as a figurative immigrant (but not a literal one). Immigration forms a bedrock layer of Braddock's history and a key to understanding its economic decline as traumatic. One of the landmarks of immigrant literature in the United States, Thomas Bell's *Out of This Furnace* (1941), is set in Braddock. Bell's semiautobiographical novel offers a number of significant contexts for *Martin*, not least of which are the traumatic aspects buried within the immigration experience that resurface when the American Dream turns sour. Bell chronicles a wave of immigration to Braddock from "the old country" earlier than the one with which Cuda came—for Bell, it is the Slovaks, beginning in the 1880s and continuing into the 1940s—but the structure is strikingly similar. *Out of This Furnace* spans three generations, just as *Martin* does (Cuda's generation, the generation of Martin and Christina's absent parents, and then the generation of Martin and Christina), with an emphasis on how the traumatic transition from Old World to New World crosses those generations. The originary trauma in *Out of This Furnace* comprises the conditions of immigration endured when the family leaves the European old country to work for American steel manufacturers in Braddock. Rather than highlighting the conventional narrative of immigration to America as the path to prosperity, Bell focuses on how the Slovaks suffered by being "exploited, ridiculed, and oppressed." The Slovak immigrants in *Out of This Furnace*, disparaged with the epithet "Hunkies," were looked down upon in their new country, despite how "the Slovaks with their blood and lives helped to build America."[9]

The vampiric bloodletting of *Martin* forms a bridge to the bloody toil of immigrant labor and its traumatic legacy in *Out of This Furnace*. Indeed, Franco Moretti has argued that Bram Stoker's *Dracula* (1897), the template for so many modern vampire stories, including *Martin*, revolves around issues of immigration, labor, and Old World versus New World tensions.[10] *Martin*'s black-and-white visions of "the old country" constantly remind us of how the past lives in the present and how Old World experiences and beliefs do not simply wash away with Americanization. This is especially true when the promises of Americanization turn out to ring hollow. If we perceive Martin as a figurative immigrant, then we can see how his figurative Americanization is incomplete. Not only does he have visions of the old country, but he also believes himself to be a vampire who is more than eighty years old. He is Americanized in the sense that he has left behind the "magic" that Cuda clings to concerning the old country's superstitious beliefs about how a vampire is supposed to act, but he still believes he is a vampire and seeks victims accordingly. In short, Martin is an embodied amalgam of unacknowledged trauma, of stories not told that shape Braddock as powerfully as anything we can see: the traumatic stories of immigration, the economic collapse of the steel mills, and the decline of the American Dream.

"A Protest Against Something Unacceptable"

Cathy Caruth, in conversation with the psychologist Arthur S. Blank Jr., an author of pioneering work on PTSD in Vietnam veterans, calls PTSD "a protest against something unacceptable."[11] Martin is a witness to Braddock's disintegration, and his traumatized and traumatizing vampirism can be seen as a protest against this disintegration. His vampirism, suspended between the "real" and the "unreal," tells the story of Braddock's decline in ways that make that story's trauma recognizable. Caruth claims that one important way in which individual trauma becomes collective is the telling of an apparently private story to the public. With the telling of this private story in a manner that highlights its public dimensions, our understanding of individual trauma shifts through "creating a collective public story that can be told and heard."[12] Blank offers a concrete example of this process when he explains how the PTSD of one Vietnam veteran went from clinically uncategorized to categorically recognized in 1980. A traumatized veteran whose illness was never properly diagnosed or treated as Vietnam-related PTSD committed suicide but was able to receive government compensation even several years after his death because his wife, working with Blank, was able to tell the story of his mental breakdown through the letters he sent home from Vietnam. His story, which Blank summarizes as describing "his mind falling apart under the impact of certain events," strikes Blank as evidence of how a private story (undiagnosed illness not officially linked to the collective trauma of the Vietnam War) becomes a public story (PTSD recognized officially as connected to the war).[13]

Of course, not every traumatized veteran has the benefit of detailed letters that can narrate his or her story after death in ways that turn private, individual trauma into collective, public trauma. But film offers an especially powerful means of transforming private stories into public stories. The inherently collective dimensions of film in terms of both its production and its reception suit extremely well the demands of converting individual trauma into collective trauma. In fact, high-profile war films such as *Coming Home* (Hal Ashby, 1978) and *The Deer Hunter* (Michael Cimino, 1978) had already thrust the private pain of Vietnam veterans into the public spotlight prior to 1980. *The Deer Hunter* in particular, with its western Pennsylvania setting, steel mills, and eastern European immigrant cultural milieu, is in some ways a secret sharer with *Martin*. But even though both films were released in the same year and contain some intriguing resemblances, *Martin* ultimately accomplishes what *The Deer Hunter* cannot. By paradoxically not referring explicitly to Vietnam at all, *Martin* reveals the systemic social complexity embedded within Vietnam trauma that eludes *The Deer Hunter*. Although *The Deer Hunter* goes to great lengths to deliver a "realistic" portrait of the Vietnam War that proves undeniably moving in its depictions of anguish on both the home front and the war front, it cannot escape the exclusivity of its realist investments. By making Vietnam so "real," *The Deer Hunter* also places Vietnam at a remove from the audience's concerns: as painful as this event might be, we know how to process it. It is "real" and can be filed safely under that label.

But what is *Martin*? Is it "real"? Is it fantasy? Is it a private story? A public one? Romero's insistence on confronting us with these questions but not providing immediately accessible answers enables us to channel *Martin*'s engagement with the wide spectrum of issues surrounding the Vietnam experience—including economic crisis and immigration histories—into translations of individual trauma as collective trauma. This work of translation occurs precisely because our conventional frameworks of "real" and "fantastic" are not available to us in our viewing of this film. As soon as we attempt to label Martin as a vampire or an immigrant or a Vietnam veteran, we must face a conundrum of interpretation that changes conventional otherness into transformative otherness. Unlike in our viewing of *The Deer Hunter*, we do not know how to process what *Martin* presents according to our routine habits of perception. We remain alive to the act of interpretation, so that we move beyond standard labels not only of Martin himself but of Braddock as a whole. Braddock cannot be just another depressed Rust Belt town that we label unthinkingly because we are now seeing it through the eyes of Martin, a vampire documentarian. The impossibility of the category "vampire documentarian" is exactly what keeps *Martin* open to Vietnam, immigration, and economic decline as intermixed elements in the story of Braddock. This story is offered to viewers at first through the lens of what appears to be individual trauma but becomes translated ultimately as collective trauma because Romero refuses to grant the story easy legibility at the level of individual trauma alone. What Romero insists upon when telling this story in this way is a reckoning with Martin, the individual as well as the film, as a matter of transformative otherness.

Martin as impossible individual—the vampire documentarian—becomes Martin as collective sign for the traumatic experience of Braddock. Romero tells this collective story of Braddock through Martin by making him not a native of the town but the relay between all of the residents there whom we come to know through his presence. For example, Mrs. Santini is a customer at Cuda's shop, but it is only through Martin's relationship with her that we are permitted to see and understand her depression and loneliness that eventually lead to her suicide. The same can be said for Christina. Even though she has lived with Cuda for quite some time, it is only through Martin that we witness her disappointment and desperation in her relationship with Arthur, whom she holds onto solely as a ticket out of Braddock. This is another way in which Martin comes to stand for Braddock—he stays, while Mrs. Santini (through suicide) and Christina (through moving) leave. It is striking that despite Cuda's insistent negativity toward him, Martin never attempts to flee Braddock. He even does his best to follow Cuda's rules about not taking victims from Braddock itself. The most elaborate sequence in the film depicting one of Martin's vampiric attacks, a home invasion gone awry when a woman's extramarital lover is unexpectedly present, takes place in Pittsburgh rather than in Braddock. So when Martin leaves Braddock, he always returns. While so many others abandon Braddock, contributing to its depopulated emptiness and economic decline, Martin remains.

How *Martin* Ends

Martin's alignment with Braddock, his ability to graft his individual trauma onto Braddock's collective trauma, becomes most heightened at the end of the film. Shortly before being murdered by Cuda, Martin joins Braddock's residents outdoors on a beautiful sunny day for a town parade. Earlier in the film, Martin would complain about how bright sunlight bothers his eyes, but here he walks freely without sunglasses as a marching band passes by in a celebratory parade (fig. 4.3). He clearly enjoys the sound of the music and the rhythm of the marchers, even smiling and falling in alongside them as they make their way through Braddock's streets. This is one of the most hopeful moments in the film, especially since it comes on the heels of Martin's devastating discovery of his lover Mrs. Santini's dead body. We learn through Martin's conversation with the talk-radio host, with whom he confides on the air, calling himself "the Count," that he has grown more self-aware and perhaps even more empathetic toward others in the wake of Mrs. Santini's suicide. Quite unlike the omnipotent vampires of the movies, Martin speaks of his powerlessness to control Mrs. Santini's actions. "In real life, you can't get people to do what you want them to do," he explains.

Martin's apparent surrender of his illusions of control over others marks a significant departure from the fantasies that have animated all of his vampiric attacks, where the drugs he administers to his victims allow him to bend them

4.3 Martin joins Braddock's town parade in *Martin*. © 1978 New Amsterdam Entertainment. All Rights Reserved. Image courtesy of Richard P. Rubinstein.

quite literally to his will. His retreat from this desire to master others frees him to be with others in a different way. This is what we see when he joins the Braddock parade—he becomes part of the town, his individuality now merged with Braddock's collectivity. For a fleeting moment, he belongs. And in this moment of belonging, Martin's story and Braddock's story meld, converting the individual trauma expressed through vampirism into the collective trauma encompassing the Vietnam War, economic decline, and immigration.

This is why Martin's death, which occurs with shocking suddenness immediately after the parade sequence, registers as such a deep loss. Cuda awakens Martin, asleep in his bedroom, by telling him he has heard about the death of Mrs. Santini. Cuda refuses to believe she committed suicide; he is convinced Martin killed her. "I warned you, Martin. Nobody in the town," says Cuda. "Your soul is damned." Cuda then hammers a stake into Martin's heart, the blood spewing out of his body and onto Cuda's clothes.

Romero then pairs two remarkable shots that mirror each other in equal but opposite ways to conjoin the individual, literal death of Martin with the collective, social death of Braddock. First, the camera zooms out slowly from Martin's lifeless face, streaked with blood, to reveal the full horror embodied by the stake implanted in his chest (fig. 4.4). This is real death in all of its ghastly materiality, not a bloodless fantasy scene from a black-and-white Hollywood vampire movie or the supernatural dematerialization of the vampire as the

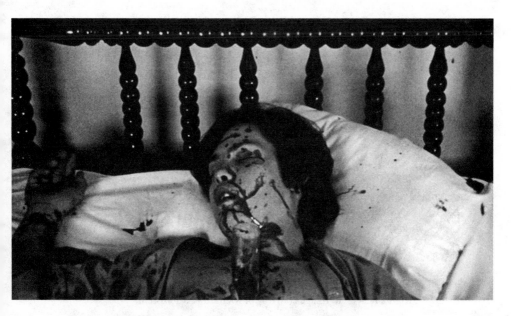

4.4 The first view of Martin's death in *Martin*. © 1978 New Amsterdam Entertainment. All Rights Reserved. Image courtesy of Richard P. Rubinstein.

sun rises in F. W. Murnau's *Nosferatu* (1922). After a cut, the camera zooms in slowly from outside toward the frontal exterior of Cuda's house, where we know a horrific murder has just taken place—and yet the house betrays no signs of disorder, even as the camera draws closer and closer to it (fig. 4.5).

These two shots, united by the formal similarity of slow zooms but differentiated by camera movement outward that discloses death (first shot) and then camera movement inward that conceals death (second shot), crystallize *Martin*'s aesthetics of trauma. We see Martin's individual trauma, captured so horrifically in the image of his body's destruction. We cannot see Braddock's collective trauma, hidden behind the faceless exterior of Cuda's house. But since Martin has become part of Braddock, with his story of individual trauma now thoroughly imbricated with Braddock's collective trauma, we do see Braddock translated through Martin; the two trauma narratives become one. Romero establishes this union not only thematically but also cinematically. The spectatorship Romero invites is summarized in these two paired zooms: to see presence where only absence appears, to see the collective where we see only the individual, to see trauma where we see only the everyday.

The sequence continues over the film's end credits, showing us Cuda sprinkling seeds over a patch of newly dug soil in his backyard. As we realize that this is Martin's unmarked grave, the soundtrack reverberates with a cacophony of overlapping radio voices that repeat the question, "What happened to

4.5 The second view of Martin's death in *Martin*. © 1978 New Amsterdam Entertainment. All Rights Reserved. Image courtesy of Richard P. Rubinstein.

the Count?" While Cuda kisses a small white crucifix and buries it in the earth that he has just seeded, the chaotic din of voices quiets down to just one. It is a gentle, hesitant male voice, not Martin's but also not unlike Martin's. The voice says, "I think I know where the Count is. I have a friend who I think is the Count." Fade to black.

Martin is dead, the film is over, and yet Martin lives on. He has been incorporated as a voice from Braddock, a figure lodged within the town's imagination as well as in our own. His story lives as a trauma narrative that enables us to see Braddock's story beyond the clichés and instead in the register of horror's transformative otherness. If "What happened to the Count?" is the spoken question that Romero leaves us with, then its unspoken corollary is "What happened to Braddock?" The experience of watching *Martin* teaches us how indivisible these questions really are and how answering them requires that our habits of perception regarding the documentary and the fantastic, the individual and the collective, the traumatic and the everyday must not remain neatly separated. They must contaminate each other, disturb each other, even contradict each other for us to see the horror of economic otherness.

Once we understand *Martin* in this way, we can begin to recognize the full dimensions of the film's genesis and afterlife. Romero's commitment to blurring the borders between documentary realism and fantastic horror, right down to alternating between color and black-and-white film, recalls the work of one of Romero's favorite directors: Michael Powell and his film *Peeping Tom* (1960) in particular. Powell spoke of his own shocking horror film as "a very tender film,"[14] and I think the same could be said of the equally shocking *Martin*. Much of this tenderness comes from the fact, apparent in just about every frame, that *Martin* is a film made by a community about the community. Nearly everyone involved with the production, filmed on a shoestring with a tiny crew on location in Braddock and Pittsburgh, does double and triple duty: special-effects maestro Tom Savini also plays Arthur and performs stunts; cinematographer Michael Gornick provides the voice of the radio talk-show host; sound technician Tony Buba (a director of important documentaries about Braddock) has a small acting role, helped to scout locations, and granted access to his mother's home to play the crucial role of Cuda's house; producer Richard P. Rubinstein appears as the husband of one of Martin's victims; and Romero not only writes, directs, and edits but also plays a young priest with a taste for good wine and an affection for *The Exorcist* (William Friedkin, 1973).

In short, *Martin* is no work for hire about some faceless place. It is a labor of love that stands as an invaluable portrait of Braddock alongside the documentaries of Tony Buba (especially his seminal film *Lightning Over Braddock* [1988], in which Romero makes a brief appearance as himself) and the photography of LaToya Ruby Frazier, who brilliantly brings to life an African American Braddock detectable only at the edges of Romero's vision in the film.[15] It is worth noting that in *Martin*'s pivotal town-parade sequence, described earlier, many of the musicians in the marching band as well as most of the onlookers watching the parade are African American. These images hint at yet another layer in the story of Braddock that Romero leaves largely unexplored in *Martin* but that will be taken up years later by Frazier. What Frazier chronicles so movingly in her work, drawn from her own experiences growing up in Braddock, is the African American specificity of Braddock's collective trauma, that trauma's connections to race alongside other forms of economic and social pain.[16] Even if *Martin* does not pursue this story, it certainly opens the door to the story's telling.[17] Indeed, the film still has many stories to tell. Not least is the story of how Romero's cinematic project, too often simplified as a series of zombie films famed for their spectacular displays of graphic gore, encompasses the translation of individual trauma into collective trauma as well as the transformations between personal and social otherness.

CHAPTER 5

THERAPEUTIC DISINTEGRATION

Jewish Otherness in the Cinema of David Cronenberg

O nce upon a time, director David Cronenberg exploded heads. Literally. His film *Scanners* (1981) features an encounter between two telepaths that results in one's skull bursting apart as if detonated by a grenade. But in the many years since *Scanners*, Cronenberg's cinema has moved from horror and science fiction into art films and highbrow literary adaptations. He no longer explodes heads. Or does he? And how does the valence of this question change when we consider alongside it a dimension of Cronenberg's work that has nearly escaped critical commentary altogether: its Jewishness?[1]

This chapter begins by examining *Scanners* alongside his Hollywood satire *Maps to the Stars* (2014) to argue that we should resist the impulse to which many critics succumb when faced with Cronenberg's bewilderingly heterogeneous body of work, which now spans five decades: dividing his career into distinct periods, usually separated by genre labels.[2] We instead need to recognize the formal and thematic discourse that has characterized his cinema from the beginnings to the present: the need for a therapy that works alongside the impossibility of ever fulfilling that need. Whether within the films as narrative and audiovisual structures or across the films as a continuing dialogue with his audience as his work metamorphoses, Cronenberg's cinema constantly reaches toward therapy as a solution to the schisms that shatter ties between mind and body but then ultimately disintegrates the possibility that therapy can heal such schisms. But the cycle of activating and then disintegrating the therapeutic impulse across roughly fifty years of films and shifting generic forms is an illumination of how we tend to imagine therapy as a bridge between the personal and the social, the brain and the flesh, the self and the other. Cronenberg, in the spirit of transformative otherness, reimagines therapy's bridge between self and other as something closer to a telepod, as in his film *The Fly* (1986): a mechanism for metamorphosis, for the struggles of indivisible and ongoing transformation rather than the solutions that maintain divisions safely separating self from other. We still have much to learn about and from Cronenbergian therapy. In the second half of this chapter, I argue that a particularly vital context for Cronenbergian therapy is Jewish-inflected philosophical thought, with its long history of contemplating otherness through the painful lens of anti-Semitism.

Therapy connotes the treatment of a physical or mental illness, a cure for some form of sickness. I am choosing the term *therapy* here instead of *psychotherapy* not because psychotherapeutic models do not matter to Cronenberg—on the contrary, his work is littered with implicit and explicit references to psychotherapy, including the historical drama *A Dangerous Method* (2011), which deals with Freud and Jung directly and will constitute this chapter's final case study—but rather because I want to highlight how much Cronenberg's conception of therapy resists traditional distinctions between psychotherapy and physical therapy. In Cronenbergian therapy, the "talking heads" conventionally associated with psychotherapy become the "exploding heads" or "imploding bodies" of a newly integrated and disintegrated body–mind. For example, the psychotherapist in *The Brood* (1979) winds up killed by a brood of "children" who are physical manifestations of the rage he has unleashed psychologically in a patient. Cronenberg calls this form of therapy "psychoplasmics," highlighting in its very name the slippage between psychotherapy and physical therapy that is then enacted cinematically as the roles of therapist and patient transform. Lodged within Cronenbergian therapy is a powerful critique of traditional psychological divisions not only between body and mind but also between self and other. Cronenbergian therapy insists on transformative otherness, where self and other are constantly metamorphosing, rather than on discrete roles that cleanly separate self from other and analyst from analysand even when processes such as transference and countertransference are acknowledged.

Before we turn to specific examples of Cronenbergian therapy, it is important to contextualize what I am calling its transformative otherness within the larger account of the horror film offered by this book as a whole. Since my own concept of horror's transformative otherness stems from a break with Robin Wood's influential definition of the horror film, and since Wood's criticism itself depends heavily on a negative assessment of Cronenberg as the director of "reactionary" horror films, a brief discussion of Wood on Cronenberg is required. Wood's "An Introduction to the American Horror Film" (1979) concludes with a section entitled "The Reactionary Wing," where politically regressive trends in the horror film come under scrutiny and are contrasted to the politically progressive trends characterized by the work of directors such as Tobe Hooper (see chapter 3) and George A. Romero (see chapter 4). For Wood, the horror film's chief reactionary is Cronenberg.

Progressive horror, according to Wood, channels Freud's return of the repressed in productively critical ways. What is repressed by social normality, namely all those manifestations of otherness that do not fit dominant bourgeois ideology's conventional norms, must be dealt with through annihilation or assimilation. Annihilation of the other entails projecting the other outward, from within the self to outside the self, in order to disown and hate it. Assimilation of the other entails converting the other into a replica of the self, with all of the other's threatening difference safely neutered. For Wood, progressive horror films resist these strategies of annihilation or assimilation of the other by defying social normality's need to repress otherness and instead allowing the repressed other to return. If a horror film is progressive, it will represent this return of repressed otherness in positive ways, such as by portraying a sympathetic monster or at least (as in the case of Hooper and Romero) by generating a critical negativity "that is not recuperable into the dominant ideology, but constitutes (on the contrary) the recognition of that ideology's disintegration, its untenability, as all it has repressed explodes and blows it apart."[3]

For Wood, Cronenberg betrays horror's progressive negativity by substituting it with a reactionary "*total* negation," an "expression of unqualified horror at the idea of releasing what has been repressed." What Wood sees in Cronenberg's *Shivers* (1975), *Rabid* (1977), and *The Brood* is "the precise antithesis of the genre's progressive potential," an antithesis where the return of the repressed can be imagined only with disgust as a matter of "unremitting ugliness and crudity."[4] What Wood misses in Cronenberg, however, in addition to the director's Canadianness, is his investment in transformative otherness: his creation of a form of horror that conceptualizes not only the return of the repressed but also the very idea of therapy through a confrontational mode of spectatorship that refuses to honor those strict divisions between self and other on which Wood's categories of "progressive" and "reactionary" horror ultimately depend.[5]

To clarify this argument, let me begin by describing briefly two examples of Cronenbergian therapy, chosen from a multitude of possible examples that could include everything from his very first short film, *Transfer* (1966), to *The Brood* to *Spider* (2002) to *Cosmopolis* (2012) and beyond. By selecting *Scanners* and *Maps to the Stars*, though, both of them less obvious instantiations of Cronenbergian therapy, I am making an implicit claim about the widespread applicability of these observations throughout his oeuvre. This claim will receive more explicit attention when the chapter considers the Jewishness of Cronenberg's work as well as Cronenberg's most sustained exploration of therapy to date in *A Dangerous Method*.

Cronenbergian Therapy: *Scanners* and *Maps to the Stars*

In *Scanners*, the therapeutic situation is epitomized by a spectacular corporate scientific demonstration near the beginning of the film. The telepathic technology of scanning, produced in certain individuals when exposed to a particular drug before birth, is here presented as a possible investment opportunity for various corporations attending in the audience. The demonstration takes an unexpected turn when the subject who volunteers to be scanned turns out to be Darryl Revok (Michael Ironside), the powerful leader of a fascistlike group of scanners who want to use scanning to lord over the "normals" of the world. Revok turns the scanning demonstration around, becoming the scanner rather than the scanned.

The results are mind-blowing—and not just in the literal sense of legendary special-effects artist Dick Smith's prosthetic wizardry that results in a stunning slow-motion head explosion. What is also mind-blowing is the transformation of therapeutic hierarchies. The doctor or analyst role, played here by the corporate scanner, is upended by Revok in his role as patient or analysand. The corporate scanner begins as a figure of authority and expertise. In his instructions to Revok, he confidently wields the psychotherapeutic vocabulary of self-disclosure and requests that Revok think of something personal, which the corporate scanner will then use his scanning to detect and reveal. He does not even close his eyes, signaling that not much concentration will be necessary.

Naturally, the corporate scanner's dominant role collapses when faced with the challenge from Revok. In the process, scanning as a therapeutic technology—a force that can probe the personal recesses of someone else's mind and offer up what is hidden there for disclosure—folds in on itself and becomes a source of vulnerability rather than authority. Therapy's status as a clinically clean cerebral exchange is also inverted through its insistently embodied translation as a bloody mess (fig. 5.1). Literally blowing the mind of the man who thought he would figuratively blow the minds of his subject and his audience by demonstrating his scanning prowess encapsulates Cronenberg's simultaneous fascination and unease with the therapeutic model as well as his awareness of how closely the theater of therapy mirrors cinema's logics of display. In *Scanners*, the therapeutic theater bears an unmistakable resemblance to the movie theater—a construct that recurs often in Cronenberg's work and can be seen especially clearly in *The Brood, Dead Ringers* (1988), *M. Butterfly* (1993), and *Crash* (1996).

The cinematic nature of therapy and the therapeutic nature of cinema are also central to *Maps to the Stars*. The grand theatrical gestures of both Havana Segrand (Julianne Moore) and Dr. Stafford Weiss (John Cusack) in a scene near the midpoint of the film are partially accounted for by characterization, but not

5.1 A head explodes in *Scanners*.

entirely. Havana, an over-the-hill Hollywood actress, is desperate to play a part originated by her own more famous deceased mother—so desperate, in fact, that she begins to see disturbing visions of her mother as the young, beautiful actress she once was rather than the woman who sexually abused her and died in a fire years later. Her therapist, Stafford, is a celebrity psychologist and best-selling author who has his own skeletons in the closet. He is secretly married to his own sister, and their daughter, Agatha (Mia Wasikowska), was horribly burned when she set fire to their home after discovering the truth about her family's incest. In this scene, a therapy session that takes place at Stafford's luxurious home, the therapeutic method involves an unsettling and blackly comedic combination of glib, self-help psychotherapy and intensively sexualized massage therapy that Stafford administers to Havana (fig. 5.2). What Stafford learns from Havana during the session is that Agatha is back in Los Angeles after years away in a clinic from which Stafford hoped she would never return and that Havana has unwittingly hired her as her new personal assistant.

Of course, we are not surprised in this scene to see a vain, hallucinating actress and a hypocritical psychologist to the stars act as if they were perform-ing for a large audience rather than engaging in an intimate therapeutic dialogue—they rely on empty quips and clichéd expressions to make themselves look like expert entertainers, not vulnerable human beings. But what is more unnerving is how genuine the private, inner need for therapy really is on the part of both Havana and Stafford while they perform so flamboyantly and

5.2 A missed therapeutic encounter between Havana (Julianne Moore) and Stafford (John Cusack) in *Maps to the Stars*.

publicly within walls made up largely by transparent windows. Both of them are deeply haunted by similar demons—young women marked by fire—so the potential for a therapeutic interpersonal connection that runs both ways is dramatically foregrounded. Here, as in many instances of Cronenbergian therapy, the need for therapeutic connection is shared just as deeply by the analyst as by the analysand; they are bound in a potential relation of transformative otherness, of conjoined needs, rather than of a doctor–self outside and above a patient–other. The fact that neither Stafford nor Havana can ever really *see* each other in this scene—once the therapeutic massage begins, their eyes never meet despite the heavily sexualized contact between them—sharpens the painful sense of a missed encounter where therapy's dichotomous roles could have undergone transformation but do not. In the end, this is an abandoned opportunity for mutual recognition, a failed therapeutic moment.

The therapeutic situation fails in *Scanners* because the doctor/patient hierarchy proves to be an illusory one. The scanner is scanned, the cerebral becomes physical, the talking head becomes an exploding head. In *Maps to the Stars*, the therapeutic hierarchy is similarly challenged—it is Havana who comes closer to blowing Stafford's mind with her revelatory news about Agatha than vice versa—and a cerebral therapeutic process is again made profoundly physical, but this time more in sexual terms than in violent ones. In the movement between *Scanners* and *Maps to the Stars*, violence recedes, and sexuality comes forward, leaving more room for a heightened sense of interpersonal need in *Maps to the Stars* than in *Scanners*. *Maps to the Stars* features no literally exploding heads, although Agatha's later murder of Havana, where she savagely bludgeons the actress with one of her award statuettes, comes close. The failure of therapy in *Maps to the Stars* is not the spectacular failure of the exploding head in *Scanners* but the more quietly cutting failure of real interpersonal needs for mutual recognition raised but gone unmet.

Thinking through these two films together and these two scenes in particular allows us to sketch some preliminary ideas about the nature of Cronenbergian therapy. In Cronenbergian therapy, the need for interpersonal connection is as vivid and powerful as the impossibility of meeting that need—hence, the restless, often ferocious desire in Cronenbergian therapy to smash conventional therapeutic hierarchies of doctor and patient, to transgress therapeutic boundaries between the psychic and the physical, to make therapy a spectacularly public and cinematic spectacle rather than a private and personal dialogue. Despite all of these efforts to refigure and transform therapy, the irresistible force that is the desire for a therapy that works ultimately meets the immovable object that is therapy's inadequacy to fulfill such desires. The result is frustration, desolation, and often a tragic sense of loss, occasioning a stalemate captured with remarkable frequency as some form of suicide; examples of his feature films with explicitly suicidal acts include *Rabid*, *Videodrome* (1983), *The Dead Zone* (1983), *The Fly*, *Dead Ringers*, *M. Butterfly*, and *Crash*, while a more metaphorical "suicide of the soul" is present in *Eastern Promises* (2007) and *A Dangerous Method*.

Scanners offers an unusually hopeful version of the suicidal figuration as the protagonist Cameron Vale (Stephen Lack) allows his body to be destroyed by his evil brother, Revok, while he transfers his own mind into Revok's body. *Maps to the Stars* is more typically Cronenbergian: Agatha and her brother, Benjie (Evan Bird), deliberately overdose on pills as they enact a doomed wedding ceremony that echoes their parents' incestuous union. The film's final, unearthly high-angle crane shot might be a suggestion of spiritual transcendence, an ascension of the soul to the stars through a redemptive act of transgressive repetition. Or maybe it is just an incredulous joke about how hollow dreams of stardom plague these Hollywood-enslaved subjects even as they die.

Perhaps, in the end, it is both. I draw attention to this double-edged option for interpretation because even though the pain of Cronenbergian therapy is undeniable, there is also something in it that is darkly funny and poignant. The anguish of interpersonal needs gone unmet collides with the absurdity of the human condition—the striving for life that must exist in the face of the inevitable failure that is certain death. It makes sense that Cronenberg has often described himself as intrigued with existential philosophy and even referred to himself as a "card-carrying existentialist" during the promotion of his science-fiction mindbender *eXistenZ* in 1999.[6]

It is also increasingly clear that Cronenberg's existential bent also bears the unmistakable marks of a Jewish sensibility. In fact, the closest thing we may have to a programmatic Cronenberg film is his short *At the Suicide of the Last Jew in the World in the Last Cinema in the World* (2007), in which Cronenberg plays the title role. Then there are the shadows of the Holocaust that haunt the central therapeutic relationship in *The Dead Zone*, and there is the keen attention in *A Dangerous Method* to how Freud's embattled Jewishness and Jung's privileged Protestantism make for a tragic mismatch. Even Cronenberg's debut novel *Consumed* (2014) includes a Jewish Canadian doctor named Barry Roiphe who bears more than a passing resemblance to the director.

The Jewish Cronenberg

Despite the aforementioned references, the Jewishness of Cronenberg's work has never been at the forefront of critical discussion concerning his films. This is perhaps understandable, especially given Cronenberg's atheism and his accounts of growing up feeling quite separate from anything resembling a conventional Jewish identity. Born in Toronto in 1943 to middle-class Jewish Canadian parents who had drifted away from traditional Judaism much earlier in their lives, Cronenberg was not raised religiously. Yet he maintains that his parents, both of them artists, "invented their own version of what it is to be Jewish" and that if he is asked if he is Jewish, his answer is "yes."[7]

Cronenberg's conviction, reached at an early stage of his career, that he "would much more likely be put in jail for my art than for my Jewishness" seems to have been recalibrated in more recent years.[8] At the heart of *A Dangerous Method* is the perception that psychoanalysis is a Jewish science, just as *At the Suicide of the Last Jew in the World in the Last Cinema in the World* foregrounds the perception that the movie industry was invented by Jews. However incomplete or erroneous these perceptions might be (they are presented ambivalently within the films), their power as perceptions speaks to how what is alluring, dangerous, and fragile about therapy and film for Cronenberg is inextricably linked to Jewishness. I want to experiment with what it could mean to place Cronenberg's work in conversation with Jewish-inflected strands of philosophical thought. My aim is not to make Cronenberg or his films more Jewish than they actually are but to see what we can learn about Cronenbergian therapy and transformative otherness by pursuing an intellectual genealogy that we might call Jewish film theory.

One thinker who may help us unravel Cronenbergian therapy is the Lithuanian Jewish French existential and phenomenological philosopher Emmanuel Levinas (1906–1995). Levinas, an important figure in continental philosophy for many years, has recently begun to be explored in the context of film.[9] He is best known for his ethical reflections on the subject's responsibility to the other, a relationship he articulates most famously in *Totality and Infinity* (1961, translated into English in 1969). Levinas's meditations on self and other have a promising potential to illuminate the interpersonal tensions that structure Cronenbergian therapy, not just in terms of subject matter but also in terms of sensibility. This claim may at first seem somewhat unlikely because Cronenberg's strictly secular Jewishness would appear to conflict with Levinas's observant Judaism.[10] Yet both of them struggle with questions of the interpersonal and otherness through the lens of Jewishness—a lens that provides them with a dark wariness about the horrors human beings are capable of as well as with a fascination regarding the possibilities of untapped human potential.

A soldier in the French army during World War II, Levinas was captured and spent most of the war as a prisoner in Nazi labor camps. Almost everyone in his family perished in the Holocaust. The book he began writing while in captivity bears a distinctly Cronenbergian title: *Existence and Existents* (1947, translated into English in 1978). In it, he formulates the concept of the *there is*, a terrifying notion of being as absolute darkness that exists when everything else, including the acts of killing and dying and even the I itself, have disappeared. Levinas writes, "The rustling of the *there is* . . . is horror. We have noted the way it insinuates itself in the night, as an undetermined menace of space itself disengaged from its function as receptacle for objects, as a means of access to beings." Although Levinas recognizes the foundational importance of the *there is*, along with how it "transcends inwardness as well as exteriority," he does not surrender to it.[11] The rest of the book as well as the rest of his work painstakingly build outward from the *there is* by contemplating what it means for the I to be with another and to face another. This is no easily won accomplishment. For Levinas, the interpersonal is not a realm without risk but rather "the fearful face-to-face situation of a relationship without intermediary, without mediations," as self and other exist in absolute, even terrifying interdependence.[12]

To be truly face-to-face with another, in Levinas's notion of that concept, might be one way of describing the goal of Cronenbergian therapy as a matter of transformative otherness. The fact that Cronenberg approaches through the mediation of cinema what Levinas describes as an unmediated state points to how the cinematic medium may have the potential to foster rather than evade the most difficult feats of interpersonal connection through the workings of transformative otherness as acts of spectatorship. We may *need* cinema's potential for transformative otherness to activate a model of the interpersonal for us by means of spectatorial experience, to teach us what the interpersonal consists of and how to access it. But even if Levinas is fond of referring to his very idiosyncratic notion of ethics as "an optics,"[13] he is not receptive ultimately to film as an aesthetic means of furthering his philosophical project. To find another thinker who is, I would like to turn to a figure whose life's work was also shaped by Jewish thought but who placed film at its center: Siegfried Kracauer (1889–1966).

My turn from Levinas to Kracauer is motivated in part by the fact that they shared a foundational intellectual mentor in Franz Rosenzweig (1886–1929). Rosenzweig, along with Martin Buber (1878–1965), was at the center of a major renaissance in Jewish thinking that took place in Weimar Germany. Kracauer, like his colleagues and friends Walter Benjamin (1892–1940) and Theodor Adorno (1903–1969), was an observer and sometimes participant in this German Jewish cultural movement. When Rosenzweig founded an adult Jewish education center in Frankfurt, the Freies Jüdisches Lehrhaus, in 1920, Kracauer was among the German Jewish intellectuals who attended its sessions. Perhaps the most significant record of Kracauer's involvement with the Freies Jüdisches Lehrhaus is "The Bible in German" (1926), Kracauer's review of a new German translation of the Hebrew Bible by Rosenzweig and Buber. Kracauer's polemical review takes particular critical aim at Buber's philosophical concept of "I and Thou," the subject and title of an influential book published by Buber in 1922. For Kracauer, Buber's distinction between a "Thou-world" characterized by nonobjectifying human relations that partake of the sacred and an "It-world" characterized by objectifying human relations that remain profane cannot grasp "what is real in the visible external world."[14]

What is striking here is how Kracauer frames his critique of Buber's concept "I and Thou," which is even more central to Jewish philosophical thought than Levinas's later face-to-face ethics, in terms that anticipate Kracauer's own magnum opus, *Theory of Film: The Redemption of Physical Reality* (1960). And perhaps what is more striking still is how even the subtitle of Kracauer's book echoes Rosenzweig's own magnum opus, *The Star of Redemption* (1921). Even though Kracauer's critique of Buber and Rosenzweig's translation of the Hebrew Bible was harsh enough to spark a heated debate with Kracauer on one side and Buber and Rosenzweig on the other—a debate that severed Kracauer's relations with Buber—Kracauer's commitment to the truth of the profane, to reality as material reality, is actually more consonant with than against Rosenzweig's *Star of Redemption*.[15] For Rosenzweig, who had his own reservations about Buber's "I and Thou" that mirror Kracauer's to some degree, redemption is anchored to everyday life in the mundane here and now, not to a divine elsewhere beyond the everyday.[16] It is this peculiarly theological-materialist notion of redemption that finds its echoes in Kracauer's *Theory of Film*. Indeed, Miriam Bratu Hansen has noted that when it came time for Kracauer to offer a German-language translation of the title for *Theory of Film*, he resisted Rudolf Arnheim's suggestion that he trade the word *Erlösung* (redemption) for another, less theologically charged term. Kracauer wrote to Arnheim, "I still think '*Erlösung*' would not be bad, precisely because of its theological connotation."[17]

Hansen provides a lens through which to understand this theological-materialist dimension to Kracauer's thought, which becomes particularly important for *Theory of Film*. She argues that what she calls Kracauer's "modernist materialism," where the material world allows "a different constitution of the subject that manifest[s] itself in that new relationship with things, in particular things modern," is inseparable from Kracauer's "materialist philosophy of death."[18] Materialism and death come together for Kracauer via Jewish Gnosticism, particularly through the concept of "tikkun" (repair). Hansen thus describes Kracauer's sense of redemption as "the idea that the intellectual's task is to furnish an archive for the possibility, even if itself unrepresentable, of a utopian restoration of all things past and present."[19]

In other words, film's redemptive function for Kracauer is to reveal reality for what it is: a world where the thingness of objects and the dead stands on equal footing with the life of subjects and the living. Through film, our stubborn insistence on distinguishing subjects from objects, the living from the dead, the present from the past, and, indeed, the self from the other falls away, and the world of full physical reality reveals itself. As Kracauer writes near the end of *Theory of Film*, "Film renders visible what we did not, or perhaps even could not, see before its advent. It effectively assists us in discovering the material world with its psychophysical correspondences. We literally redeem this world from its dormant state, its state of virtual nonexistence, by endeavoring to experience it through the camera. And we are free to experience it because we are fragmentized." Earlier in the book, Kracauer builds this notion of the film spectator's fragmentation in this way: "With the moviegoer, the self as the mainspring of thoughts and decisions relinquishes its power of control."[20]

Kracauer's fragmentation and Cronenberg's imagination of therapy as a form of therapeutic disintegration, where the real need for therapy and the impossibility of therapy ever fulfilling that very need exist in constant tension, have much in common. Both believe that cinema has the potential to shatter our habits of perception, our routines of thinking and feeling. Both believe that horror and death play privileged roles in this shattering. For Kracauer, there is redemption in the shattering. But what about for Cronenberg? Perhaps not at first glance. After all, suicide as the central gesture in Cronenberg's cinema points toward the opposite of redemption. But if we consider the Jewish Cronenberg, as I have attempted to do here, the twinned desire for therapy and insistence on therapy's failure become something other than a suicidal standstill. In the very repetition of desire/failure across so many films over so many years, Cronenbergian therapy becomes a vision of transformative otherness lodged precisely in the lived thingness and it-ness of who we are as embodied beings (self and other merged through materialism) rather than in a divine transcendence dependent upon whom we could be beyond those bodies (self and other separated through idealism). Even when Cronenberg is at his most openly redemptive—for example, at the conclusion of *Scanners*—the materiality of the body (Revok) counters any idealist transcendence accomplished by the mind (Vale). We are left not with an ideal self who has simply triumphed over the material other but with an other–self, a Revok–Vale, an embodied being still undergoing transformation.

At first, Cronenberg's often spectacularly fantastic films might seem impossibly distant from Kracauer's valorization of cinema's "realistic tendency" in *Theory of Film*, but there are telling moments where Kracauer, especially when gesturing toward the trauma of the Holocaust, appears to make room for films that are cousins of Cronenberg's cinema to come. When mentioning classic horror films of the 1930s and 1940s, Kracauer admits that they often devolve into "uncinematic staginess" but also that sometimes the "fantastic monsters" in these films "may be staged and manipulated so skillfully that they merge with their real-life environment and evoke the illusion of being virtually real. Is nature not capable of spawning monsters?"[21] Kracauer returns to this line of thinking in his book's conclusion, when the author of *From Caligari to Hitler: A Psychological History of the German Film* (1947) connects the horror of Georges Franju's brutal slaughterhouse documentary *Blood of the Beasts* (1949) with documentaries depicting the Nazi concentration camps: "The mirror reflections of horror are an end in themselves. As such they beckon the spectator to take them in and thus incorporate into his memory the real face of things too dreadful to be beheld in reality. In experiencing the rows of calves' heads [in *Blood of the Beasts*] or the litter of tortured human bodies in the films made of the Nazi concentration camps, we redeem horror from its invisibility behind the veils of panic and imagination."[22]

Kracauer and Cronenberg demonstrate a shared commitment to horror's transformative otherness, rather than to conventional subject/object or self/other distinctions, as the substrate of reality they hope that cinema can reveal. For Kracauer, as we have seen, the stakes of such revelation involve new perceptions about relations between the living and the dead, past and present. For Cronenberg, the stakes are more interpersonal than historical. In the repetitive, even obsessive shuttling between desire and failure in Cronenbergian therapy, the call to imagine an alternate set of interpersonal relations asserts itself: relations that cease battling for dominance between mind and body, self and other, but instead dwell in the leveling, redemptive transformation of life lived as experience rather than life analytically compartmentalized as interpretation. Does Vale's mind "cure" Revok's body in *Scanners*? Do Agatha and Benjie "cure" themselves of their family's pathologies in *Maps to the Stars*? The inadequacy of these questions underlines how the films favor the metamorphoses of experience over the diagnosis of explanation and hold transformative otherness above all.

For all of the Jewish thinkers this chapter has considered thus far, the face or the head—usually a symbol for selfhood, not for the other—crystallizes the redemptive potential of transformative otherness. For Levinas, a version of this leveling, experiential otherness is expressed through the face-to-face encounter where the self and responsibility for the other merge as one. For Rosenzweig, the worldly as the divine can be found in what he calls "the face of man," where the nose and ears as receptive organs and the eyes and mouth as expressive organs point toward how "man has an above [divine] and a below [worldly] in his own corporeality."[23] In *Theory of Film*, Kracauer describes the cinema as analogous to Perseus's shield when it reflects the head of Medusa. This comparison allows Kracauer to speculate, in an echo of his friend Walter Benjamin (who, unlike Kracauer, did not survive Nazism) and Benjamin's concept of the "death's-head," that "perhaps Perseus' greatest achievement was not to cut off Medusa's head but to overcome his fears and look at its reflection in the shield. And was it not precisely this feat which permitted him to behead the monster?"[24] In Cronenberg's films, the head explodes—whether literally on-screen or figuratively in terms of our "blown minds" as we see, in the ashes of therapy's disintegration, a glimpse of what transformative otherness might look or feel like: where self and other, mind and body no longer stand divided but metamorphose constantly as other–selves and body–minds.

A Dangerous Method: Returning Again to the Repressed

At first glance, *A Dangerous Method* looks like the least "Cronenbergian" film ever made. Of course, by 2011 it had already been years since we expected a new Cronenberg film to deliver anything resembling the director's early signature horror spectacles: the wriggling phallic-fecal parasites of *Shivers*, the exploding head of *Scanners*, the gut-spewing television set of *Videodrome*. Still, *Crash* had its wound sex, *A History of Violence* (2005) its bone-crunching physical combat, and *Eastern Promises* its stabbed eye. The only times blood spills in *A Dangerous Method* are when a woman loses her virginity and when she cuts the cheek of the lover who has spurned her.

Yet *A Dangerous Method* revolves around themes central to the director's previous work. The film's male protagonists, Sigmund Freud (Viggo Mortensen) and Carl Jung (Michael Fassbender), fit neatly into the long line of doctors and scientists who populate Cronenberg's cinema from *Stereo* (1969) through *eXistenZ*. They are men who wish to liberate humanity from the bodily, social, and imaginative constraints that cage it but who fail to see how their work tragically misunderstands the very people—themselves included—they want to set free. The resulting monstrosity and death horrifically pervert the original impulse to unchain or, more accurately, fulfill the blindness that clouded that impulse from the outset. In other words, Cronenberg's films have always been about the return of the repressed. *A Dangerous Method*, which explores the early years of the psychoanalytic movement that would popularize the very concept of the return of the repressed, is no exception in this regard. But con-tra Robin Wood's conviction that Cronenberg's early work portrays the return of the repressed in reactionary ways, *A Dangerous Method* epitomizes Cronen-berg's career-spanning engagement with therapy as an undeniable need equally impossible to meet; the consequent therapeutic disintegration is enacted as transformative otherness. Like never before in Cronenberg's oeuvre, *A Danger-ous Method* demonstrates how the director's investments in transformative otherness incorporate Jewishness.

What is conspicuously absent from *A Dangerous Method* is what Cronen-berg has called the "demon in the corner" in his cinema—the irrefutable fasci-nation and galvanizing energy that accompany the horrifying return of the repressed.[25] This is where Cronenberg's films come to life most memorably, where they create the astonishing images of bodies transformed by sex and violence that have granted the adjective *Cronenbergian* its cinematic distinctive-ness. When the repressed returns in *A Dangerous Method*, it is barely percep-tible. It appears in an averted gaze, a word in a letter, a haunted stare. Even when it does take on a more emphatically somatic form, such as Jung's bleeding cheek, Freud's fainting spell, and the hysterical convulsions of Jung's patient and then lover Sabina Spielrein (Keira Knightley), what we sense is how discreet this imagery feels. In the Cronenberg universe, it hardly registers as imagery at all. We are left with a reticent film about repression.

But, paradoxically enough, *A Dangerous Method* accrues stunning power precisely through its restraint. By turning his attention to the absence, loss, and emptiness of repression triumphant as intensively as he usually focuses on the shock, horror, and ambivalent ecstasy of repression overturned, Cronenberg has sharpened the tragic pain that has always characterized his cinematic vision. The danger of *A Dangerous Method* is not just the risk surrounding the experi-ments in psychoanalytic therapy that the film depicts but also Cronenberg's decision to radically revise his own cinematic method. Somewhat unexpect-edly, the gamble pays off. But how? Why? What can we learn about Cronenberg's cinema as a whole through the inversion and distillation that is *A Dangerous Method*? And about Cronenberg's engagement with transformative other-ness and with Jewishness in particular?

Cronenberg's sources were John Kerr's nonfiction book *A Most Dangerous Method: The Story of Jung, Freud, and Sabina Spielrein* (1993) as well as Chris-topher Hampton's related play *The Talking Cure* (2002). The book, the play, and the film dwell on the intersecting lives of Freud, Jung, and Spielrein between 1904 and 1913. During these years, Freud (based in Vienna) and Jung (based in Zurich) forge a professional alliance and personal friendship that promises to expand the sphere of psychoanalysis and install the younger man as Freud's self-appointed heir. But Jung's affair with Spielrein, a highly educated young Rus-sian Jewish woman and his first patient treated according to Freud's "talking cure," exacerbates the mounting tensions between the two men. Spielrein, whose hysteria is cured so successfully that she eventually becomes a noted psychoanalyst, turns to Freud when Jung decides to end their affair and deny its existence. She forces Jung to admit the affair to Freud, an action that drives the men farther apart and inflames their intellectual, cultural, and class differences. Spielrein's attempt to mend fences between them proves an impossible task. As Jung (quoting *Hamlet*) puts it in a letter to Freud in 1913 that is quoted in Kerr's book, Hampton's play, and Cronenberg's film, "The rest is silence."

Hampton wrote the screenplay of *A Dangerous Method*, and the film tends to follow the play quite closely in its dialogue and narrative arc. In fact, the film's detractors might complain that the whiff of the theatrical remains too strong, that the film feels stubbornly uncinematic. It is true that this repressed film refuses to show when it can suggest or conceal instead, knowing full well that the sort of showing it might do is something at which cinema (and Cronenberg's cinema in particular) excels. But the repression here is rigorously strategic, not artificial or thoughtless.

Note, for example, how Cronenberg chooses to deflate rather than inflate one of the play's most graphic moments. In the play, an infuriated Spielrein reacts to Jung's abrupt decision to break off their romantic relationship by slashing him with a paper knife and then smacking the banknote he demands as payment for her therapy to his bleeding cheek, where it sticks. The scene ends with Jung reaching up to peel away the bloody money. In the film, Cronenberg retains the slashing but omits the banknote. Spielrein instead slams the cash down on Jung's desk and storms out—another evasion cloaking the physical violence that just preceded it. Even the film's sex scenes, which are more explicit than anything mentioned in the play and involve Jung whipping an ecstatic Spielrein, function as dress rehearsals after the fact for the more spectacularly Cronenbergian sex in films such as *Videodrome*, *Crash*, and *A History of Violence*. There, Cronenberg lavishes all the powers of cinematic inspection on each body part, on every twist and turn of the lovers' exposed flesh. Here, Jung and Spielrein do not even shed most of their clothing when they are at their most physically intimate.

Otto Gross (Vincent Cassel), a brilliant psychoanalyst but also a drug-addicted libertine whom Freud sends to Jung for treatment, utters one of the most Cronenbergian lines in the film: "Never repress anything." Although Gross plays a decisive role in seducing Jung into pursuing the affair, his presence in the film is symptomatically marginal. There is little space in *A Dangerous Method* for such an unrepressed force. The nude drawings, chaotic mess, and open window (in a film of closed windows) that adorn his room can only hint at what Gross represents. The queer tension attached to the return of the repressed that pervades so many of Cronenberg's films (Cassel plays a closeted gangster in *Eastern Promises*) never materializes between Gross and Jung. After a brief sexual encounter with a female nurse, Gross vaults the wall of Jung's hospital—out of the film, never to be seen again.

But perhaps the most telling repression featured in *A Dangerous Method* involves converting dialogue exchanged between characters in Hampton's play into letters read through voice-over in the film. Cronenberg privileges the distance and disconnection of letters written and received in solitude rather than the dynamism of face-to-face encounters. The film's opening and closing title sequences present the inked script of words on paper in partial and magnified views that cause them to resemble Rorschach blots. Like the film itself, these blots never resolve into a revelatory "answer" about the secret truth of the writing or the writer, a code decoded. Whatever we learn about the correspondents instead remains indirect, masked, sometimes even off-screen.

The film concludes with four intertitles that briefly summarize the fates of Gross, Freud, Spielrein, and Jung in the years following the film's conclusion. Of the four, only Jung will survive the two world wars about to engulf Europe when *A Dangerous Method* ends. Gross starves to death in Berlin in 1919. Freud, a Jew living in exile due to the rise of Nazism, dies of cancer in London in 1939. The intertitle devoted to Spielrein tells us something without visuals that Hampton's play dramatizes as a showstopping flashforward: Spielrein's murder in Russia in 1942 at the hands of the Nazis. Again, Cronenberg opts to restrain the play rather than unleash it. But the impact of reading that intertitle, like the impact of hearing the carefully chosen words included in the film's letters, delivers searing emotional pain. The anguish flows from the unspoken, the unshown—and all of this from the director who once proclaimed that his artistic mission was "to show the unshowable, to speak the unspeakable."²⁶

A Dangerous Method is not the first time Cronenberg has entered the territory of the biopic, nor is it his first adaptation of a play. In *Naked Lunch* (1991), Cronenberg gains purchase on William S. Burroughs's experimental novel, widely considered "unfilmable," by incorporating thinly veiled fictionalizations of Burroughs and his literary companions Jack Kerouac, Allen Ginsberg, Paul Bowles, and Jane Bowles. In *M. Butterfly*, Cronenberg works from a screenplay by David Henry Hwang, who (like Hampton) adapts his own play for the film. But what emerges most sharply in a comparison of these predecessors to *A Dangerous Method* are the differences, not the similarities. *Naked Lunch* visualizes the writing process in the idiom of shocking presence rather than haunting absence—the film's typewriter–insect–anuses engage in all manner of sex and violence to embody the act of writing rather than, as in *A Dangerous Method*, using writing as a means to disembody the characters. We leave *Naked Lunch* with a vivid sense of how writing sets loose desires unacknowledged by these famous writers, especially the conflicted sexuality of Bill Lee/Burroughs (Peter Weller). In *A Dangerous Method*, writing affords just one more remove from genuine self-expression for the historical figures, despite their pioneering efforts in mapping the psyche.

By the same token, *M. Butterfly* cinematizes Hwang's play in the opposite direction of *A Dangerous Method*. Cronenberg highlights the broad historical sweep surrounding China's Cultural Revolution by incorporating key scenes of the masses, those teeming crowds impossible to place on a stage but possible to film as the true agents and victims of history. The masses are never seen in *A Dangerous Method*; Cronenberg focuses with microscopic intensity on the film's main characters to the exclusion of the countless lives touched by psychoanalysis. For example, when Freud visits Jung at the psychiatric hospital where he works in Zurich, neither man looks very closely at the patient about whom they offer dueling diagnoses. She shares the same room with them, but Jung buries his head in his notebook, while Freud physically distances himself from her. Like so many other meticulously orchestrated frame compositions in the film, this one accentuates the opportunity lost when people so close spatially live worlds apart psychologically. The fact that the patient is forced to soak in a treatment bath identical to the one Spielrein must endure earlier in the film speaks volumes about how spatially close these men can be to their patients and still not truly see them (fig. 5.3).

5.3 Jung (Michael Fassbender, *left*) and Freud (Viggo Mortensen, *right*) discuss a patient whose presence is never fully recognized by them in *A Dangerous Method*.

Repression and Vision: Echoes of *The Brood*

The absence of the masses from *A Dangerous Method* is not a coincidental by-product of psychoanalytic therapy's one-on-one structure but rather an underlining of the film's emphasis on the blinding power of repression. To recognize this choice on Cronenberg's part as a purposeful one, consider once more how significant the therapeutic situation has been to his cinema from the beginnings to the present. His very first short film, *Transfer*, depicts a psychiatrist and his patient conversing across a dinner table located in the surreal setting of a snowy field. Therapeutic or quasi-therapeutic scenes appear in almost all of Cronenberg's films after *Transfer*, but none features them more prominently than *The Brood*—at least until *A Dangerous Method*.

Both *The Brood* and *A Dangerous Method* present therapy sessions at regular intervals as major narrative and thematic devices, but, as with *Naked Lunch* and *M. Butterfly*, the differences overshadow the similarities. *The Brood* begins with a therapy session between Dr. Hal Raglan (Oliver Reed) and his patient, Mike (Gary McKeehan). The startling intimacy of the session reaches a climax when Raglan exhorts Mike to show him the anger Mike speaks about; Mike responds by tearing open his shirt to reveal the bloody welts and sores that cover his body (fig. 5.4). Raglan, the inventor of a radical psychotherapeutic approach

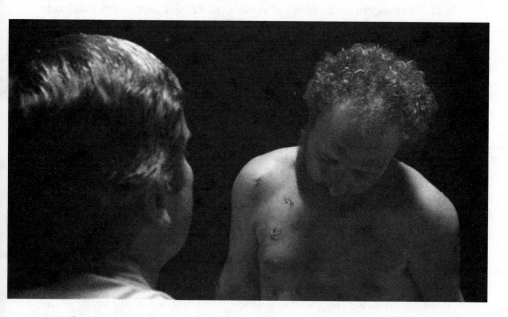

5.4 Mike (Gary McKeehan) reveals the welts that cover his body in a therapeutic session with Dr. Raglan (Oliver Reed) in *The Brood*.

called "psychoplasmics" that enables patients to externalize their inner rage as bodily manifestations, beholds Mike's ghastly self-display with approval, telling him he can now "see" him fully. Patient and therapist embrace—and the lights go up, shifting our attention to the audience of visitors to Raglan's institute who have been observing this painfully personal therapeutic dialogue as a public performance.

The striking juxtaposition of psychotherapy's private examinations and public implications characterizes *The Brood* throughout. Nola Carveth (Samantha Eggar), Raglan's prize patient, stretches psychoplasmics to its limits by giving birth to a brood of parthenogenetically produced "children" that then murder the people Nola channels her anger toward in therapy. The relentless alternation of Nola's private therapy sessions with the brood's savage public murders grants the act of therapy a social presence that *A Dangerous Method* converts into absence. In the latter film, aside from Spielrein, whose patient status soon gets superseded by her identity as a lover and then as an analyst, the public world that patients represent remains nearly invisible—and completely invisible to Jung in particular. When Jung and Spielrein, acting as his analytic trainee, test on an audience of hospital patients the therapeutic effects of listening to Wagner, Jung again quite literally does not see them—he has eyes only for Spielrein as she records the patients' reactions.

The tragedy of *The Brood* is that neither Nola nor Raglan realizes what the brood are capable of until it is too late. Raglan dies when the creatures turn on him. Nola dies when her estranged exhusband, Frank (Art Hindle), kills her to neutralize them. And at the film's end, their beloved young daughter, Candy (Cindy Hinds), carries on her body the trauma of her own experiences with the brood and her family: *The Brood* concludes with a sequence that includes a zoom-in close-up of the welts on Candy's arm that show us the outer evidence of her inner anguish. We see her as clearly as Raglan and the public audience saw Mike when the film began and as clearly as we see Nola's grisly birthing process near the film's end. The tragedy of *A Dangerous Method* is that neither Jung nor Freud ever really sees his patients or himself in the light of painfully self-implicated understanding—when they get close to any such recognition, they retreat from it or destroy it.

At the end of *A Dangerous Method*, Jung and Spielrein meet one last time at Jung's lakeside estate. Spielrein, now married, pregnant, and a professional psychoanalyst, faces away from the lake while Jung stares out across its surface (fig. 5.5). So even though they now exchange intimate confessions about how much their past relationship meant to each of them, they do not face one another. In fact, the distance between them now seems greater than ever before, despite moving beyond the therapeutic positioning of Jung behind a seated and hysterically convulsive Spielrein or the sexualized positioning of Jung behind a kneeling and ecstatically convulsive Spielrein. The failure to see in *A*

5.5 Sabina Spielrein (Keira Knightley) and Jung meet one last time but face away from each other in *A Dangerous Method*.

Dangerous Method may not provoke the stomach-churning horror that the insistence to see gives birth to in *The Brood*, but the films share a cumulative sense of devastating loss associated with a poisoned future.

Children figure crucially in those visions of a sabotaged future in both *The Brood* and *A Dangerous Method*. When Candy's father reassures her at the film's end that "we're going home," it is the impossibility of that sentiment that cuts to the bone. What kind of home can exist for Candy after the things she has seen, experienced, and (as her marred flesh testifies) internalized? What sort of future can she look forward to? The conclusion of *A Dangerous Method* also annihilates our sense of the future as a place of hope, where children constitute a sign of renewal. Although Jung and Spielrein's final meeting occurs in the presence of children—Spielrein calls Jung's frolicking kids "glorious," and she looks radiant in her pregnancy—the aura of loss dominates nonetheless. When Jung makes the shattering remark that Spielrein's unborn child should have been his, she agrees with him. He is surrounded by beautiful children he never really wanted, while she carries a child she wishes had a different father. These children belong to a future already betrayed, not to one ripe with potential for growth and change. Like Candy, they are condemned to a future suffocated by the present. The closing intertitles of *A Dangerous Method* spell this out for us in the grim logic of history: when the Nazis execute the Jewish Spielrein, they also kill her two children.

To say that *The Brood* shows us the horror of a future lost whereas *A Dangerous Method* tells us about that future is true but not as simple as it sounds. Among Jung's last words to Spielrein is his recounting of an apocalyptic vision that has possessed him: a tidal wave of blood carrying thousands of drowned corpses surges across Europe and crashes down into the lake he lives beside. Jung admits that he has no idea what this vision means, but of course we know its meaning all too well. What Jung hallucinates as a sort of natural disaster will become man-made mass death during the two world wars to come. What Cronenberg provokes by not showing us Jung's vision in images is our capacity to substitute, all too readily, our own images of historical horror. Photographs of the corpses from the Great War's trenches, from Auschwitz, from Hiroshima flood our consciousness as mercilessly as Jung's tidal wave overwhelms his own.

Yet what *A Dangerous Method* also intimates, perhaps to even more painful effect, is the glimmer of an alternative history, one that could have been but never was. In this other history, Jung, Freud, and Spielrein would see each other and the world they attempt to enlighten in more generous and empathetic terms. Perhaps a different sort of psychoanalysis would have been born, one capable of showing the world to itself in ways that made catastrophes such as global warfare and the Holocaust avoidable rather than inevitable. But this sort of alternative history is ultimately as illegible to us as Jung's vision is to him. And it is this failure of sight as well as insight on the part of the film's characters, this heart-sinking disappearance of self-recognition magnified against the backdrop of cataclysmic history, that makes the absent images of *A Dangerous Method* as harrowing as the graphic images of Cronenberg's earlier films.

Repression and Anti-Semitism

If *A Dangerous Method* devotes much of its creative energy to imagining the powers and consequences of repression, then it reserves a special interest in that especially hateful form of repressive blindness known as anti-Semitism. In a number of key scenes, Freud's keen awareness of social persecution as a Jew contrasts with Jung's blithely privileged Protestantism in ways that color both the personal tensions between them and the historical canvas on which their relationship unfolds. When Freud and Jung first meet, Freud marvels at Jung's inability to comprehend how the psychoanalytic movement's roots among Jews leaves it particularly vulnerable to attack by anti-Semitic opponents in the medical establishment. But the younger man's blindness on this count gets established as a telling pattern, one that stems from his class as well as his cultural background. When the two doctors sit side by side at dinner (a striking instance of spatial parity between individuals within the frame in a film where it occurs very rarely), Jung does not look up to realize that their seating arrangement responds to the presence of Freud's large family joining them at the table. Only belatedly does Jung recognize that the food he has been piling thoughtlessly on his plate was meant not just for him, but for everyone. Still, he does not apologize.

Jung's persistent obliviousness to how his own social advantages and wealth grate against Freud's Jewishness and more modest means does not make him an anti-Semite, but it does emphasize his blindness on a subject where history will prove Freud horribly, unbearably correct. Nevertheless, when Freud uses Jewishness as a wedge to drive Spielrein farther away from Jung's sphere of influence and closer to his own, he cannot escape his gesture's self-serving aspects. Even so, Freud's reminder to Spielrein that they are and always will be Jews receives confirmation during the film's closing intertitles with a tragic finality that overrides the interpersonal jealousies shaping his comment.

Cronenberg's turn toward more explicitly geopolitical subject matter in *A History of Violence* and *Eastern Promises*, films that wrestle with themes of national, subnational, and international conflict in the post-9/11 global landscape, continues in *A Dangerous Method*.[27] This film differs from the previous two in its status as a historical period drama, but its investment in history, like its investigation of Jewishness and the fearful hatred that Jewishness can ignite, feels very much of the present. One powerful formal link between all three of these films is that each one ends with variations on the same shot: a close-up on the face of a man who has overcome great obstacles but who has somehow lost everything that matters most to him in the process. All three films hold the desolate stare of its protagonist long enough for us to register the devastation he feels before cutting away. In *A Dangerous Method*, however, that look haunts us in a new manner because we know that Jung is not just staring out at us from the screen—he is also somehow staring ahead toward a traumatic future that now belongs to the audience as their historical past. Jung may only stumble toward this history as an apocalyptic premonition, but we see it as a tragic, macrocosmic outcome of the relationships among Jung, Spielrein, and Freud that the film presents microcosmically.

The promise of progress shimmers for a moment when Spielrein leaves Jung's estate in a car, essentially reversing the film's opening sequence where a screaming Spielrein must be restrained inside a horse-drawn carriage on her way to Jung's hospital for treatment. But that promise of progress, of cure and growth and enlightened modernity, disintegrates when we realize that the future Spielrein moves toward is a deathly modernity of technologized warfare and concentration camps. In the car, an emotionally ravaged Spielrein moves forward with the automobile's motion but simultaneously looks back to the past—to Jung, to what was lost, to what could have been. Jung's defeated stare in the film's final shot, paired with Spielrein's sorrowful reflection back, suggests that she feels what lies ahead and behind at least as deeply as he does.

But is her vision like his? Spielrein ultimately sees more clearly than Jung. She may lack his second sight, his premonition of a future yet to come, but at nearly every stage of the film she sees and feels more fully than either Jung or Freud. When Spielrein first goes into treatment, she appears grotesquely out of control: her body lurches in the spastic fits of hysteria, her words struggle to escape her contorted jaw. Later, as she progresses toward a cure, her body can still tremble with hints of muscular spasms when she feels overwhelmed. Indeed, one might be tempted to interpret Spielrein's slashing of Jung's cheek as a sort of regression. Her body, which she has fought so hard to master, seems to race ahead of her mind and act primitively, instinctively.

However, I think it would be closer to the truth of Cronenbergian therapy to say that what Spielrein demonstrates in this moment, as in so many others, is the capacity to fuse her body's feeling and her mind's thinking with stunning force. She literally cuts through Jung's self-deluding hypocrisy and cowardice about the nature of their relationship with a speed, directness, and honesty he never attains, just as she draws courage from her love for Jung to corner Freud into admitting a rift with his protégé that he refuses to acknowledge (when Freud compliments her for tending to choose his side when he and Jung disagree, she reminds him that he just denied having any disagreements with his protégé). Spielrein's sex scenes with Jung, in which she often employs mirrors to see herself feeling, crystallizes her ability to live physically and mentally with a simultaneity that eludes the male psychologists. Even Gross, who encourages Jung to cross the line of sexual involvement with his patient and connects Freud's obsession with sex to the fact that he "doesn't get any," lacks her balance of intellect and sexuality. Where Gross descends into addiction and madness, Spielrein gains modes of expression that make interchanges between her body and mind increasingly fluid.

Spielrein's pregnancy epitomizes this progression, especially when she reveals that she would prefer a girl. She wisely rejects the masculine game of fathers and sons, kings and heirs, that has played out so disastrously between Freud and Jung. Likewise, her decision to become a child psychologist frees her from emulating her male mentors and opens up a professional world she can inhabit on her own terms. When Jung's wife, Emma (Sarah Gadon), who displays an impressive amount of clear-eyed vision of her own regarding her husband and his relations with Spielrein and Freud, asks Spielrein if she would treat Jung, Spielrein declines rather than bringing that relationship full circle. She does not fall into the trap that ensnares so many of Cronenberg's past female characters: the desire to follow the pathways to experience and knowledge designed by men rather than creating their own. In The Brood, Nola's body travels far beyond the expectations set by Raglan's theory of psychoplasmics, but her actions (inseparable from those of the brood) conform all too literally to Raglan's ideas of how therapy should "show" the rage it uncovers. Even later figures, such as the heroic video game designer Allegra Geller (Jennifer Jason Leigh) of *eXistenZ*, want to win a game that is ultimately revealed as made and managed by men.

Perhaps Spielrein's closest relative in Cronenberg's oeuvre is Claire Niveau (Geneviève Bujold) in *Dead Ringers*, the successful actress who maintains a steadfast identity of her own while her lovers, the identical twin gynecologists Elliot and Beverly Mantle (Jeremy Irons), disintegrate beside her. But Claire seeks out the Mantles in the first place because she is desperate for them to cure her of the condition that cripples her sense of self-worth: her childlessness. They cannot make her fertile, and it is finally Beverly who leaves Claire behind to die alongside his brother in the film's concluding scene. Claire is left alone, wanting a man who loves her but cannot be with her because his bond with his brother transcends reason, subjectivity, and life itself. The Mantle twins die together in an enactment of what Freud would call the death drive.

In *A Dangerous Method*, Spielrein provides Freud with a theory of sex and death's mutual imbrication that leads Freud toward his formulation of the death drive. In other words, Spielrein helps to invent the very concept that bewilders Claire when faced with the suicidally interdependent Mantles. Although both Spielrein and Claire initially possess masochistic desires that draw them to the men in their lives, Spielrein chooses to walk away from Jung, while Claire finally has no say in Beverly's preference for death with Elliot rather than life with her. Of course, Spielrein's fate, as revealed in the closing intertitles, is doomed, but the impression of her we take with us is a woman who sees and feels in ways that the men who "cured" her cannot imagine. Given how many of Cronenberg's films end with literal or figurative suicides, Spielrein represents a bracing alternative stance toward the "demon in the corner" of his cinema. If we define that demon as a version of the death drive, then Spielrein sees clearly enough to learn from this demon without surrendering to it, whereas Jung and Freud suffer the consequences of failing to integrate the demon's existence into their own self-perceptions.

In *Beyond the Pleasure Principle* (1920), Freud's groundbreaking attempt to theorize the death drive as he grappled with the personal and social horror of World War I, he mentions Spielrein in a footnote that quietly conveys the tragedy that *A Dangerous Method* dissects so masterfully: Freud commends Spielrein's work as "instructive and interesting" but confesses that it is "unfortunately not entirely clear to me."[28] Cronenberg's purposefully repressed film drives home the cost of blindness encapsulated in Freud's textual repression of Spielrein. To understand Freud in this way, to reckon with all that he leaves unsaid, indicates just how much *A Dangerous Method* allows us to see—and how so often what we are shown is, in this director's terms, almost nothing at all.

What *A Dangerous Method* shows us, ultimately, is the promise of Cronenbergian therapy—particularly through the figure of Spielrein—for our understanding of transformative otherness. Since the links between Cronenbergian therapy and transformative otherness inexorably encompass Jewishness, it should perhaps come as no surprise that Cronenberg's Freud is very much a Jewish Freud. In fact, the last word on Freud in *A Dangerous Method*, given to us through the film's concluding intertitles, identifies him as a Jewish exile, a man who, despite and because of his stunning intellectual accomplishments, must flee his home and die in a country that is not his own; he must live in the age of Hitler as a persecuted Jew.

The book that Freud publishes during that period of exile, *Moses and Monotheism* (1939), is a startling and poignant testimony to Freud's own struggle with his Jewish identity. Freud argues that Moses, the biblical hero of the Jewish people who led their exodus from Egypt, was not a Jew at all but an Egyptian. The Jewish people have repressed not only the Egyptian origins of Moses but also the fact that they eventually turned on him and killed him. So the biblical story of heroic Moses is accomplished only through imagined identity, anguished guilt, and shameful horror—an act of repression at the heart of Judaism that influences the concept of monotheistic religion and shapes the survival of the Jewish people throughout history against all odds.

Freud begins *Moses and Monotheism* in Vienna but completes it in London. He admits that the book has required a torturous process of coming into being very much attached to his own Jewishness: "In the certainty of persecution—now not only because of my work, but also because of my 'race'—I left, with many friends, the city which from early childhood, through seventy-eight years, had been a home to me."[29] In *Moses and Monotheism*, Freud rewrites the origins of the Jewish people as a return of the repressed while he faces his own persecution as a Jew; he rewrites the exodus in exile, deeply aware of his own Jewish otherness. Freud begins the book with this sentence: "To deny a people the man whom it praises as the greatest of its sons is not a deed to be undertaken lightheartedly—especially by one belonging to that people."[30]

I hope that Freud's words, in light of this chapter's experimental rather than exhaustive genealogy of a Jewish-inflected film theory running from Rosenzweig to Levinas and Kracauer and finally to Cronenberg and back to Freud, can help us hear something we may have missed otherwise. It is there in Freud's *Moses and Monotheism*; in Kracauer's *Theory of Film*, written with great difficulty by an exiled Jew in a language and a country not originally his own; and in Cronenberg's *A Dangerous Method*, as one of horror's masters turns his own directorial method inside out to reimagine both the return of the repressed as well as Jewish otherness. What we can hear, as we listen to these voices together, is a statement of purpose for transformative otherness as a form of both therapy and horror. It is the declaration by Freud, by Kracauer, by Cronenberg, each in his own time and in his own way but with shared recognition of that declaration's pain and promise: "I am a Jew."

PART III

TRANSFORMING HORROR'S OTHER VOICES

CHAPTER 6

GENDERED OTHERNESS

Feminine Horror and Surrealism in Marina de Van, Stephanie Rothman, and Jennifer Kent

There is an unforgettable sequence in Marina de Van's extraordinary film *In My Skin* (*Dans ma peau*, 2002) where Esther (de Van), a successful young woman struggling with tensions that haunt her personal and professional lives, becomes simultaneously disconnected from and newly connected to her own body. During a stressful business dinner where she needs to impress both her senior colleagues at an international marketing firm and a prospective client, Esther suddenly finds that her left forearm has detached itself from her body and now lies frozen on the table, as lifeless to her as the plates and silverware beside it (fig. 6.1). Mortified, she attempts to reattach her forearm as inconspicuously as possible but finds she must stab herself surreptitiously with a knife and fork before any real feeling of wholeness can return. Although she eventually succeeds in regaining the sense that her forearm belongs to her, she can no longer concentrate on the business being discussed. Her imagination instead drifts toward a nearby hotel, where she checks in after the dinner's conclusion. Alone in the room, she begins to eat herself— literally consuming her own flesh and blood in an ecstatic, eroticized frenzy.

What this sequence captures so vividly is how *In My Skin* stands at the crossroads of a number of important discourses that are rarely considered together: horror, feminism, surrealism, and the "New French Extremity," a renaissance of graphic sex and violence in French art cinema beginning in the late 1990s and led by directors such as Catherine Breillat, Bruno Dumont, Philippe Grandrieux, Gaspar Noé, and François Ozon. The alarmed critic James Quandt,

6.1 Esther (Marina de Van) reaches for her detached forearm in *In My Skin*.

who includes de Van in this group, coined the term "New French Extremity" in 2004 to describe

a cinema suddenly determined to break every taboo, to wade in rivers of viscera and spumes of sperm, to fill each frame with flesh, nubile or gnarled, and subject it to all manner of penetration, mutilation, and defilement. Images and subjects once the provenance of splatter films, exploitation flicks, and porn . . . proliferate in the high-art environs of a national cinema whose provocations have historically been formal, political, or philosophical (Godard, Clouzot, Debord) or, at their most immoderate (Franju, Buñuel, Walerian Borowczyk, Andrzej Zulawski), at least assimilable as emanations of an artistic movement (Surrealism mostly).[1]

Whereas Quandt rules out surrealism as a meaningful context for the New French Extremity, I argue that analyzing *In My Skin* as a film that practices a particular kind of surrealism permits us to see the hidden intersections between horror and feminism that subtend certain forms of the New French Extremity but also lead beyond it.[2] I call this critical terrain that is mined so productively by *In My Skin* "feminine horror": the adaptation and transformation of horror genre tropes and affects for female-focused concerns. These transformations invite us to recognize gender's significance for our understanding of horror's transformative otherness.

By using the term *feminine horror*, I do not wish to suggest that its opposite is *masculine horror* or that the genre can be neatly subdivided by these two labels. What I want to signal is a new critical space that grows out of but ultimately departs from influential formulations such as Carol J. Clover's Final Girl, Barbara Creed's monstrous-feminine, and Linda Williams's nonphallic woman/monster.[3] What Clover, Creed, and Williams accomplish, each in her own way, is a means to imagine the horror film beyond the long-held clichés of all-encompassing misogyny and/or irrelevance to the progressive interests of women. Although none of them wishes to endorse the genre as essentially feminist in its conventional practices (neither do I), feminine horror does step outside the "representations of women" model that underwrites their approaches to the horror film to reveal a rich feminist potential in the genre's form. Feminine horror considers not only the matter of women on-screen but also the issue of female authorship. Perhaps most significantly, feminine horror focuses squarely on film aesthetics and cinematic modes of confrontation to posit *feminine* and *horror* as intimately connected and mutually enriching terms, not exceptions that prove the (masculine) rule. In other words, feminine horror provokes us to acknowledge the vast if too often untapped feminist power of the horror film.

Given the historical marginalization of women from key roles in film production and the especially glaring underrepresentation of women as directors of horror films, my turn to feminine horror aims to connect this book's explorations of horror's transformative otherness with women's authorship and experience.[4] There is no monolithic "women's horror film" that automatically results every time a woman earns the rare chance to direct a feature-length horror film, but I submit that we can detect an emergent alternative tradition of feminine horror when we focus on certain horror films directed by women. At the heart of this alternative tradition is surrealism, an aesthetics and a politics I analyzed in chapter 2 as central to horror's transformative otherness. Surrealism aids us in recognizing how horror can refigure the distinctions between self and other as a matter of ongoing metamorphosis rather than discrete identities as well as how feminine horror can actualize the horror film's feminist potential. For example, the scene from *In My Skin* described at the beginning of this chapter (to which I return later) depends on spectators reckoning with Esther's forearm as both a part of her body and apart from her body. Esther is neither a conventionally embodied, whole self nor a monstrously disembodied, fragmented other. As she moves between seeing her own body as attached to her or detached from her, we, too, must constantly see her anew: not solely an integrated self, not solely a disintegrated other, but rather an other–self, always in a state of transformation. This reckoning with Esther extends to our understanding of her as a woman, how the horror that accompanies her gendered inhabitation of transformative otherness is not just some fantastic dream but a poignant expression of lived reality.

As we will recall, André Breton defined surrealism in 1924 as "the future resolution of these two states, dream and reality, which are seemingly so contradictory, into a kind of absolute reality, a *surreality*, if one may so speak."[5] Surrealism
may seem an unlikely avenue for pursuing feminine horror, given that the
movement, at least in its canonical guise centered on Breton in France during
the interwar years, is usually considered a misogynistic, homophobic collective
with precious little room for women other than as objects of fetishistic fascination.[6] But recent scholarship has made more room for the significance of women
artists within the surrealist orbit, and de Van benefits from consideration in this
context, especially when *surrealism* is often an oddly incidental or minimized
term in most discussions of the New French Extremity.[7] In order to situate de
Van at the center of a feminine-horror tradition that incorporates surrealism,
we must first look back to one of her predecessors: Stephanie Rothman.

Looking Back: Stephanie Rothman and *The Velvet Vampire*

As I mentioned in chapter 1, Stephanie Rothman was the sole female director
invited by Robin Wood to participate in "The American Nightmare" retrospective in 1979. Wood's laudable investments in feminism are apparent not only in
his invitation to Rothman but in his appreciation of her horror-related films
The Velvet Vampire (1971) and *Terminal Island* (1973). Indeed, Wood and Rothman developed a friendship based on mutual admiration in the wake of "The
American Nightmare," with Rothman appreciating Wood's writing about horror films such as *The Texas Chain Saw Massacre* (Tobe Hooper, 1974) and *The
Last House on the Left* (Wes Craven, 1972) that she herself did not care for.[8] In
a reflection on "The American Nightmare" published in 1980, Wood praises *The
Velvet Vampire* as "imaginative and audacious, gaining a strong impetus from
Rothman's interest in Surrealism (in her seminar she expressed a debt to and
great admiration for Jean Cocteau and Georges Franju), but riven by contradictory impulses and confusions."[9]

Like Wood's account of the connection between surrealism and horror in
general (see chapter 2), this characterization of Rothman as influenced by surrealism is both significant and limiting: significant in that he calls attention to
an important affinity between surrealism and horror in Rothman's work, but
limiting in that, for him, this affinity cannot resolve the "contradictory impulses
and confusions" he finds in her films. A closer look at the surrealism of *The
Velvet Vampire*, however, particularly with regard to the film's activation of
transformative otherness, reveals a powerful vision of feminine horror where
Wood sees incoherence.[10]

The Velvet Vampire traces the encounter of the married couple Susan (Sherry
Miles) and Lee (Michael Blodgett) with the mysterious vampire Diane (Celeste

Yarnall). After they initially meet in a Los Angeles art gallery, Diane invites the couple to her desert home. In a series of erotically and violently charged episodes, both Lee and Susan are seduced by Diane. After Diane kills Lee, Susan flees to Los Angeles. Diane pursues her but meets her demise when Susan convinces a crowd of onlookers to join her as she corners Diane with crucifixes and exposes her to the sunlight. Susan then takes refuge with the art dealer Carl (Gene Shane) but learns in the end that Carl not only knew Diane well but is also a vampire.

What this basic plot summary cannot capture is how ambitiously and creatively Rothman visualizes the relationships that unfold among Susan, Lee, and Diane. In a complex network of exchanged looks and actions pulsing with graphic sex and violence—the film's status as a product of famed exploitation producer Roger Corman's New World Pictures is never in question—Rothman deploys surrealism to both prefigure and refigure feminist film theorist Laura Mulvey's landmark claims concerning cinema's reliance on a "male gaze." I return to Mulvey in more detail during my discussion of de Van, but for now I want to emphasize how Rothman, four years before Mulvey's "Visual Pleasure and Narrative Cinema" (1975) is published, uses surrealism and horror to disrupt the conventional workings of an active male gaze and a passive female "*to-be-looked-at-ness*" that Mulvey finds characteristic of mainstream narrative cinema.[11]

For Rothman, the primary visual tools for staging this disruption are the surrealist icons the mirror and the dream. In Diane's house, Susan and Lee's guest bedroom includes a two-way mirror. This mirror permits Diane to watch the couple's most intimate and sexual moments without their knowledge, but it also opens a gateway to their dreams. In repeated dream sequences shared by both Susan and Lee, Diane walks through a mirror to enter an outdoor desert "bedroom" inhabited by the couple (fig. 6.2). In the dream, Diane initially "steals" Lee from the bed where he lies with Susan. But Diane eventually abandons her seduction of Lee in order to join Susan in the bed, where she tenderly cuts Susan's breast. The knife she uses is the same one she employed during the day to save Susan's life by sucking the poison out of her thigh after Susan was bitten by a rattlesnake.

Through this stunning set of visual links, enabled by the surrealist logic of the dream that refuses to divorce itself from reality and by the mirror that refuses to simply reflect but also serves to transport, *The Velvet Vampire* establishes Diane as a healer as well as a monster, a lover for Susan as well as a sexual rival. In fact, Rothman goes even further by suggesting that Susan's process of transformation during the film is precisely her ambivalent but unmistakable movement from perceiving Diane solely as a monstrous rival to recognizing her differently: as *both* healer and monster, lover and rival, a teacher of new ways of knowing herself rather than just a vampiric other out to destroy

6.2 The desert "bedroom" in a dream sequence in *The Velvet Vampire*.

her. Rothman conveys Susan's transformation not only or even primarily through narrative structures but through the visual vocabulary of surrealism and horror in the register of transformative otherness.

When Diane tells Susan that Lee is "not very observant," she alerts the spectator to *The Velvet Vampire*'s engagement of transformative otherness as a matter of recalibrating male and female desire. Looking closely at the film uncovers a network of female desire and becoming that ultimately supersedes male desire, but one that we risk missing if we are not observant enough. Consider, for example, the looks that unite Diane and Susan: Diane watches Susan and Lee make love through the two-way mirror; Susan watches Diane and Lee make love while Lee believes Susan is asleep. But Susan already senses Diane behind the mirror before she discovers the mirror's two-way capability, and Diane locks eyes with Susan while she has sex with Lee. In this way, Lee's role is revealed as peripheral, a unit of exchange between the two women that inverts how women are so often exchanged between men.[12] Even though Diane seduces Lee, Susan is the true object of her desire, and Lee is finally shrugged off almost as casually as Diane quickly dispatches the male rapist who attempts to assault her in the film's opening sequence. Rothman structures *The Velvet Vampire*

around the fact that Lee, as a man, assumes himself to be the central connection between Diane and Susan, when in actuality it is the connection between
the two women that constitutes the dramatic essence of the film. Diane encourages Susan to think about the two of them together, united by "the pleasure we
have, that only we can have," a pleasure that triggers the envy and hatred of
men "because they can never know what it's like."

Indeed, *The Velvet Vampire*'s climax dispenses with Lee altogether after
Diane kills him. The climax instead focuses on Diane's pursuit of Susan. Again,
this pursuit may at first appear straightforward and one-sided: Susan flees the
murderous threat of Diane, attempts to evade her, enlists the aid of others to
help combat her, and finally defeats her. But a closer look reveals something
else entirely—namely, that Susan is not so much fleeing and then vanquishing
Diane as transforming her understanding of Diane gradually from an other
who threatens her to a teacher who offers her a new form of self-recognition.
When Susan is mortified to see Diane in the back of the bus she boards to escape
the desert for Los Angeles, she quickly turns away from her as if to deny her
presence. But eventually it is Susan who turns around to look at Diane. Similarly, Susan's flight from Diane in the Los Angeles bus station is less about hid-
ing from Diane and more about keeping herself visible to Diane. Susan "hides"
from Diane in a bank of brightly lit, transparent glass phone booths and then
in the broad daylight of the city streets. Even when Susan seems to attack Diane
with crucifixes and sunlight, her order to the crowd to help her remove Diane's
cape is also a means of undressing her sexually—a point emphasized when
Rothman dwells on Diane's revealing top beneath her cape—so her breasts are
nearly exposed. Diane's final demise, her disintegration in the sunlight's glare,
is visualized fleetingly as a transformation into Susan—Diane's black hair
becomes Susan's blond hair, Diane's face becomes Susan's face. In these ways,
Susan's flight *from* Diane doubles as Susan's flight *to* Diane, a process that brings
her ever closer to acknowledging her desire for Diane and incorporating Diane's
otherness into herself.

The conclusion of *The Velvet Vampire* brings this process full circle. Again,
what appears initially as a common "surprise" epilogue at the narrative level—
Susan suddenly realizes that Carl's sanctuary is illusory and that she is now subject to yet another vampiric threat, this time male—becomes something quite
different when reckoning with Rothman's surrealist imagery. In one last powerful burst of visuals that collapse dream and reality, Susan slits her own hand
with a replica of the knife that Diane used earlier in the film to cut Susan's thigh
and breast. This is also the knife that Susan stabs Diane's hand with during her
escape from the desert. Shortly before the knife draws blood from Susan's hand,
the image of Diane floods her consciousness: they are reunited in the dream,
Diane cutting Susan's breast with this same knife. So when Carl delicately sucks
the blood from Susan's wound, just as Diane did when she saved Susan from

snake poisoning, the visual suggestion is that he is participating not in Susan's death but in her rebirth. Susan can finally cease fleeing the vampire by awakening to the vampire within herself. At last, she and Diane are together; they are one. Rothman ends the film with an extreme close-up of Susan's wide-eyed stare during this transformation. The stare certainly signals fear and shock, but awareness as well; it also evokes a very similar zoom-in close-up of Diane's eyes earlier in the film when she stares with such deep longing at Susan through the two-way mirror. It is as if Susan and Diane have finally stepped through the mirror together, returned to their shared dream, and transformed it into a reality of frightening but fulfilled desire.

This interpretation of *The Velvet Vampire*'s conclusion gains added weight from Rothman's allusions to the queer legacies of vampire literature and surrealism throughout the film. Carl's last name is Stoker, after *Dracula* (1897) author Bram Stoker, and Diane's last name is Le Fanu, after *Carmilla* (1872) author Joseph Sheridan Le Fanu. Both Stoker's novel and Le Fanu's novella are widely known for their homoeroticism, with *Carmilla* an especially striking exploration of lesbian vampirism.[13] The surrealist who presides most prominently over *The Velvet Vampire* is Jean Cocteau, in particular his images of moving through mirrors in his films *The Blood of a Poet* (1932) and *Orpheus* (1950). Cocteau's homosexuality often complicated his relation to the surrealist movement, but Rothman reclaims his imagery for surrealism in *The Velvet Vampire* as compellingly as the woman avant-gardist Maya Deren does in her classic *Meshes of the Afternoon* (1943).

Even though Deren did not become familiar with *The Blood of a Poet* until after she completed *Meshes of the Afternoon*, she was "struck by similarities to her own work" once she became acquainted with Cocteau.[14] Like Rothman, Deren seems drawn specifically to the surrealist trope of the mirror that is more than a mirror, a trope that Cocteau excels in visualizing as his characters pass through mirrors as if they were a pool of water or an open window. At the climax of *Meshes of the Afternoon*, a young woman (played by Deren) throws a knife at her male partner, but at the point of impact the knife shatters a mirror image of her partner rather than the man himself. The shards of this broken mirror return soon in the film's final shot, depicting the young woman with a bloodied slit throat surrounded by splintered mirror fragments. Deren describes her film's conclusion, with its shocking convergence of surrealism and horror, in terms that serve remarkably well when applied to the ending of *The Velvet Vampire*: "The film is culminated by a double-ending in which it would seem the imagined achieved, for her, such force that it became reality."[15] But whereas *Meshes of the Afternoon* concludes with an image of life terminated, *The Velvet Vampire* opts for a life reborn, however terrifying in its implications. Still, the women in both of these films have passed through the mirror in the surrealist sense and found themselves on the other side, where the strictures dividing reality from dream as well as patriarchal expectations from feminist desires no longer hold. These women confound Mulvey's influential deployment of psychoanalyst Jacques Lacan's mirror stage as a means for understanding the male spectator's wishful attainment of an ego ideal through films that valorize male agency in contrast to female passivity.[16] They instead smash the mirror or walk right through it.

By tracing these mirror moves that connect Cocteau, Deren, and Rothman as well as surrealism, horror, and feminism, I have been sketching a genealogy for feminine horror that gathers women directors from seemingly quite different traditions and periods under a common rubric. In this mapping of feminine horror, Deren's avant-garde and Rothman's horror become less distant from each other via the shared traits of surrealism. In fact, Rothman emerges as indebted to *both* Corman and Cocteau, without that debt being an impediment to Rothman being Rothman.

Indeed, even in Rothman's early days of training with Corman, when she cowrote and codirected the low-budget vampire film *Blood Bath* (1966) with Jack Hill, her unique visual sensibility can be detected in the film's dreamlike images. In *Blood Bath*, the painter Salvador Dalí's stark natural landscapes littered with strange figures and objects stand beside Cocteau-like cinematic images of statues (here corpses) coming to life. Even in this codirected quickie, which Rothman insists does not count as one of her own films, her voice in relation to how she channels these surrealist influences is unmistakable.[17] By *Terminal Island* in 1973, she had proven herself to be an innovative force in horror every bit as promising as George A. Romero at that juncture. But where Romero was able to soldier on after the commercial and critical disappointments that came between *Night of the Living Dead* in 1968 and *Martin* in 1978, Rothman felt forced to quit the film business altogether. Just one year and one film after *Terminal Island*, she stopped directing features. As Rothman explains while reflecting on her career in 2010, "I was a woman. No one told me directly, but I often learned indirectly that this was the decisive reason why many producers wouldn't agree to meet me. If that sounds exaggerated, remember that I worked in the American film industry from 1965 to 1974, and some of those years I was the only woman directing feature films."[18]

In the light of Rothman's foundational and woefully underrecognized achievement in feminine horror, we can see a space where avant-gardists such as Deren and Nelly Kaplan find common ground with more genre-oriented or art-film-influenced narrative filmmakers such as Jennifer Kent and Karyn Kusama. What unites them all is a commitment to feminine horror that transcends avant-garde, art film, and genre labels—a commitment boldly enacted by Rothman in 1971, amplified by de Van in 2002, and expanded by Kent and others in the 2010s and thereafter in ways that we are only beginning to grasp.[19] If we place

Rothman, de Van, and Kent alongside each other, the outlines of feminine horror beyond the conventional oppositions between genre and art begin to take shape.

Marina de Van and *In My Skin*

When Esther "loses" her forearm in *In My Skin*, de Van reactivates a classic surrealist image seen in *Un chien andalou* (Luis Buñuel, 1929), *The Exterminating Angel* (*El ángel exterminador*; Luis Buñuel, 1962), and *The Beast with Five Fingers* (Robert Florey, 1946)—the latter a horror film to which Buñuel contributed an uncredited sequence design where a disembodied hand moves of its own accord (see chapter 2). But this image is merely de Van's most overt, knowing nod to surrealism. Far more compelling is the film's refusal to romanticize the juncture between dream and reality—the collision on which surrealism depends—as anything other than embodied, materialist, and female. In this way, the surrealism of *In My Skin* is closer to that of Breton's materialist critic and sometime rival Georges Bataille than to Breton's, but perhaps even closer still to the surrealism of women surrealist artists such as Meret Oppenheim, whose confrontationally tactile surrealist objects often draw their power from specifically feminine icons and themes. My goal here is not to categorize de Van as a surrealist but to describe *In My Skin* as an example of feminine horror that achieves its effects by turning to strategies of spectator engagement usefully understood through the lens of surrealism.

In My Skin tells the story of Esther's awakening to her body as both a distant, depersonalized object and the intimate, irresistible subject of her identity. From the outside, Esther appears to "have it all": a good job where she is valued and promoted; a handsome, professionally accomplished boyfriend, Vincent (Laurent Lucas), who is committed to a relationship of deepening seriousness with her; and a female best friend, Sandrine (Léa Drucker), who helps her find employment, works with her, and knows her well. But beneath the enviable exterior—and the film might be seen as a series of invitations to the viewer to go deeper and deeper under the surface, into Esther's skin—these markers of success aren't quite what they seem. The atmosphere of the office where Esther works is cutthroat and competitive, so her progress there requires a tricky balance of self-promotion and self-erasure that can (and does) leave others estranged from her, including the ultimately jealous Sandrine. Vincent, although concerned for her, is too defensive and judgmental to be trusted as a full confidante.

So as soon as Esther discovers, through an accident at a party, that she feels what should be searing pain in her body not first and foremost as unpleasurable, we have an intuitive sense that she is not merely a sick individual hopelessly out of touch with herself. We instead feel that she is an exceptionally intelligent, ambitious woman who perceives quite accurately that the price of "having it all" is a sort of self-denial that must return to inhabit the very site where the irresolvable tensions structuring her private and public personae take shape: her body. In other words, Esther is a woman whose conflicts are heartbreakingly familiar, not a freakish deviant from whom we can easily dissociate ourselves. Even if the spectacle of her increasingly deliberate and extreme self-mutilation grows more and more difficult to stomach—de Van rarely shrinks from the sort of graphically horrific detail that comes from either (or, more accurately, both) clinical detachment or passionate fascination—we never lose sight of her ability to make visible on her body the typically unseen pressures that often circumscribe a late-capitalist Western woman's personal and professional existence.

By allowing us into Esther's skin in all the literal, metaphorical, and gendered senses of that phrase, de Van creates a portrait of a woman that is harrowing but not pathologizing, tender but unrelenting, and horrific but not fantastic. Despite the gut-wrenching images of self-mutilation taken far beyond the realm of conventional medical diagnoses and into the unlikely stratosphere of autocannibalism, Esther is real in a way that surrealism helps us to recognize.[20] She is real in that she enables us to see a reality that everyday habits of perception hide from us: the costs of being a woman who "has it all." In this sense, there is nothing at all fantastic about In My Skin. In fact, the film calls to mind Breton's praise for M. G. Lewis's feverish British gothic novel The Monk (1796): in its "unforgettable intensity" there is "no longer anything fantastic: there is only the real."[21]

If surrealism often served to obscure rather than reveal the realities of female experience, usually by reducing women to the status of idealized muses or immature hysterics, then the achievements of the women who managed to channel the energies of surrealism for their own artistic purposes should be valued especially highly. Female artists associated with surrealism, such as Leonora Carrington, Léonor Fini, Frida Kahlo, Jacqueline Lamba, Lee Miller, Meret Oppenheim, Kay Sage, Dorothea Tanning, Toyen, and Remedios Varo have received more serious critical consideration in recent years, but the attention devoted to their work still pales before the criticism lavished on their male counterparts. The fact that many of these women were the partners or lovers of more famous male surrealists seems to have impeded the desire to study the female artists on their own terms, with the additional complication that a number of these women artists either renounced their connections to surrealism at some point or insisted that studying the female artists apart from the men is entirely counterproductive. Even though Oppenheim rejected the possibility that the work of female artists deserves focused critical attention so that historical patterns of overlooking or dismissal may be redressed, I turn to her in particular because I believe her work proves especially illuminating when analyzing the feminine horror of *In My Skin*.[22] Oppenheim, like de Van, stages female embodiment as an opportunity to confront the spectator's own body at the level of sensation.

Although Meret Oppenheim (1913–1985) was still a teenager when she moved to Paris from Switzerland in 1932, she quickly impressed the surrealists Alberto Giacometti and Hans Arp, who invited her to exhibit her work alongside that of other surrealist artists.[23] She also gained notoriety through the striking nude photographs of her taken by Man Ray, one of two surrealists with whom she would become romantically linked (the other was Max Ernst). Oppenheim maintained connections to surrealism throughout her life, but her most famous contribution to the movement is one of her earliest and most well-known artworks: a teacup, saucer, and spoon covered in fur entitled *Object (Le déjeuner en fourrure)* (1936) (fig. 6.3). Breton selected Oppenheim's piece for inclusion in the very first surrealist exhibition of object art in 1936, and he also reportedly bestowed the subtitle *Luncheon in Fur* on it (with its possible allusions to Leopold von Sacher-Masoch's novel *Venus in Furs* [1870], Edouard Manet's famous painting *Le déjeuner sur l'herbe* [1863], and Ernst's variation on Manet, a painting also entitled *Le déjeuner sur l'herbe* [1936]). That same year, *Object* was

6.3 Meret Oppenheim, *Object (Le déjeuner en fourrure)*, 1936. © 2021 Artists Rights Society (ARS), New York/ProLitteris, Zurich. Digital image © The Museum of Modern Art/ Licensed by SCALA/Art Resource, NY.

acquired by the Museum of Modern Art in New York and featured in curator Alfred H. Barr Jr.'s important exhibition there, *Fantastic Art, Dada, Surrealism* (1936–1937). Barr singled out *Object* for its remarkable impact on the public: "Few works of art in recent years have so captured the popular imagination . . . the 'fur-lined tea set' makes concretely real the most extreme, the most bizarre improbability. The tension and excitement caused by this object in the minds of tens of thousands of Americans have been expressed in rage, laughter, disgust, or delight."[24]

Why would Oppenheim's *Object* generate such strong reactions? Barr's words suggest but do not make explicit the arresting jolt of embodied feminine energy delivered by the piece. Few objects come with as many connotations of traditional feminine elegance and polite refinement as the tea set—*to serve* and *to entertain* might as well be its watchwords. As a result, the fur encasing it acts as a shocking revolt against such classical notions of the feminine by substituting a sign of animal savagery or human primitivism for one of civilized manners;[25] uncouth sexualization for restrained taste; and a tactile, feminine embodiment that repulses for a distant, feminine disembodiment that attracts. But what gives *Object* an unmistakably surrealist spark is its capacity not only to switch one reality (the tea set) for another (the fur) but also to demand that we see how these two realities are actually inseparable, how they have always infected each other in ways we have simply failed to recognize. Oppenheim applies the fur to the tea set very deftly, so alternations in the color, thickness, and patterning of the fur are matched carefully to the contours of the saucer, cup, and spoon. The effect on the spectator maximizes sensory awareness of how the tea set's "refinement" lies just beneath its "savagery" as well as how indivisible the tea set's refined and savage dimensions really are.

What Oppenheim does for the tea set, de Van does for the skin. Female skin is another time-honored marker of feminine elegance, refinement, and allure, so when de Van literally peels away that outer layer of traditional femininity to expose the blood, viscera, and self-mutilating carnal appetite beneath it, she insists that we see femininity with new eyes. Eyes that do not merely exchange our habitual enchantment with feminine surfaces for newfound disgust with what lies beneath the female skin but that confront us with the inextricability of the appealing exterior we wish to see and the frightening interior we do not. The eyes, in other words, of surrealism—shocked eyes embedded in shocked bodies that must refigure the reality of "femininity." Instead of an impoverished, stereotypical notion of femininity that goes only skin deep, we must consider a femininity that affords the female skin a whole new depth.

At the heart of this confrontation with the spectator, for both Oppenheim and de Van, is a recalibration of the positions of observer and observed. Oppenheim once wrote that whether "there are lines, spots, or a bouquet of flowers on a painting is unimportant; but one absolutely must have the impression that 'something is looking at you'—a meaning that isn't described in the painting, but rather emanates from it, floats around it."[26] Although Oppenheim's *Object* is not a painting, it surely "looks at you" in precisely the way she suggests. So, too, does *In My Skin*. The frisson delivered by these artworks stems from their uncanny skill in forcing us to feel observed when we are used to doing the observing, uneasily embodied when we are accustomed to being comfortably disembodied. The surrealist Marcel Jean gestured toward this power when he noted that spectators of the fur-lined teacup "immediately imagine themselves drinking their chocolate from this vessel."[27] We don't just observe the teacup from a distance; we become the observed who drinks from the teacup.

In My Skin performs a similar transmutation of observer and observed, even before its more graphically horrific sequences. De Van's very first images of Esther depict her at home, working at her desk. She is framed in a frontal medium close-up, so we can see only her face, neck, and shoulders. Her boyfriend Vincent enters the shot to peek at what Esther is doing, which is not visible to us. He chides her gently for working at such a slow pace, but we can hear her writing nearly constantly in longhand before and after their conversation—a brief talk where physical affection is interlaced with references to salaries, expenses, and the prospects of moving in together. De Van then cuts to an unusual low-height shot that tracks upward from near the floor, capturing Esther's bare leg bathed partially in shadow beside the metallic leg of the chair she sits on. The slow tracking movement allows us time to notice the texture of Esther's skin—its pores, bumps, and indentations—as well as how the shape of her leg mimics the shape of the chair's leg. In fact, de Van composes the shot in such a way that what we see is not so much the leg of Esther beside the leg of the chair but a single leg of fused flesh and metal, simultaneously animate and inanimate, subject and object. De Van reveals that the effect of this shot was deliberately constructed, so that the female leg and the chair leg blend visually to form a "hybrid body" that "permanently connects our image of the body with the setting," conjoining living flesh with "barren" inorganic material.[28] Through this "hybrid body," *In My Skin* introduces us to Esther with a visualization of transformative otherness that sets the tone for the entire film.

De Van's "hybrid body" defamiliarizes our sense of what is alive (human subject) and what is inanimate (material object), making it difficult for us to maintain our customary stance as observers. What could have been a probing, voyeuristic shot that permits us to spy on exposed female flesh caught unawares becomes instead a disorienting encounter with something not quite skin and not quite metal yet also both skin and metal. Instead of knowing confidently what we are observing, we find ourselves feeling observed—"something is looking at you." We feel observed because de Van, like Rothman before her, reverses so thoroughly those habits of looking at the feminine body that Mulvey calls the "to-be-looked-at-ness" of the cinematic female image: a well-established series of voyeuristic or fetishistic gestures rooted in narrative cinema's visual vocabulary that presents the woman as an erotic spectacle to be viewed for a spectator who is catered to by the film's organization of looking relations.[29] Again and again, *In My Skin* robs viewers of their ability to understand Esther's body along these lines, effectively choking off the conventional byways upon which spectatorship of the female figure tends to travel. We cannot be sure of what we are looking at or how to look at it or even where to look; our routine visual consumption of the female body, based on the privilege of disembodiment or on an erotic embodiment choreographed by the film itself, is interrupted and replaced by a profound uncertainty about the nature and practice of looking.

The consequent estrangement from our habits of seeing manifests itself as a turning of the tables on the mechanics of to-be-looked-at-ness. The standard cinematic logic of "woman as embodied image" and "spectator as disembodied (or pleasurably embodied) viewer" no longer holds. Instead of just doing the looking, we feel looked at—the film rotates our senses inward by severing access to the familiar forms of bodily address we are accustomed to as viewers, leaving us confusingly and uncomfortably embodied. De Van accentuates this confusion about what we are looking at (and who/what is doing the looking) by situating our first visual impressions of Esther within a split-screen credit sequence that often juxtaposes a clear, legible image of everyday places and things with an accompanying "negative" image that makes those same places and things strange, discolored, distorted. Like Oppenheim, de Van aims to "double" our vision along surrealist lines of confrontation and transformation—by blurring boundaries between teacup and fur, between skin and metal, between everyday and strange, between observer and observed, between self and other.

Although de Van begins this process of confronting the spectator quietly, she steadily escalates the horrific stakes. The first time Esther injures herself, we are as surprised as she is. When she uses a secluded upstairs bathroom at a party, she is shocked to find bloody tracks on the white carpet. Like her, we see the blood before we realize whose blood it is—her own. When Esther then inspects her wounded leg, which she unknowingly gashed outside the party while wandering through a construction area, she vacillates between repulsion and fascination. So do we. De Van films the wound in unsparingly explicit detail but with a tone of matter-of-fact curiosity rather than agitated terror. Again, we are not sure how to look or where to look. Toward the wound? Away from it? With concern for Esther? With bewilderment about her numbed reaction? The fact that we are again staring at Esther's leg, the same leg already "hybridized" for us earlier through a visual alchemy of skin and metal, makes this an especially surreal spectacle. Is the "real" leg made of unbroken skin? Brushed metal? Torn flesh?

The questions about how and where to look constantly posed to the spectator of *In My Skin* can be detected especially clearly in a scene where Esther
bathes herself at home after her leg has been treated at the hospital. In an uncom-
mon high-angle tracking shot that reveals Esther's full-frontal nudity as dis-
passionately as the blue plastic bag that insulates her wound from the bathwa-
ter, the spectator's attention is drawn not to her exposed body parts but to her
skin. Esther stretches the loose folds of flesh near her inner thigh in a strangely
detached manner, like a child at play or a surgeon at work on a body that is not
her own. She distends the skin beyond conventional limits, causing us to twinge
as we imagine what might happen to our own skin if we attempted to experiment with it as she does. By utilizing the high-angle framing that highlights
Esther's act of stretching her skin rather than the nudity of her body, de Van
short-circuits Esther's to-be-looked-at-ness and transforms it into an embodied awareness, a being-looked-at, on the part of the viewer.

But de Van is not through yet. After a cut, Esther appears in a blue bathrobe
that nearly matches the color of the plastic bag from the previous shot, height-
ening our sensory confusion about the layers and textures of matter we are
perceiving—bathrobe, bag, and skin intertwine. Is skin like plastic? Is a bathrobe like a bag—a body bag? Where does the (living) skin end and the (dead)
coating begin? The following shots overlay graphic horror onto these impressions as Esther unwraps the bandage around her wound and we see, in close-
up with minimal editing and without any nondiegetic sound, the mutilated
flesh of her leg (fig. 6.4). We cannot help but flinch, as even Esther herself does,
when she uses a scissor to separate the bandage from the sticky gauze, dried
blood, coarse stitches, and half-formed scabs beneath. Again, we feel the spectacle of Esther's skin "in here," in our own bodies, rather than observing it solely
as an image "out there," safely removed from us for our viewing pleasure. When
Vincent then bursts into the bathroom to greet Esther with a lover's familiarity, his warmth dies as soon as he sees the wound. He does not know how to
look at her; she in turn seems unsure how to look at him (or present herself to
him); and we, too, emerge from this scene with our habits of looking badly
shaken. We have absorbed a surrealist shock to the senses.

I have already mentioned how the image of Esther's detached forearm evokes
a series of related surrealist images made famous in the cinema by Buñuel.[30]
But when Esther retires to the hotel to feed upon herself, de Van includes an
illuminating variation on the most notorious image in surrealist film: the eyeball slashed with a razor in the opening moments of *Un chien andalou*. Esther,
lying prone, cuts open her upper thigh and brings her leg toward her mouth,
so that the blood leaking from the wound drips onto her face—and into her
eye. Where *Un chien andalou* mounts an attack on the spectator's vision—"You
will see differently, even if I have to slice your eye to accomplish it," the film
seems to state—*In My Skin* directs that attack not only outward at the spectator

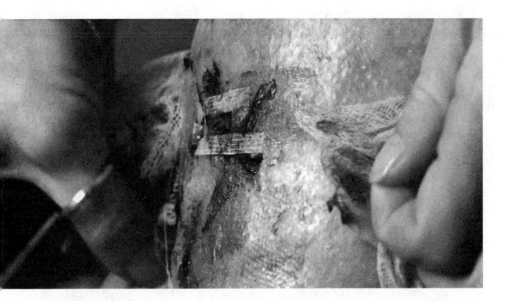

6.4 The mutilated flesh of Esther's leg in *In My Skin*.

but inward at Esther's own eye. It's as if *In My Skin* reformulates *Un chien andalou* to state, "You *will* see differently, and I am putting my own vision at risk to accomplish this." This is one of many scenes in the film where de Van's decision to cast herself as Esther enhances the confrontation with the spectator in striking ways. Again, the comparison with *Un chien andalou* is instructive: Buñuel cast himself as the slasher of the eyeball, lending a menacing literalness to his role as "cutter" of the film and a physical exclamation point to the film's desire to reach out and shock its audience. But Buñuel only enacts the violence; he is not its recipient. De Van, in contrast, enacts the violence *and* absorbs its effects, aligning herself with both the assaultive director and the assaulted spectator. Buñuel, on-screen and off-screen, observes from the outside while he unleashes violence on others. De Van, like us, is inside as well as outside the violence, observer and observed, self and other.

Surrealist film departs somewhat from surrealist painting in that appearances by the surrealists themselves within the films are more common than in the paintings.[31] But as the art historian Whitney Chadwick notes, this pattern does not hold true for female artists associated with surrealism: "Among women artists there is a persistent anchoring of their imagery in recognizable depictions of the artist, even when the subject of the work is not the self-portrait per se."[32] *In My Skin* resembles these self-depictions by female surrealists (paintings such as Fini's *The Alcove: An Interior with Three Women* [c. 1939], Kahlo's *The Broken Column* [1944], and Varo's *Titeres vegetales* [*Vegetarian Puppets*, 1938] as well as films such as Deren's *Meshes of the Afternoon*) not only through de Van's physical presence as the lead actress but also in her characterization of Esther as someone invested in recording and preserving her self-mutilation photographically. I am not suggesting that *In My Skin* is autobiographical in any direct manner but that de Van, like a number of female surrealist artists, invites spectators to reckon with how personally invested she is in addressing them in a bodily way.[33] De Van risks exposing her own body to the potentially objectifying gaze of viewers in order to confront those same viewers, at the level of bodily sensation, about how they see.

In My Skin ends with Esther retreating to another hotel room, where she engages in her most extended session of self-mutilation yet. For the first time, she uses a camera to photograph the damage inflicted on her body. These photographs are at once brutally detailed, with every bloody wound caught in sharply focused close-up, and impossibly abstracted because we cannot tell what part of the body we are looking at. In addition to the photographic record of her body's transformation, Esther also creates a bodily record: she removes a sizable patch of her own skin and attempts to preserve it using chemicals. In a poignant gesture, she presses this disembodied slice of skin against her breast, kissing it with a maternal tenderness that captures how violently her concepts of a whole body and a unified self have been shattered and how much she wishes to transform or invent a new sense of this sort of wholeness. Her gesture recalls the words of the female surrealist artist Leonora Carrington in a piece entitled "What Is a Woman?" from 1970:

> Am I that which I observe or that which observes me?. . . If I am my thoughts, then I could be anything from chicken soup to a pair of scissors, a crocodile, a corpse, a leopard or a pint of beer. If I am my feelings, then I am love, hate, irritation, boredom, happiness, pride, humility, pain, pleasure, and so on and so forth. If I am my body, then I am a foetus to a middle-aged woman changing every second. Yet, like everybody else I yearn for an identity although this yearning mystifies me always. If there is a true individual *identity* I would like to find it, because like truth on discovery it has already gone.[34]

Like Carrington, Esther cannot imagine a wholly integrated self that smoothly combines her thoughts, feelings, and body into an individual identity rooted in the descriptor "Woman." She attempts to be a certain kind of woman for Vincent, another for Sandrine, and yet another for her business associates, but the conflicting needs and expectations of these roles take on physical form when she mutilates her own body. The self-mutilation, as destructive as it is, also functions as a form of self-making—there is relief and even satisfaction for Esther when she can cut herself to her own specifications in a way she cannot with others. Abstracting herself from her body allows Esther to inflict chilling physical harm on herself, but it also permits her to give birth to herself. When Esther "nurses" her severed skin against her breast, just as she lovingly moisturizes another remnant of her own rended flesh with lip balm earlier in the film, she nurtures a part of herself that has been split off from her identity. She may see her own skin as an outside observer might when she mutilates her body, but she also reacts to these shards of her flesh with deep feelings of sadness, affection, and even protectiveness—the kinds of feelings that indicate she also feels observed by these supposedly "dead" fragments of herself.

In other words, Esther's identity is split into subjective and objective relations to herself in the register of transformative otherness—a fact that de Van visualizes by returning to split-screen framing and adding discontinuous diegetic sound during the climactic self-mutilation sequence. This sequence also includes a set of extraordinary shots in which Esther contorts her body in the mirror in ways that spin her self-image alternately closer to and farther away from recognition as a whole, unified body. It is fitting, then, that *In My Skin* concludes by confronting us with two Esthers: one who leaves the hotel to go to work (still an active subject, an observer, a self) and another who remains behind on the hotel bed, staring unblinkingly into the camera as the room rotates disorientingly around her (now an object, an observed component of the surroundings, an other perhaps dying or already dead). Yet in classic surrealist fashion, it is the observed Esther who stares directly back at us, daring us to see the "real" Esther as one or the other of these two variants when, of course, she is both (fig. 6.5). This is the face of feminine horror as transformative otherness: a cinematic portrait of gendered subject/object relations reimagined through horror's endlessly metamorphosing self/other relations.

But calling Esther, as written, directed, and acted by de Van, the face of feminine horror does not mean she is alone. One of the most exciting and distinguishing features of the New French Extremity is how many women directors are connected to it, including (in addition to de Van) Diane Bertrand (*The Ring Finger* [*L'annulaire*, 2005]), Catherine Breillat (*Fat Girl* [*À ma souer!*, 2001], Hélène Cattet (*Amer*, 2009; codirected with Bruno Forzani), Claire Denis (*Trouble Every Day*, 2001), Julia Ducournau (*Raw*, 2016), Coralie Fargeat (*Revenge*, 2018), and Lucile Hadzihalilovic (*Innocence*, 2004). As Tim Palmer points out, these women are just a few of the female filmmakers who have played important roles in the flourishing of contemporary French cinema, a production context where "many French women filmmakers are simply going about their business, finding audiences, working in an industry accommodating them on an unprecedented and increasingly proportionate scale."[35] So de Van has good company not only in terms of the number of female directors in recent French cinema more generally but also in terms of how women filmmakers are mining the New French Extremity for visions of feminine horror more specifically. Indeed, when we place *In My Skin* alongside films such as those listed here, we

6.5 Esther stares back at us at the conclusion of *In My Skin*.

can see in late twentieth- and early twenty-first-century France a golden age for feminine horror.

De Van joins Rothman, Deren, Nelly Kaplan (*A Very Curious Girl* [*La fiancée du pirate*, 1969]), Hélène Cattet (*The Strange Colour of Your Body's Tears*, 2013; codirected with Bruno Forzani), Julia Ducournau (*Titane*, 2021; whose earlier film *Raw* appears directly indebted to *In My Skin*), Veronika Franz (*Goodnight Mommy*, 2014; codirected with Severin Fiala), Lucile Hadzihalilovic (*Evolution*, 2015), and Agnieszka Smoczynska (*The Lure*, 2015) as women directors whose contributions to feminine horror evince the powerful influence of surrealism.[36] But de Van and Rothman also help us to see how a number of women directors closer to horror genre filmmaking rather than to surrealism also seem less atypical and worthy of further consideration alongside their peers in feminine horror who lean more heavily toward the arthouse or the avant-garde. These women directors include, among others, Amy Lynn Best (*Severe Injuries*, 2003), Angela Bettis (*Roman*, 2006), Kathryn Bigelow (*Near Dark*, 1987), Anna Biller (*The Love Witch*, 2016), Antonia Bird (*Ravenous*, 1999), Zandashé Brown (*Blood Runs Down*, 2018), Xan Cassavetes (*Kiss of the Damned*, 2013), Aislinn Clarke (*The Devil's Doorway*, 2018), Nia DaCosta (*Candyman*, 2021), Elisabeth Fies (*The Commune*, 2009), Gigi Saul Guerrero (*Culture Shock*, 2019), Catherine Hardwicke (*Twilight*, 2008), Mary Harron (*American Psycho*, 2000), Tiffany Jackson (*The Field Trip*, 2010), Natalie Erika James (*Relic*, 2020), Jennifer

Kent (*The Babadook*, 2014), Jackie Kong (*Blood Diner*, 1987), Karyn Kusama (*Jennifer's Body*, 2009), Karen Lam (*Evangeline*, 2015), Mary Lambert (*Pet Sematary*, 1989), Issa López (*Tigers Are Not Afraid*, 2019), Alice Lowe (*Prevenge*, 2017), Barbara Peeters (*Humanoids from the Deep*, 1980), Yolanda Ramke (*Cargo*, 2017; codirected with Ben Howling), Juliana Rojas (*Good Manners*, 2018; codirected with Marco Dutra), Katt Shea (*Dance of the Damned*, 1989), Jen and Sylvia Soska (*American Mary*, 2012), and Jovanka Vuckovic (*The Captured Bird*, 2012).[37]

As I mentioned earlier, feminine horror does not simply stand apart from the horror film writ large. It instead both incorporates the influence of male directors and exercises influence upon them in turn. Feminine-focused horror films such as *Repulsion* (Roman Polanski, 1965), *Ginger Snaps* (John Fawcett, 2000; written by Karen Walton), *Teeth* (Mitchell Lichtenstein, 2007), *Inside* (*À l'intérieur*; Alexandre Bustillo and Julien Maury, 2007), and *Swallow* (Carlo Mirabella-Davis, 2020) attest to this relationship, but so do the evolving roles of women in the work of some of the horror genre's most notable male auteurs. Persuasive arguments in this regard have been mounted for David Cronenberg and George A. Romero, directors whose more recent films make these cases even more compelling.[38] I am thinking in particular of Cronenberg's *A Dangerous Method* (2011), discussed in chapter 5, which gives the film's heart to Sabina Spielrein (Keira Knightley) rather than to the two powerful men on either side of her, Carl Jung (Michael Fassbender) and Sigmund Freud (Viggo Mortensen), who are directly descended from the "mad" scientists who dominate Cronenberg's earlier horror films, and of Romero's *Season of the Witch* (1973), *Day of the Dead* (1985), *Diary of the Dead* (2008), and *Survival of the Dead* (2009), where women, both living and undead, give the films their sharpest moral standpoint as well as their most affecting energy. Cronenberg (whose film *Rabid* [1977] was remade by Jen and Sylvia Soska in 2019) almost certainly influenced the embodied horror of *In My Skin*, and Brian De Palma (whose film *Sisters* [1972] was cowritten by Louisa Rose) also appears to be a touchstone for de Van—not only does she make emphatic use of the split screen, a device De Palma is famous for, but also the name of the hotel where Esther first mutilates herself is the "Hotel Palma."[39]

Alfred Hitchcock also makes his presence felt in *In My Skin*, especially in the hotel-room settings of Esther's self-mutilations and the shots of her eyes that evoke the famous visualization of Marion Crane's (Janet Leigh) dead eye as a graphic match for blood running down the drain in *Psycho* (1960)—an image that riffs on *Un chien andalou* and testifies to Hitchcock's well-known admiration of surrealist film (see chapter 2). De Van's channeling of Hitchcockian imagery reminds us that Hitchcock, although often taken to task as the antithesis of feminine horror, also blazed trails for feminine horror to explore in more depth. Revisiting *Psycho* alongside *In My Skin* highlights how Marion's dead eye, Norman Bates's (Anthony Perkins) peeping eye, and Mrs. Bates's empty, mummified eye sockets are not isolated subject or object positions but a conjoined network of horrific images that reach out toward and involve the spectator as both observer and observed—one of the hallmarks, as de Van demonstrates so powerfully, of feminine horror as transformative otherness.

Looking Forward: Jennifer Kent and *The Babadook*

The critical and commercial success of Jennifer Kent's *The Babadook* in 2014 represents a breakthrough for feminine horror. Garnering the kind of widespread public attention that eluded *The Velvet Vampire* and *In My Skin* upon their original releases, *The Babadook* demands consideration here at the conclusion of this chapter for its signaling of possible future directions in feminine horror. As an Australian film alongside Rothman's American work and de Van's French work, *The Babadook* also reminds us of the global reach of feminine horror.[40]

The *Babadook* focuses on the life of Amelia (Essie Davis), a single mother living with her six-year-old son, Samuel (Noah Wiseman), in a middle-class Australian suburb. Amelia lost her husband in a car accident while he drove her to the hospital to deliver Samuel. The trauma of this loss haunts Amelia's world in ways that deeply affect both her and her son. Because Samuel is a constant reminder of her husband's death, Amelia struggles to be affectionate toward him, while Samuel acts out with socially inappropriate and aggressive behavior. Their tense life together becomes worse when a mysterious children's book entitled *Mister Babadook* makes its way into their home through unexplained means. The book, in menacing pop-up illustrations, tells the story of a malevolent spirit called the Babadook that promises to terrorize the lives of those who refuse to "let him in." Amelia tries to hide the book and then even burn it, but it keeps returning. The arrival of the book is accompanied soon after by what appear to be manifestations of the Babadook's threatening presence. In a spiral of anxiety, sleeplessness, and prescribed sedatives, Amelia becomes more and more unhinged. After Samuel withdraws from school and Amelia loses her job as a nursing-home aide, the two spend more and more isolated time together in their small home, with the Babadook increasingly omnipresent and eventually possessing Amelia. In her possessed state, Amelia becomes neglectful and violent toward Samuel and kills the family dog. Samuel must eventually fight back by keeping his mother tied and bound, but he never loses sight of his love for her. Amelia uses the strength of Samuel's love to exorcize the Babadook from her body. At the film's end, she and Samuel are living a happy life together, but the Babadook has not been completely banished. It lives in the basement among the dead husband's belongings, still potentially fearsome but now seemingly content to be fed with the worms from the garden collected for it by Samuel and delivered to it by Amelia.

Even though *The Babadook* begins with a dream (a nightmare depicting the traumatic car accident), what is striking about the film when placed beside *The Velvet Vampire* and *In My Skin* is how little it depends on iconic surrealist imagery. If *The Velvet Vampire* channeled Cocteau beside Corman and *In My Skin* conjured Buñuel and Bataille beside Cronenberg and De Palma, then *The Babadook* opts for the visual vocabulary of the horror genre in a more classical sense. Indeed, the television programming that consumes Amelia draws largely on iconic horror images from Georges Méliès to Lon Chaney to Mario Bava, while Samuel's ingenious tinkerings with homemade weapons and traps as well as the Babadook's Freddy Krueger–like, knife-shaped fingers and assaults on sleep evocative of *A Nightmare on Elm Street* (1984) bear the stamp of Wes Craven. The fact that the television programming also includes naturalistic images of Australian wildlife (or as naturalistic as *Skippy the Bush Kangaroo* [1968–1970] can get) gestures toward Kent's investments in a more naturalist-based rather than surrealist-based horror.

But *The Babadook* is fully aligned with feminine horror nevertheless. Whereas *The Velvet Vampire* and *In My Skin* deployed surrealism to upend the categories of observer and observed, self and other, *The Babadook* turns to a horror-infused psychological realism. But the result is very similar: our desires to lean on clear distinctions between an observing self and an observed other become frustrated, especially regarding Mulvey's male gaze and female to-be-looked-at-ness. As we will recall, Mulvey theorizes the distinction between these two registers as a matter of gendered and sexualized difference (the active male looks at a passive, sexually objectified female), but what *The Babadook* insists upon, with remarkable power, is how Amelia suffers from female to-be-looked-at ness not as a sexual object but as a mother. Motherhood is as central to *The Babadook* as it is peripheral to *The Velvet Vampire* and *In My Skin*, so it is not surprising that Kent's intervention in feminine horror revolves around the maternal.

Again and again, Amelia is looked at by others in ways that judge her as an inadequate, incompetent, failing mother. Nearly all of Amelia's interactions with the world outside her home transpire along these lines, whether in the form of the scolding officials at Samuel's school, the doctor who disapproves of but reluctantly grants her desperate request for a children's sedative, the privileged mom friends of Amelia's sister who cannot fathom her problems, the police officers who doubt her story, or even the man whose car she runs into while driving in a distracted daze. This man, at first incensed that Amelia has damaged his brand-new car, alters the tone of his anger completely when he spies Samuel in the backseat of Amelia's car. He is more enraged with Amelia for endangering her child than for hitting his car, cursing her as a "crazy bitch" as she drives away. What the man vocalizes is precisely what so many of the film's looking relations convey: that to be a struggling mother is to be judged as a "crazy bitch."

The Babadook mounts a strong feminist critique of this misogynistic antipathy toward anything but the most safely idealized and policed version of motherhood. As Kent explains when discussing the originating impulses for her film, "We're all, as women, educated and conditioned to think that motherhood is an easy thing that just happens. But it's not always the case."[41] If *Rosemary's Baby* (Roman Polanski, 1968) uses horror to tell the unacknowledged truth about the stubbornly taboo subjects of difficult pregnancies and postpartum depression, as Lucy Fischer has argued,[42] then *The Babadook* extends this critique to the situation faced by single working mothers in particular. Amelia's job as a nursing-home aide in the dementia ward requires her to be properly "maternal" even at the workplace, with no recognition of how hard it is to meet such expectations in general, let alone when the responsibilities for mothering at home are so exhausting. Amelia's supervisors glare at her with equal venom when she must take a call at work from her son's school and when an exhausted Amelia treats the nursing-home patients as unresponsive "children" during a bingo game she administers distractedly. Amelia must absorb the withering looks directed at her as a failing mother, only this time these looks follow her to work from home and back again. There is no space that offers her refuge from the to-be-looked-at-ness of being a maternal figure.

Indeed, it is striking that Amelia's one brief moment of escape, her visit to a shopping mall made possible when her kindly coworker Robbie (Daniel Henshall) offers to cover her shift, is ultimately revealed as no escape at all. Kent brilliantly captures Amelia's desire to become invisible, to become transparent to the judging looks of maternal to-be-looked-at-ness, by framing Amelia at the mall against blank white walls, bright white light, reflective glass surfaces, and faceless mannequins clad in mostly white clothing (fig. 6.6). "There is nothing to look at here," Amelia seems to be telling the world that is always so eager to inspect her maternal qualifications. With no child in tow, she even allows herself to eat the ice cream (white vanilla, of course) usually reserved for her son; the real luxury is not so much the ice cream itself but reveling in the rare absence of looks usually directed at a mother for seeing how responsibly she handles her child's consumption of a treat like ice cream (too indulgent? too strict? what would a "good mother" do?).

The feminine horror of *The Babadook* comes through when even this fleeting moment of escape for Amelia exacts a steep price in terms of maternal judgment. While at the mall, she misses a series of frantic calls from her sister, who is distressed by how much Samuel is frightening her daughter while in her temporary care. "Where have you been? You weren't at work," her angered sister scolds, as if surveillance rather than support of Amelia were her top priority. Even her coworker Robbie contributes to this elevation of surveillance over support by showing up at Amelia's house unannounced shortly after her visit to the mall, with flowers for Amelia and a gift for Samuel. Suddenly, it becomes

6.6 Amelia (Essie Davis), whose desire to become invisible is made visual in *The Babadook*.

all too apparent that Robbie's kindness, however well intentioned and clumsily romantic, is given less in the spirit of selfless assistance and more in the spirit of obligatory reciprocation. Robbie, who assumes that covering for Amelia at work will allow her to have more time at home with her sick son and thus make Robbie himself more attractive to her romantically since she will value his recognition of her maternal needs, has his idealized visions of Amelia's motherhood quickly scuttled. Samuel reveals he was not sick at all, it becomes clear that Amelia was not tending to him in the ways Robbie had assumed, and quite obviously the flowers are far less useful for Amelia than her vibrator (and even the vibrator cannot compete with Samuel's endless need for attention, as shown in an earlier scene of interrupted masturbation). In short, Robbie's assumptions about Amelia's motherhood, even after his hopeful assertion to her that she doesn't always "have to be fine," proves no match for the realities of Amelia's motherhood. He has never really seen Amelia at all, and we never see him again.

The sophistication of *The Babadook*'s approach to feminine horror resides in its ability to show how the film's conflicts are not only about others looking at Amelia and passing judgment on her motherhood but also about how she internalizes these maternal judgments. All too often, Amelia looks at herself through the eyes of others and finds herself failing as others imagine her to be failing. She even grows hostile toward the one woman who truly sees her generously and without judgment, the elderly next-door neighbor, Mrs. Roach (Barbara West), because she fears becoming the older woman. When Amelia looks at Mrs. Roach, she sees a nightmare version of herself: alone, lonely, helpless, glued to the television, a potential victim of the Babadook. It is significant that Mrs. Roach's name conjures the cockroaches that haunt Amelia while she is under the spell of the Babadook, an imaginary infestation that again triggers self-judgments about her inadequacy as a mother who can't keep a clean home.

Redemption arrives for Amelia when she quite literally vomits out these internalized maternal judgments of others, simultaneously expelling the Babadook's presence inside her. In this redemptive moment, Amelia converts her most horrifying gesture while possessed by the Babadook—strangling Samuel nearly to death—to her most physically maternal gesture of her own: holding Samuel close to her own body with fierce protectiveness after shouting to the Babadook, "If you touch my son again, I'll fucking kill you!" (fig. 6.7). Then Amelia screams so intensely, so full of rage and love, that the Babadook crumples. Yet the Babadook's final retreat comes not through Amelia's scream but because of what she does next: she reaches out to it with concern and tenderness, as a mother would toward her wounded child.

What Amelia achieves in this act of redemption is ultimately a recognition of transformative otherness concerning her motherhood that is as powerful for the audience as it is for her. In this moment, Kent's emphasis on the entwined nature of Amelia's two physical gestures (one violently aggressive, the other violently protective) expresses how "bad" motherhood and "good" motherhood are not polar opposites but intimately interdependent. The rage undergirds the love and vice versa. The terror and the joy of motherhood are rooted in the inextricability of these forms of attachment, their shared emotional substance, their horrifying *and* redemptive capacity to transform into each other. When Amelia realizes this, she sees herself—and we see her—not as a mother who is "bad" or "good" but as a mother who no longer fears the looks of others from

6.7 Amelia protects her son in *The Babadook*.

without or within that adhere to these categorizations in the first place. Like Susan and Esther before her, she has stepped through the mirror.

The Babadook's epilogue hammers home Kent's refiguring of motherhood through feminine horror. The transformative otherness of Amelia's new relation to being a mother is underlined by not having the Babadook destroyed ("bad" mother replaced by "good" mother) but by keeping it carefully, cautiously, perhaps even tenuously domesticated ("good" mother and "bad" mother in constant negotiation, one metamorphosing into the other until the lines between them disappear). Notice how Amelia will not permit Samuel to accompany her into the basement when she feeds the Babadook ("one day, when you're bigger") as well as how the bruises on Samuel's neck from her strangulation of him are fading yet still visible as the film ends. But Amelia no longer attempts to hide or cringes in shame when such signs of "bad" motherhood emerge. She is no longer beholden to the to-be-looked-at-ness of maternal judgment. When the social workers return to her home to do an inspection of her maternal fitness, an event that terrified and shamed her earlier in the film, it is no longer Amelia who feels observed but the social workers. She and Samuel are so forthright in their ownership of their pain—they openly admit to the social workers that this is the first birthday Samuel will celebrate on the proper date because his father died on that same day—that it is the social workers who feel self-conscious and uncomfortable. Amelia has turned the observers into the observed by finally seeing herself as fully and generously as Mrs. Roach (now a valued caretaker for Samuel while Amelia works) has always seen her.

When *The Babadook* performs this transformation of observer and observed, it achieves the ends of feminine horror through means other than surrealism. What *The Velvet Vampire* and *In My Skin* accomplish by wedding surrealism and horror comes to fruition in *The Babadook* by juxtaposing motherhood and horror. Early in the film, Kent captures Amelia's horror when she reads this line in *Mister Babadook*: "You start to change when I get in, the Babadook growing right under your skin." In that moment, Amelia fears she already is or will soon become the Babadook, the "bad" mother incarnate. But by the film's conclusion, she clearly understands that line from *Mister Babadook* as a source of strength, not a threat. Amelia has become the Babadook, at least in the sense of acknowledging that the rage of the Babadook is part of her just as much as the love of a "good" mother is part of her, that these two parts are not parts at all but a single, transformative whole.

Samuel's fascination with magic and his steadily increasing (Babadook-enabled?) mastery of it remind us that, as Samuel himself puts it, "life is not always as it seems." We may still need magic in order for society to see motherhood in terms beyond the "good" and "bad," but *The Babadook*'s feminine horror allows us to see Kent generating that magic through cinema. This is a feat

Kent will achieve even more impressively in *The Nightingale* (2019), another extraordinary meditation on traumatized motherhood through the vocabulary of horror (now rape revenge rather than ghostly possession). Kent invites us, along with Amelia, to feel the Babadook growing right there, under our skin, just as de Van invites us into Esther's skin and Rothman into Susan's skin. Together, these women show us the power and the promise of feminine horror.

In a curious but revealing postscript, part of *The Babadook*'s ascent into popular culture's consciousness involved its appropriation as a queer allegory. In 2017, a "queer Babadook" internet meme went viral. "Haunting a small white family in an Australian suburb is a radical act, and the Babadook did that," noted the journalist John Paul Brammer while commenting on the queer Babadook phenomenon. Another journalist, Alex Abad-Santos, said that the Babadook "is queer in the most empirical sense," that "its existence is defiance, and it seeks to break down the borders of acceptability and establishment."[43] Although space does not permit an extended study of the queer Babadook here, its suggestive intersection between different forms of otherness, namely feminine and queer horror, are explored in the following chapter in relation to Blackness and Jewishness.

CHAPTER 7

RACIAL OTHERNESS

Horror's Black/Jewish Minority Vocabulary, from Jordan Peele
to Ira Levin and Curt Siodmak

The writer-director Jordan Peele geared up for the premiere of his
breakthrough horror blockbuster *Get Out* (2017) by programming
a slate of films that influenced him at New York's Brooklyn Academy of Music under the series title "The Art of the Social Thriller." The films
Peele selected were *Night of the Living Dead* (George A. Romero, 1968), *Rosemary's Baby* (Roman Polanski, 1968), *The Shining* (Stanley Kubrick, 1980), *Candyman* (Bernard Rose, 1992), *The 'Burbs* (Joe Dante, 1989), *Scream* (Wes Craven, 1996), *Rear Window* (Alfred Hitchcock, 1954), *Funny Games* (Michael
Haneke, 1997), *The Silence of the Lambs* (Jonathan Demme, 1991), *The People
Under the Stairs* (Wes Craven, 1991), and *Guess Who's Coming to Dinner* (Stanley Kramer, 1967). It's a striking and telling array of influences, but only one of
the two films that hang most heavily over *Get Out* is included: *Rosemary's Baby*.
The other, as this chapter illustrates, is *The Stepford Wives* (Bryan Forbes, 1975).
Both are famous modern horror films, but they began as best-selling novels
(published in 1967 and 1972, respectively) by the Jewish American author Ira
Levin (1929–2007). In fact, Peele has spoken openly about *Get Out's* debt to what
he calls "the Ira Levin school of writing."[1]

The fact that *Get Out* would find so much inspiration in a Jewish author's
work is fascinating in its own right and suggests that the horror genre may have
some important things to teach us about how social minority positions have
more in common than we might imagine—that those who lack social power
and suffer from majority prejudice can find common ground in horror. This
commonality extends not just to Jews and Blacks but also to women: *Rosemary's*

Baby reads like a Jewish nightmare of anti-Semitic oppression in the same way that *The Stepford Wives* reads like a feminist nightmare of gender oppression.[2]

Get Out's African American protagonist, Chris Washington (Daniel Kaluuya), is apprehensive about meeting his white girlfriend Rose Armitage's (Allison Williams) parents for the first time. She reassures him that their trip from the urban city to the exurban country to meet them will be just fine because her parents are liberal and accepting people. But the visit becomes increasingly nightmarish as Chris's suspicions grow about the strange, unspoken racism of Rose's family and friends as well as of Rose herself. Ultimately, Chris learns the shattering truth: the Armitages are the leaders of a secret society that lures Black people into their clutches so they can be subjected to a terrifying medical procedure that inserts aging white brains into young Black bodies, erasing Black subjectivity in the process. Chris realizes that he is the next target and that his life is on the line. Through courageous strength and cunning, Chris manages, with some last-minute help from his Black friend Rod (Lil Rel Howery), to escape the white nightmare of the Armitages with his body and mind intact.

What Peele gets from Levin is that when you are a social minority, paranoia can be real, lived horror even if it is treated only as absurd fantasy by the social majority. As Rosemary Woodhouse says in the novel *Rosemary's Baby* when she tries to convince others who refuse to believe that she has become the victim of an elderly band of Satanists, "Now and then there *are* plots against people, aren't there?"[3] What Rosemary voices here is the horror of minority experience within a majority society that marginalizes the legitimacy of that horror, that dismisses real pain as imagined paranoia. In Levin's fiction and in *Get Out*, being paranoid is not a delusional state but an anguished way of waking up to the way things actually are.

This chapter begins by exploring the affinities between *Get Out* and Levin's work to theorize what I call modern horror's minority vocabulary: the genre's ability to articulate the experience of social minorities as real pain rather than just paranoid fantasy. The horror film has often been regarded as thriving negatively on otherness, usually by aligning its monstrous threats with social others. As we will recall, Robin Wood's landmark claim that the structure of horror films can be boiled down to the formula "normality is threatened by the Monster" assumes that the monster resembles the minority others that majority society fears—those deemed different in terms of race, class, gender, sexuality, nationality, ethnicity, or political beliefs.[4] What Wood and those in his wake have been less willing to argue is that horror's relation to social otherness may be closer to acknowledging actual minority experience rather than converting it into fantastic monstrosity. This is precisely what a closer look at the relationship between Peele and Levin reveals—the power of horror as a vocabulary for the illumination, not the demonization, of the pain endured by social minorities.[5] Levin and Peele, each on his own but even more emphatically together, show us horror as transformative otherness in conjunction with race. Indeed, they demonstrate how the notion of transformation has always been foundational for the horror film and how closely horror's imagination of transformation has been connected to racially inflected allegories of becoming Black or becoming Jewish. In this chapter's second half, these issues of transformation are pursued through another Jewish writer whose impact on Peele is not as explicit as Levin's but whose legacy for *Get Out* is equally important: Curt Siodmak, writer of both *Donovan's Brain* (1942) and *The Wolf Man* (George Waggner, 1941).

From *Get Out* to *Rosemary's Baby* and *The Stepford Wives*

Get Out is at least as much a product of 1968 as it is of 2017. Peele's use of horror as a minority vocabulary stems directly from two watershed modern horror films released in 1968: *Rosemary's Baby* and *Night of the Living Dead*. Although both of these films have long been considered central to shaping modern horror cinema, they have most often been perceived as inhabiting opposite ends of the horror spectrum. *Rosemary's Baby* is the glossy, big-budget, star-studded, Hollywood-produced, auteur-driven horror film that paved the way for *The Exorcist* (William Friedkin, 1973), *The Omen* (Richard Donner, 1976), *The Silence of the Lambs*, *The Sixth Sense* (M. Night Shyamalan, 1999), *Zodiac* (David Fincher, 2007), and *The Shape of Water* (Guillermo del Toro, 2017). *Night of the Living Dead*, as discussed in this book's introduction, is the gritty, low-budget, starless, independently produced, unknown-directed horror film that opened the doors for *The Last House on the Left* (Wes Craven, 1972), *The Texas Chain Saw Massacre* (Tobe Hooper, 1974), *Shivers* (David Cronenberg, 1975), *Halloween* (John Carpenter, 1978), *The Blair Witch Project* (Daniel Myrick and Eduardo Sánchez, 1999), *Paranormal Activity* (Oren Peli, 2007), and *Get Out*. What is lost when focusing on these differences, however, is how much the two films share in terms of their investments in social otherness.[6] *Night of the Living Dead* features an African American protagonist, Ben (Duane Jones), who survives the zombie onslaught only to be murdered by the all-white militia that has supposedly come to his rescue. *Rosemary's Baby* is less straightforward in its presentation of social otherness, but pairing Polanski's film with Levin's source novel uncovers just how much *Rosemary's Baby* is rooted in the dynamics of a Jewish nightmare.

In Levin's novel, one of Rosemary's friends reacts to her emaciated appearance during her pregnancy with a telling line: "You look like Miss Concentration Camp of 1966" (154). A hint, among others, that Rosemary's struggle is not limited to being sold out by her husband to a coven of Satanists and impregnated with the Antichrist. Her struggle also transforms her from a literal Catholic into a figurative Jew. Already a sort of fish out of water in the New York of the 1960s due to her midwestern background and residual attachment to the Catholic faith, Rosemary becomes truly other as she draws closer to the Jewish elements in her life. First, her ostensibly Protestant husband, Guy Woodhouse, is already tainted in the eyes of her midwestern Catholic family for having divorced parents and a mother who married again, this time to a Jew no less. It's even possible that Guy changed his name from Sherman Peden for reasons not solely to do with his acting profession. After all, he criticizes his fellow actor Donald Baumgart for holding on to his Jewish-sounding name, a name Guy makes a point to ridicule; it is Baumgart, moreover, whom Guy blinds with the help of the coven in order to secure his own break in the acting business. Like the Jewish Bobbie Markowe in Levin's novel *The Stepford Wives*, who changes her surname from Markowitz to Markowe in order to conceal her Jewishness, it's possible that Guy's background is not Protestant at all. Although Levin does not make this suggestion explicit, he makes it clear that one of Guy's partners in the coven, Abe Sapirstein, is a Jew. Sapirstein, the famous obstetrician who becomes Rosemary's doctor at the behest of the coven, is praised by the coven's leader, Roman Castevet, as "brilliant, with all the sensitivity of his much-tormented race" (110). The characterization of the Jews as a "much-tormented race" who might have something to gain from Roman's promises that Satan "shall redeem the despised and wreak vengeance in the name of the burned and the tortured!" (236) is underlined by having Roman hide behind his own false name ("Roman Castevet" is, as Rosemary discovers, an anagram for his true name, Steven Marcato, son of the infamous Satanist Adrian Marcato). Rosemary, who is as uncertain about her own name (she veers between her married name and her maiden name, Reilly) as she is about the name of her unborn child, at one point tells Sapirstein that she wants to name her baby after him. Sapirstein's response: "God forbid" (184).

Sapirstein's reply is emblematic of Levin's humorously ironic but cutting juxtaposition of the fantastic and the realistic in his work. On the one hand, Sapirstein as Satanist is suggesting to Rosemary, "If only you knew how little agency you will have in the identity of your baby and how little God will have to do with it." On the other hand, Sapirstein as Jew is also saying, "Why would you saddle your child with such a Jewish-sounding name when it will undoubtedly result in social suffering?" The fact that the names "Adrian," "Andrew," and "Abe" begin with the same letter and compete as possible names for Rosemary's baby points toward a certain interchangeability between the positions of Satanist and Christian (Adrian dies in a stable, Christ is born in a manger) as well as of Satanist and Jew (Sapirstein, named after the father of the Jewish people, delivers babies for others, while his namesake was willing to kill his own miraculously born child to prove his faith in God). It's as if Levin, with his nearly obsessive exchanging of "true" and "false" names (even Rosemary's trustworthy friend Edward "Hutch" Hutchins writes adventure stories for boys under three different pseudonyms), is arguing that everyone is in danger of becoming an other—Christ is only so far from the Antichrist, the Christian only so far from the Jew, the God-fearing believer only so far from the Satanist. Simply scratch out one name and put in another, and a different identity appears. In this logic of precarious naming, Rosemary as figurative Jew makes alarming sense—there *is* a plot against her, she *could* suffer the fate of those condemned to the concentration camps. She is not a Jew, but she has come to occupy the social position of Jew as persecuted other.

It may seem surprising at first that writer-director Roman Polanski, as both a Polish Jew and a Holocaust survivor, drains much of Levin's explicitly Jewish content from the film adaptation of *Rosemary's Baby*. Gone is the "Miss Concentration Camp" line, Guy's Jewish-tainted family history, and the explicit identification of Sapirstein as a Jew. But since Polanski's own survival as a child depended in part on concealing his Jewishness, it makes sense that it is not really until *The Pianist* (2002) that he grapples with Jewishness in any overt, straightforward way.[7] But nearly all of his films draw much of their power from channeling precisely the sort of paranoia that anchors Levin's Jewish-inflected vision. In fact, Levin has called Polanski's *Rosemary's Baby* "possibly the most faithful film adaptation ever made."[8] Levin may foreground Jewishness in a way that Polanski does not, but both men convey the pain of paranoia's reality for the social other. In short, there is a shared feeling for Jewishness as a persecuted minority position in both Levin and Polanski, even if one expresses it explicitly and the other implicitly. For example, it is noteworthy that Polanski replaces Levin's description of Minnie Castevet's "hoarse midwestern bray" (24) with the actress Ruth Gordon's nasal, stereotypically New York Jewish cadences. Gordon's voice suggests that Polanski wishes to retain, at least on an implicit level (neither Minnie nor Gordon is Jewish), the presence of Jewishness in the mixed brew of identities presented by the film.

Get Out nods to *Rosemary's Baby* in a number of ways, including the naming of the patriarch of the white Armitage clan "Roman," but perhaps the most powerful connection between the two texts (and here I am combining Levin's novel and Polanski's film as a collective reference point) are the affinities between Chris and Rosemary (Mia Farrow). Both protagonists veer between knowing and not knowing what is happening to them, between trust and distrust of their own gut feelings, between wishful desires about those who surround them and steely recognition of the dangers they pose. In short, they oscillate between denying their observations, feelings, and experiences as paranoid and embracing them as truth.

Of course, there are dissonances between Chris and Rosemary as well. Chris fights and even kills some of his enemies (although he relents from strangling his betraying girlfriend, Rose, to death), whereas Rosemary's knife-wielding revenge on her tormentors is cut short by her maternal instincts toward her baby

7.1 Chris (Daniel Kaluuya) avenges himself against his enemies in *Get Out*.

7.2 Rosemary (Mia Farrow) prepares to avenge herself against her enemies in *Rosemary's Baby*.

(figs. 7.1 and 7.2). Rosemary loses her only real ally in the conspiracy against her when the coven places her perceptive friend Hutch (Maurice Evans) in a coma, resulting in his eventual death. Chris's Hutch, his friend Rod, a Transportation Security Administration officer, not only uncovers the conspiracy against Chris but also saves him from it when he arrives to rescue him at the film's conclusion. Naming Chris's girlfriend "Rose" suggests that Peele is aware of both the similarities and differences between Chris and Rosemary. For much of *Get Out*, we believe that Rose is Chris's ally, confidante, and partner. But Rose is not Rosemary, as Peele reveals in the film's final act. So even if Peele mobilizes Rose's apparent closeness to Chris early on, he ultimately warns us not to simply equate Rose with Rosemary or Chris with Rosemary.

In fact, the biggest difference between Chris and Rosemary emerges when Chris, accompanied by Rod, is able to leave the nightmare of the country behind and return to a community in the city. Where *Rosemary's Baby* concentrates its horror in the seemingly civilized urban setting of a stately Manhattan apartment building, *Get Out* discloses the exurban space of the country—with its isolation, wealth, emptiness, and whiteness—to be much more frightening than the city. In fact, Chris's foundational trauma, the loss of his mother in a hit-and-run accident when he was a child, is about this divide: in the racially diverse city, you are connected to other people and *should* call for help (which Chris as a child was too frightened to do); in the racially homogenous country, you (especially when you're nonwhite) are alone, and no one will help. When Rod saves Chris, the city comes to the country, where the sense of a Black community finally gets established, against all odds, in a place that is entirely inhospitable to it.

The dissonances between Chris and Rosemary diminish when Chris is placed alongside Joanna Eberhart, the heroine of Levin's *The Stepford Wives*. Joanna is a stronger, more self-aware version of Rosemary. She is an accomplished professional woman, successful homemaker, and awakened feminist who moves with her husband and two children from New York City to the suburb of Stepford, Connecticut. The conspiracy against Joanna and the other women of Stepford is a plot hatched by the men of the town to replace their wives with animatronic robots that desire only to indulge the husbands' decidedly prefeminist whims. Joanna, like Chris, is a photographer, and the two even share some of the same photographic subject matter. Chris's intimate portraits of urban African American life are anticipated by one of Joanna's most prized photographs: a well-dressed young Black man attempting to hail a ride but ignored by an empty taxicab that passes him by. Joanna captures not only the scene but also the expression of the Black man "glaring venomously" as the cab drives away.[9]

Joanna's photograph, which she later titles *Off Duty*—paired with her deep friendship with the Jewish Bobbie Markowe and her budding friendship with Stepford's first Black resident, Ruthanne Hendry—posits her, like Rosemary, as a figurative racial minority. Joanna's figurative role is compounded not only by her literal status as a gendered minority (she is a feminist woman in an environment where women are subordinate to men and feminism is treated like an infection) but also by the symbolic transference of her anticonspiratorial mission to Ruthanne in the novel's final act. Ruthanne, who already shares with

Joanna an artist's sense of observation concerning her surrounding social reality (she is an author and illustrator of children's books), becomes the final chance for Joanna's discoveries about the true Stepford to come to light. One of Joanna's last thoughts before she succumbs to robotic replacement is that she must warn Ruthanne, and it is through Ruthanne's eyes that we see the transformed Joanna at the end of the novel. If Joanna's soul lives on, then it is through Ruthanne's Black body.

Chris must be understood, in the final analysis, as a composite of Joanna and Rosemary. Through his connections to them, he inherits horror's vocabulary of social otherness as a fabric interwoven across Black, Jewish, and female strands. By extension, Peele's *Get Out* must be understood as building on Levin's earlier creations through an expanded articulation of minority paranoia as lived pain in the horror vernacular. What Peele achieves in *Get Out* by making Blackness the explicit subject rather than the implicit subtext of minority otherness is comparable to the move Levin makes in his novel *The Boys from Brazil* (1976) and in his play *Cantorial* (1988), where Jewishness moves from the background to the foreground.[10] *The Boys from Brazil*, like *Rosemary's Baby*, includes a conspiracy against the innocent: this time the conspirators are Nazis who survived World War II. And like *The Stepford Wives*, *The Boys from Brazil* includes a technological plan to put minorities back in their place: genetic engineering masterminded by Josef Mengele produces newly born clones of Adolf Hitler.

In both *The Boys from Brazil* and *Get Out*, a past that is not even past returns to haunt and humiliate the minority protagonists. Jews who survived the Holocaust must face the prospect of reliving it through a new genetically engineered Hitler; Chris as a modern Black man is sold to the highest bidder in a slave auction and must resort to "cotton picking" (plugging his ears with it to ward off hypnosis) in order to escape. These ghostly revivals of the traumatic past underline how much minority "paranoia" in the present is not a matter of hysteria but a reckoning with how the unresolved past shapes today's world. Levin and Peele speak the language of horror precisely because they want to convey how minority paranoia is not paranoia at all. The true monster for Levin is not a genetically engineered Hitler clone but the world's inability to comprehend how anti-Semitism did not die in Hitler's bunker. The true monster for Peele is not a white neurosurgeon who resuscitates slavery but today's systemic racism that still objectifies Blacks as if they were something less than fully human. This connection between Peele's *Get Out* and Levin's *The Boys from Brazil* can be seen even more clearly in light of Peele's subsequent involvement with the television series *Hunters* (David Weil and Nikki Toscano, 2020–), a thriller featuring Jewish Holocaust survivors banding together with a racially diverse set of allies to battle Nazis in America in the 1970s. I return to *Hunters* in this book's conclusion.

Shadow and Act

When Ralph Ellison meditated in 1949 on the state of Black representation in American films of the 1940s, he turned to the distinction between "the shadow" and "the act." Film is the shadow, the realm of the image, and the act is history, the realm of action. For Ellison, the act precedes the shadow and cuts a sharp divide between the two; to treat the shadow as if it were the act would be "to confuse portrayal with action, image with reality."[11] Distinguishing shadow from act allows Ellison to find symptomatic value and emotional power in social problem films that address race, such as *Home of the Brave* (Mark Robson, 1949) and *Pinky* (Elia Kazan, 1949), no matter how blinkered or even absurd they might be in their imagining of actual Black experience and subjectivity. The fact that these films are focusing on race at all strikes Ellison as worth noting, despite their many limitations. Their value stems from the opportunity they provide especially for white viewers to connect to "the deep centers of American emotion" touched by the films. As Ellison observes, "One of the most interesting experiences connected with viewing [these films] in predominantly white audiences is the profuse flow of tears and the sighs of profound emotional catharsis heard on all sides. It is as though there were some deep relief to be gained merely from seeing these subjects projected upon the screen."[12]

What happens when we move from social problem films such as *Home of the Brave* and *Pinky* to a horror film such as *Get Out*? When tears, sighs, and relief become screams, gasps, and discomfort? Do the shadow and the act remain as neatly distinct as Ellison suggests? Or does the shadow, accruing the full power of its darkest connotations, which horror understands as a matter of course, transform our very relation to the act rather than separating itself from the act? Perhaps we feel the act through the shadow in a way that horror makes visceral, through fear and unease, in a territory of the imagination where social problem films do not dare to tread. By availing themselves of the particular resources of horror, of minority paranoia made experientially real, Peele and Levin bring the shadow and the act into an affective proximity that Ellison cannot yet detect in the films he studies.

What we can see in Levin and Peele together as they reconfigure the boundary between Ellison's shadow and act is a definition of minority experience as not only human but also *shared*—something carried collectively (even if unequally) by Blacks, Jews, and women. The unequal yet shared quality attached to this burden of otherness is something Toni Morrison addresses in *The Origin of Others* (2017), discussed in this book's introduction. Morrison, reflecting on the pain of Black experience in both literature and life, is as keenly attuned as Ellison and Peele are to how Black otherness must be reckoned with as a specific form of anguish in its own right. As Morrison reminds us so power-fully, the African American experience of slavery and its poisonous racist leg-acies distinguishes Black otherness from the othering of groups such as Jews and women in America. "The narratives of slaves, both written and spoken, are critical to understanding the process of Othering," Morrison insists.[13]

Yet Morrison also observes that "racial identification and exclusion did not begin, or end, with Blacks."[14] She begins her study of otherness by connecting America's obsession with racial difference not only to slavery but also to the centrality of immigration for American history and identity. For Morrison, the waves of immigration to the United States, in particular those from southern and eastern Europe during the late nineteenth and early twentieth century, helped set a standard that equated Americanness with whiteness. As Morrison states, "These immigrants to the United States," which included millions of Jews, "understood that if they wanted to become 'real' Americans they must sever or at least greatly downplay their ties to their native country, in order to embrace their whiteness." Of course, this act of "embracing whiteness" is itself an unequal proposition, a possibility open to European (white) Jews and white women in ways that are unthinkable for Blacks. Morrison is deeply aware of this inequality and never loses sight of its intractability: "The definition of 'Americanness' (sadly) remains color for many people."[15]

But Morrison also recognizes the value and the need to connect Black oth-erness to the othering of groups also considered apart from the white Ameri-can standard. All of her theoretical categories in *The Origin of Others*, such as "belonging," "stranger," "foreigner," and of course "Otherness" itself, are con-cepts that encompass Blackness but also hold open the possibility of placing Blackness in conversation with different forms of othering. When I refer to the unequal yet shared relations between Blacks, Jews, and women across the work of Peele and Levin, I am attempting to channel Morrison's call for us to listen for the sounds of shared otherness—not to *equate* different forms of otherness but to *learn* from how they might harmonize.

One way that Levin and Peele accomplish this feat of illuminating shared otherness is by modulating the dynamics of voice and silence so that minority positions become figurative instead of solely literal. We have already seen how Rosemary and Joanna become figurative Jews in Levin, how the plots against them attempt to relegate their own voices and their own pain to paranoia and then to silence. Some of *Get Out*'s most powerful scenes generate a similar effect by operating deftly between silence and voice. When Chris's body is put up for auction as a vessel for the surgical transplant of an aging white brain afflicted with blindness, it is quite literally a silent auction. Rose's father, the auctioneer, does not speak; the participants indicate their bids by raising their bingo cards wordlessly; and Chris himself is silent as he is represented only by a large framed photographic portrait that stands in for his physical presence (fig. 7.3).

7.3   The silent auction over Chris's body in *Get Out*.

The silence lends a genteel air to the proceedings, almost as if the horror of a slave auction could somehow be ameliorated by simply not speaking its racism—reducing the act of the auction to a silent shadow. But Peele, utilizing the logic of what I have called horror's "allegorical moment," makes the silence curdle, turning its gentility into uncanniness as viewers face the silence as an historical act of racism's horror, not just its fantastic shadow.[16] Chris as a silent, disembodied photograph accurately conveys the white bidders' attitude toward him: he is not human at all, only property to be purchased or traded, much like the exchangeable bodies of Rosemary (impregnated against her will) and Joanna (replaced with a robot). And the bidders' silence in turn relieves them of the distasteful task of speaking—admitting—their racism.

But because Peele intercuts the auction with shots of Chris speaking with Rose about his suspicions concerning the true nature of her family and friends, we are reminded of the voice under the silence. We think again of Chris's earlier exposure to "the sunken place," a mental pit of quicksand to which Rose's mother is able to send Chris by hypnotizing him and where Chris's consciousness would reside forever if the surgical replacement of his brain with the brain of an old white man were performed successfully. In the sunken place, you are aware but powerless; you become a spectator of your own body, your own life, and your own words and actions are now beyond your control. This is the essence of horror's minority vocabulary as developed by Levin and Peele, for what could be scarier than knowing what's happening to you without the ability to convince others that it is happening to you? To try to speak, but for your listeners to hear only silence rather than a Black, Jewish, or female voice?

This is what Chris experiences not only in the supernatural sunken place but also at all of those times when he wearily, resignedly faces the familiar, everyday social humiliations that surprise only others, not himself: the racist cop who demands Chris's identification even when it's his white girlfriend who is driving the car; his polite acceptance of Rose's parents' liberal but still racist "open-mindedness" about his Blackness; and finally the sinking feeling we share with him near the end of the film when a police car pulls up to him amid the carnage of the dead and dying bodies of those who have been trying to kill him. The sinking feeling, which transports *us* to the sunken place vicariously, comes because we, like Chris, do not yet know that Rod is driving the police car. What Chris knows as well as we do is that the chances of a Black man explaining the corpses that surround him as a sign of his innocence rather than his guilt are just about nil when faced by the white law and the white-majority privilege of "rational" explanation versus minority "paranoia." When Rod reveals himself, we are as exhilarated as Chris is dumbfounded. "How did you find me?," he asks Rod incredulously.

In that moment, we understand Chris's question as a variation on Rosemary's question about the existence of plots against people, a question tinged with the desperation of minority experience where pain gets dismissed as paranoia. For those who feel invisible or unacknowledged, who live in a world that they are told does not truly belong to them or in a body that they are told is not valued as fully human, the possibility of being seen and even saved is all too often beyond imagining. But we need to imagine it. What Peele and Levin show us is that one of the places we can go to imagine it is a place that may at first seem very unlikely indeed: the horror genre.

What Levin and Peele accomplish in terms of horror's minority vocabulary is as critically sophisticated as it is affectively powerful and forces us to question the conventional wisdom surrounding horror's relation to social otherness. When Peele and Levin deploy horror's transformative otherness—the genre's ability to upend self/other distinctions—they convey to spectators not the monstrosity of the other but the experience of minority pain that majority society dismisses as paranoia. To communicate such experience is an impressive and important accomplishment, but it does not come without a certain price. Peele's decision to abandon the original ending of *Get Out*, where Chris ends up in prison rather than making a getaway with Rod, indicates one kind of price: the need for an audience escape hatch, for shadow and act to diverge rather than converge. But the price I want to conclude this section by considering is something we might call the "mathematics of difference," where forging affinities between Blacks, Jews, and women, as we see across the work of Levin and Peele, comes with a need for another other: the Asian.

Among the white bidders at the auction in *Get Out* is a lone Asian man named Hiroki Tanaka (Yasuhiko Oyama). Hiroki does not win the auction, but he gets a brief moment in the spotlight earlier that same day when he asks Chris in Japanese-accented English, "Do you find that being African American has more advantage or disadvantage in the modern world?" Chris does not answer the question, but Hiroki's presence is striking in that he provides a rare moment within the film where the "modern world" is not divided into exclusively Black and white dimensions (a Latino police officer, Detective Garcia [Ian Casselberry], also appears briefly at one point).[17] Is this Peele's gesture toward acknowledging racial difference as something more than a Black/white issue? If so, then why does Hiroki occupy such a fleeting, tokenistic, perhaps even borderline cartoonish role (the stereotypical Asian accent)? At least one Asian American critic has accused Peele of disappointing insensitivity in his portrayal of Hiroki,[18] but another way of analyzing Hiroki's presence in Get Out is as yet one more echo of Rosemary's Baby.

Just as Peele includes Hiroki among the bidders in Get Out, Levin also includes a Japanese man named Hayato among the Satanists who celebrate the birth of the Antichrist at the end of Rosemary's Baby. Hayato's presence seems slightly more motivated than Hiroki's in that Levin wants to convey the worldwide reach of the Satanists, but his portrayal comes off as similarly cartoonish. Hayato speaks in the same heavily accented English as Hiroki and reproduces another common Asian stereotype: a touristic obsession with taking photographs. In fact, Hayato's photos of Rosemary and her child are the note on which Levin ends his novel. Why?

Perhaps the need for another other at the conclusion of Rosemary's Baby is necessitated by the disappearance of Rosemary herself. She has struggled mightily throughout the novel as the minority protagonist, the exploited woman and figurative Jew, but her acceptance of her maternal role finally aligns her with the very Satanists who have oppressed her. In transferring the point of view from Rosemary to Hayato, Levin preserves a minority perspective even as his minority protagonist is absorbed into the majority. A similar move occurs at the end of The Stepford Wives as we see the robotic Joanna through the eyes of her Black friend Ruthanne Hendry. The move is stronger and more meaningful in The Stepford Wives because Ruthanne is someone we know; Hayato barely registers as a person in Rosemary's Baby because he is sometimes referred to simply as "the Japanese" (245).

But here is where looking at Peele and Levin as conjoined, in the manner this chapter has argued throughout, reveals something potentially deeper than the tokenistic impressions of Asians in their work. Hiroki lacks the camera wielded by Hayato, but Hayato's function as a photographer is taken on by Chris. Indeed, shortly after Chris's brief exchange with Hiroki, he photographs the one other Black man attending the party and inadvertently frees the man's surgically imprisoned subjectivity from the "sunken place" through the flash of a phone camera. For a brief moment, this man's suppressed Black consciousness returns to inhabit his own body and warns Chris to "get out," to avoid the same fate. In a complicated series of exchanges performed in the poetics of horror's minority vocabulary as transformative otherness, Chris's photographic gesture as an amalgam of Rosemary and Joanna animates Hayato as Hayato animates Hiroki. The liberating flash of the camera, its ability to unmask minority paranoia as pain, is enacted by Chris but prefigured by Joanna and suggests how Hayato's photographic vision of Rosemary may have points of contact with Chris. Hiroki's presence, then, initially so jarring, becomes not just an intertextual cue between *Get Out* and *Rosemary's Baby* but an invitation to connect the dots among Chris, Rosemary, Joanna, Ruthanne, Hayato, and Hiroki as those who see the horror of minority experience for what it is. None of them alone can see the big picture; they need each other's visions, just as we need theirs. Just as Peele needs Levin and vice versa.

Analyzing Levin and Peele together shows us why horror matters for experiences of minority otherness, how horror can transform our understanding of such experiences. Horror can awaken us to fearful experiences that are our own but that we may not have the courage to face or to fearful experiences that are not our own but that we don't have the courage to acknowledge. In Peele as in (and through) Levin, we can see the struggle and the opportunity to imagine the pain of minority experience in an American society where social justice for all is still a dream awaiting fulfillment. This is a dream that matters, and horror is a genre that matters to that dream.

From *Get Out* to *Donovan's Brain* and *The Wolf Man*: Introducing Curt Siodmak

Horror's minority vocabulary, what I have described as the genre's ability to speak in the register of transformative otherness, can be seen especially clearly when juxtaposing *Get Out* with Ira Levin's work. Jordan Peele has acknowledged his debt to Levin, but there are other, less straightforward influences on *Get Out* that go back further in history and solidify our understanding of the Black/Jewish foundations of horror's investments in transformative otherness. The figure who enables us to dig deeper into this history is the screenwriter and novelist Curt Siodmak (1902–2000), creator of the novel *Donovan's Brain* (1942) and the screenplay *The Wolf Man* (1941).

Siodmak was a German Jew who, like so many of his contemporaries (including his brother Robert Siodmak, a noted director in his own right, and the film theorist Siegfried Kracauer, as noted in chapter 5), was forced to flee Germany when Hitler came to power. After finding only temporary refuge in Switzerland, France, and England, Siodmak eventually immigrated to the United States in 1937 and found work as a screenwriter and novelist. Although he succeeded in establishing a wildly varied and prolific career for himself, primarily in the horror and science-fiction genres, he never left behind his experience of traumatic Jewishness as an exile who narrowly escaped the Holocaust. Traumatic Jewishness haunts much of Siodmak's work, including his two most famous creations, the thrice-filmed novel *Donovan's Brain* and the screenplay for the iconic horror film *The Wolf Man*. In fact, the dedication that opens his autobiography, *Wolf Man's Maker: Memoir of a Hollywood Writer* (2001), testifies to Siodmak's traumatic Jewishness in ways that vault us ahead to Jordan Peele: "Dedicated to America, the country that was good to me, a stranger—the only country that told me 'Come in' and not 'Get out.'"[19]

Siodmak's dedication, when placed alongside Peele's film, illuminates the shared language of Jewish and Black otherness (without suggesting, of course, that the Jewish and Black experiences of America are equivalent). But this sharing is not limited to a mere coincidence of phrasing—it is rooted more deeply in minority otherness and its articulation through horror. So it should not be entirely surprising that *Get Out*, many years after *Donovan's Brain* and *The Wolf Man*, still inherits the legacy of Siodmak's traumatic Jewishness, however indirectly.

Donovan's Brain is usually referred to as a science-fiction novel, but its sci-fi premise unfolds as horror. Patrick Cory, a brilliant but troubled doctor fascinated with experimental brain research, stumbles into the research opportunity of a lifetime when he rescues a man from a disastrous plane crash. The man, who turns out to be the cruel, wealthy tycoon W. H. Donovan, is so grievously injured that his body cannot be saved; only his brain can be salvaged through the unorthodox surgery that Cory performs unbeknownst to the authorities. Under Cory's care, Donovan's brain not only survives but becomes increasingly powerful as a telepathic force. It eventually possesses Cory and forces him to engage in murderous behavior on behalf of the psychopathic, megalomaniacal Donovan. Cory ultimately defeats Donovan, but Siodmak concludes the novel by suggesting that "Donovan's unquenchable energy still roams this mortal world."[20]

The "energy" Siodmak refers to at the end of *Donovan's Brain* is precisely the kind of fascistic, mind-controlling energy that Siodmak experienced in Hitler's Germany. On one of his last days in Germany before fleeing the country for good in 1933, Siodmak, along with many other luminaries in the German film industry, attended an event at the invitation of Dr. Joseph Goebbels. According to Siodmak's memoir, Goebbels, as the Nazi "minister of propaganda and national enlightenment," informed Siodmak and his colleagues, many of them Jewish, that the German film industry was about to change: it would no longer depict the world "as pictured in the brains of Jewish film directors or writers," and Germany's films would cease to be "softened by Jewish decadence" (*Wolf Man's Maker*, 114–15). The shock of this meeting, accompanied by an official letter from the National-Socialistic Authors Union that explained to Siodmak how his writings were no longer permitted to be published in Germany, caused Siodmak to feel that "the ground under my feet had given way" (114). That feeling of being cut adrift, of traumatic Jewishness as essential otherness, haunted Siodmak for the rest of his life, even in America.

It is there in *Donovan's Brain*, albeit if only as an implicit, allegorical presence. The novel contains no mentions of Jews or Nazis. But the theme that dominates it, a mind possessed by an external psychopathic subjectivity to the point of self-erasure, has deep resonances with both Siodmak's experience of traumatic Jewishness and Peele's conceptualization of "the sunken place" in *Get Out*. For Siodmak, Hitler's rise to power makes Siodmak's own country unrecognizable to him, with even people he knows well having their brains washed so thoroughly by anti-Semitic Nazi propaganda that he senses "the meaning of ethics had changed overnight" (*Wolf Man's Maker*, 115). For Peele, white supremacy also emerges in a horrifically literal form of brain washing, with the surgical implantation of a white brain in a Black body resulting in the exile of Black subjectivity to "the sunken place." Peele's visualization of possession by an alien brain that results in becoming a spectator of one's own body is strikingly prefigured by Patrick Cory's description of possession by Donovan's brain in Siodmak's novel:

> As always, I was aware of everything I did, but for the first time I was a prisoner in my own body, with no power to do anything except what I was commanded . . . the brain could walk my body in front of a car, throw it out of the window, put a bullet through my head with my own hands. I could only cry out from the despair of my imprisonment, but even the words my mouth formed were those the brain wanted to hear. A wave of terror engulfed me as I realized I was like a man fastened in a machine which moves his hands and feet against his will.[21]

The horror of possession, of colonization by the brain of another, is the bottom line for both Siodmak and Peele. They differ in that Peele is explicit (white-supremacist brain possesses Black victimized body), whereas Siodmak is implicit (Cory is no Jew and Donovan is no Nazi, nor is Cory a German Gentile possessed by anti-Semitic Nazi thought). But like Levin's movement from implicit to explicit portrayals of anti-Semitism between *Rosemary's Baby* and *The Boys from Brazil*, Siodmak also converts what is implicit in *Donovan's Brain* to something explicit in its sequel *Hauser's Memory* (1968). In *Hauser's Memory* (adapted as a television film in 1970), the subject who must endure the possession of his mind and body by an alien subjectivity is Hillel Mondoro, a religiously observant Jewish American scientist. Karl Hauser, the dead German scientist who possesses Mondoro, is not a Nazi, but he is anti-Semitic, and his wife is a Nazi sympathizer whom Mondoro must confront through Hauser's influence. Indeed, when Hauser forces Mondoro to leave America for Germany so that Hauser may settle old scores, the parallels to Siodmak's own experience of returning to visit Germany in 1962 are unmistakable.

Siodmak, visiting Germany with his wife to pursue a film project after nearly thirty years in exile, described the return to Germany as "a traumatic experience" (*Wolf Man's Maker*, 413). In one harrowing incident, Siodmak was accosted by a man drinking with a group of friends in a restaurant in Hamburg. The man asked him if he was Jewish, and when Siodmak admitted he was a German Jew, he responded, "Didn't we catch you?" The man went on to explain that he and his friends had been in the SS and now worked together at a large insurance company in Hamburg. Siodmak was able to defuse the potentially threatening incident by joking with the man that he could make much more money in the insurance business if he came to America, with this caveat: "But you have to be Jewish." Siodmak explains that the man laughed but also "painfully squeezed the skin of my belly, obviously knowing body torture points." Even though the man and his friends then insisted on buying drinks for Siodmak and his wife, Siodmak felt that "the varnish of postwar democracy disappeared, and I was transported back into Hitler's world" (*Wolf Man's Maker*, 416).

This sort of possession of the mind, where Siodmak feels helplessly "transported" from postwar Germany to Hitler's Germany and reexperiences his Jewish otherness as traumatic, is precisely what haunts *Donovan's Brain* and *Hauser's Memory*. Indeed, Siodmak admits that these novels, along with their companion *Gabriel's Body* (1992), were born of autobiography, with his "private thoughts" wrapped in a "cloak of entertainment" (*Wolf Man's Maker*, 434). Siodmak captures the power and pervasiveness of this possession of his "private thoughts" when he reveals that he often struggled with depression and that up until the end of his life he suffered from nightmares concerning experiences that were not his own: "Today, many decades after my forced exodus from Germany, I still suffer from nightmares about concentration camps. I never experienced them, but I have met the nattily dressed men in uniform, wearing high shiny boots, whose duty it was to cleanse the world of inferior races and for whom every life, except their own, was expendable" (129).

In short, Siodmak's experience of racial otherness, of anti-Semitism as traumatic Jewishness, forms the core of his "private thoughts," which are then expressed in his work, although surrounded by a "cloak of entertainment." No wonder the theme that Siodmak returns to again and again in his creative work is possession: his life was possessed by direct exposure to the anti-Semitic hatred that would result in the Holocaust. *Donovan's Brain* and *The Wolf Man*, as works of the early 1940s, are pre-Holocaust but postemigration. As Siodmak explains, "There is a similarity between death and emigration. . . . Being banned from a country of one's birth under the threat of death, not for a crime committed but for a racial bias, is like the sentence of death by a tribunal with preconceived judgment" (*Wolf Man's Maker*, 128–29). In his work, Siodmak fashions a mode of expression for this experience of racial otherness through the vocabulary of horror. It is this vocabulary that Peele inherits and enlarges in *Get Out* by connecting it to the African American experience of racial otherness. Again, I am not arguing that Siodmak was a conscious influence on Peele in the way that Levin was but rather that all three of these artists are speaking a shared language of horror and racial otherness.

The fact that Peele includes in *Get Out* a subplot concerning the white patriarch Roman Armitage (Richard Herd), Rose's grandfather, and the Berlin Olympics in 1936 is a reminder of how this language of horror and racial otherness is shared between Black and Jewish experience. Armitage loses his opportunity to compete in the Olympics when he is beaten during the trials by Jesse Owens, the legendary African American track athlete who goes on to win four gold medals in Berlin and thus deals a blow to Hitler's white-supremacist assumptions in the heart of Germany. In his new Black body stolen from the groundskeeper, Walter (Marcus Henderson), Armitage continues to train as if he can somehow return to 1936 and replace Jesse Owens after all. What Peele suggests so chillingly through this subplot is that if white supremacy still operates today according to racist logics stubbornly unchanged since 1936, then in many ways it is still 1936 for Blacks, Jews, and all nonwhite others. At the end of *Get Out*, Walter manages to vanquish Armitage's brain and regain agency over his body, just as Cory regains his body from Donovan at the conclusion of *Donovan's Brain*. But these victories come at a high price: Walter commits suicide, and Cory cannot escape the feeling that despite the destruction of Donovan's brain, his "energy" still lives on. As Cory reminds us, "Energy cannot be destroyed."[22]

What Peele and Siodmak ultimately suggest is that the dynamics of possession that animate the victimization of racial others cannot be defeated so directly. White supremacy's desire to possess the bodies and minds of the racial others it deems inferior is an energy impossible to destroy so long as racism exists. As Siodmak ruefully observes near the conclusion of his autobiography, "I believe that human genes carry roots of discrimination, of racism and intolerance, that explode through the ages into wars. Blood has been spilled endlessly, and still is, now called 'ethnic cleansing,' a term that camouflages a holocaust" (*Wolf Man's Maker*, 440). Siodmak's pronouncement appears to be possessed by the eugenic logics of white supremacy even while reversing it, with human genetic predispositions toward racism substituting for white-supremacist claims of subhuman genetic predispositions in Jews, Blacks, and nonwhite others. So, for Siodmak, as for Peele, the entire notion of "getting out," even at the levels of thought and language, is both essential and illusory. Getting out of Germany saves Siodmak's life, just as getting out of the clutches of the Armitages saves Chris's life. But don't all signs point to the likelihood that Chris, standing in for so many Black survivors of racism and for Peele himself,[23] will have a life that is just as haunted as the lives of Siodmak and his fellow Jewish survivors of anti-Semitism?

By converting the experience of racial otherness that possesses them into a language of horror about possession that sustains their art, Siodmak and Peele access a deeper and wider genealogy for horror's minority vocabulary. Both Jewish and Black folk traditions prominently feature horror stories about possession. In the Jewish tradition, the dybbuk is a spirit of the dead who refuses to rest and so possesses the body and mind of a living person.[24] In the Black Afro-Caribbean tradition, a dead human is similarly possessed by a life beyond death, a living death, and thus becomes a zombie.[25] It is worth noting that Siodmak contributed to the screenplay for Val Lewton's film *I Walked with a Zombie* (Jacques Tourneur, 1943), one of Hollywood's most ambitious explorations of the zombie in its Black Afro-Caribbean context. It is also worth noting how *Donovan's Brain* resembles a dybbuk story, just as *Get Out* resembles a zombie story,[26] and that Ira Levin writes his own version of a dybbuk tale in his play *Cantorial*. But taking all of these connections seriously is not always or even primarily a matter of tracing direct lines of influence. It is instead an invitation to build an alternate understanding of the horror film and its minority vocabulary, to see horror as transformative otherness by recognizing the genre's deployment of self–other constructions as a matter of constant metamorphosis rather than discrete divisions. This chapter concludes with a consideration of one last example from this genealogy of horror's engagement with Black and Jewish otherness as transformative otherness: *The Wolf Man*.

The Wolf Man's Transformations of Jewish Otherness

When Curt Siodmak wrote *The Wolf Man* in 1941, he was still a Jew on the run from Hitler's Germany,[27] not in the literal sense, as he had emigrated in 1933 and arrived in America in 1937, but psychologically and spiritually. Siodmak was grateful that his job as a screenwriter employed by Universal Studios kept him busy, but he admits that "writing motion pictures had also become a drug, an escape from my still undigested past and the suppressed fears that haunted me since the country of my birth had murdered its native culture" (*Wolf Man's Maker*, 259). He describes the process of writing *The Wolf Man* and *Donovan's Brain* during this period in terms of plugging in to his subconscious: *The Wolf Man* "poured painlessly into my typewriter, scene by scene, without the need of much of a change," while *Donovan's Brain* was written "as if that book already existed, copying it from my subconscious" (273). Since Siodmak was given nothing more than the title *The Wolf Man* by Universal when he was assigned to create the film's screenplay, he had a significant degree of freedom to imagine it as he wished. In short, there was nothing impeding and everything encouraging

Siodmak to create *The Wolf Man* in the shape of his own haunting experience as a Jew on the run.

Of course, this is not to say that Siodmak invented *The Wolf Man* out of whole cloth. By 1941, Universal was well established as the studio that had made the horror film legible as a recognizable genre category. *The Wolf Man* was following in the footsteps of *Dracula* (Tod Browning, 1931), *Frankenstein* (James Whale, 1931), *The Mummy* (Karl Freund, 1932), and *The Invisible Man* (James Whale, 1933) as Universal horror films successful enough to spawn sequels and franchises that are still with us today. Siodmak himself worked on sequels to all of these films with the exception of *The Mummy*, which was directed by Siodmak's fellow German Jewish colleague and brilliant cinematographer Karl Freund. As a relatively late addition to this lineage and the last of the great Universal horror series until *Creature from the Black Lagoon* (Jack Arnold, 1954), *The Wolf Man* came with a set of horror genre expectations conditioned by Universal's previous horror films.[28] Siodmak was certainly familiar with these films as well as with their antecedents in Weimar Germany, most notably the Jewish-folklore-derived *The Golem* (Paul Wegener, 1920) for *Frankenstein* and *Nosferatu* (F. W. Murnau, 1922) for *Dracula*. Universal had attempted a werewolf film prior to *The Wolf Man* in *Werewolf of London* (Stuart Walker, 1935), and Siodmak has written of his acquaintance with werewolf-related stories and case studies ranging from Ovid to Petronius to Freud. This is to say nothing of the many other werewolf poems and tales that preceded *The Wolf Man*, from Virgil's eighth Eclogue (39 BCE) to Marie de France's "The Lay of the Bisclaveret" (circa twelfth century) to Guy Endore's *The Werewolf of Paris* (1933).[29] But the fact of the matter is that before *The Wolf Man*, the werewolf did not have a powerful hold on the popular horror imagination. Siodmak not only gave shape to the popularly iconic form of the werewolf as we know it today but forged that shape in the crucible of his own traumatic Jewishness. In other words, Siodmak gave birth to the Wolf Man as a fundamentally Jewish cinematic monster.[30]

Again, when I call the Wolf Man "a Jewish monster," I am referring to the work of Siodmak's subconscious imagination, not to his conscious intentions. Nor am I suggesting that Siodmak is the sole creator of *The Wolf Man*, for without George Waggner's direction, Jack Pierce's makeup, and especially Lon Chaney Jr.'s inimitably vulnerable portrayal of Larry Talbot, the film would not have succeeded. But to see *The Wolf Man* through the Jewish lens that Siodmak provides is to reckon with Jewish otherness as essential for the horror film in its classical form. Weimar Germany had already generated a number of important visual alignments of Jewish otherness with horror, often tinged with anti-Semitism: the prominent use of a Jewish cemetery made infamous by the fabricated anti-Semitic screed *The Protocols of the Elders of Zion* (1903) in *The Student of Prague* (Stellan Rye, 1913); the threatening Jewish giant made of clay and animated through black magic in *The Golem*; the grotesque exaggeration of stereotypically Jewish physical and cultural characteristics attributed to the vampire and his henchman (the latter played by a prominent Jewish actor) in *Nosferatu*.[31] What makes *The Wolf Man* so remarkable in contrast to these antecedents is how Jewish-coded otherness becomes more a matter of lived pain and anguished victimization than of repellent monstrosity infused with anti-Semitism. In short, *The Wolf Man* is closer to the landmark Yiddish Polish horror film *The Dybbuk* (Michal Waszynski, 1937) and *Get Out* than it is to *Nosferatu* in terms of activating horror as a Jewish-inflected transformative otherness.

How does *The Wolf Man* use horror to generate transformative otherness in relation to implicit Jewishness? Siodmak constructs the film's story not only as a horror tale but also as a narrative of emigration, exile, and displacement. Larry Talbot (Lon Chaney Jr.) is born into an aristocratic English family but immigrates to America because his father, Sir John Talbot (Claude Rains), favors his brother over him so completely that Larry feels he has no real place in the family. The film's action begins after Larry's brother dies, causing Larry to return to England from America after many years away for an awkward reunion with his father and a country no longer his own. Shortly after his arrival, Larry becomes attracted to the engaged Gwen Conliffe (Evelyn Ankers) and joins her and her friend Jenny Williams (Fay Helm) on a nighttime visit to a Gypsy fortune-teller. When Jenny is attacked by a wolf that night, Larry fights and kills the wolf but is wounded in the struggle. Jenny dies, as does the Gypsy fortune-teller, Bela (Bela Lugosi), whose corpse mysteriously replaces that of the wolf's. Larry eventually learns that Bela was a werewolf and has passed on the werewolf's curse to him through his wound. Larry soon transforms from an innocent man into a murderous wolf, without retaining any conscious control over his actions or any memories of those actions when he regains his human form. Horrified by his powerlessness over his fate, he ultimately provides his father with the means to destroy him: the silver-tipped cane that Larry used to kill the wolf/Bela. When Sir John employs the cane to kill a wolf attacking Gwen, the dead body transforms from the wolf's into Larry's.

Siodmak's plot for *The Wolf Man* emphasizes Larry's powerless victimization by a curse he never deserved but must endure rather than his fearsome monstrosity as a werewolf. He is more often the hunted than the hunter. Larry is as much a figurative Jew as Ira Levin's Rosemary Woodhouse and Joanna Eberhart, but even more so in that his victimization is never something he can fully understand. The plots against Rosemary and Joanna are confirmed and understood, but Larry must become the very thing that he cannot comprehend without ever understanding why. Larry's transformation is not just from man into wolf but from a figurative Jew who passes for Gentile into a figurative Jew whose race is exposed and can no longer pass for Gentile. In one of the film's most powerful scenes, Larry joins the rest of the town for church services. He is deeply troubled; he has just experienced his first transformation into a were-wolf the night before and has attempted to tell his father about it. But Sir John dismisses Larry's concerns as mere superstition or perhaps, at worst, delusions caused by Larry's psychological distress. As Sir John and all of the town's citizens file into the church and take their places in the pews, Larry hesitates in the entryway. In a striking tracking shot, each row of townspeople successively turns around to stare at Larry, who stands paralyzed by everyone's gaze. When even Sir John turns to look at him questioningly, Larry leaves the church.

Given the unusual tracking shot and the highly choreographed actions of the townspeople, it is possible to interpret this scene as a fantasy projection of Larry's inner psychological agony, much like an earlier dream sequence. But prior to Larry's arrival at the church, we hear the mother of Jenny Williams, who blames both Gwen and Larry for her daughter's death, speaking of Larry as a "wild animal, with murder in his eyes." One of Mrs. Williams's companions tries to calm her, warning her that she is guilty of "slander" by speaking of Larry in this way. So alongside the possibility of psychological projection is the reality of slanderous hatred; alongside Larry's fears that he has become a were-wolf is the persecution of the figurative Jew who has no place in a Christian church. Indeed, shortly before arriving at the church, Larry discovers the sign of the werewolf on his own skin: a pentagram over his heart where he was bitten (fig. 7.4).

The pentagram, a five-pointed star often associated with witchcraft and Satanism, of course also bears a strong resemblance to the six-pointed Jewish Star of David. By 1939, the Nazis were using yellow badges in the shape of the Star of David to identify Jews in public, so it is quite possible that Siodmak was aware of this practice when he wrote *The Wolf Man* in 1941.[32] In his memoir, Siodmak describes his own vexed relation to Jewishness in terms similar to Larry's curse: "I was born a Jew, wearing the invisible Star of David all my life" (*Wolf Man's Maker*, 3). But whether this association was recognized by Siodmak or by the film's viewers in 1941 is less important than the fact that Larry, like Rosemary, Joanna, and Chris after him, must suffer the fate of minority persecution by a majority that refuses to acknowledge his pain as real. Larry has been marked not only by the sign of the werewolf but by the sign of the other.

Larry's otherness, his figurative Jewishness, is solidified through his connection to the Gypsies. Our first glimpse of the pentagram as the sign of the werewolf etched into flesh comes through Bela, the Gypsy fortune-teller who carries the sign on his forehead and sees it in the palm of Jenny Williams shortly before he kills her while in werewolf form. Bela's mother, Maleva (Maria Ouspenskaya), plays a crucial role in the film as the one who explains the curse of the werewolf to Larry, provides him with a pentagram charm to protect him, intervenes to save him when he is wounded, and finally mourns his death. Like Larry, Maleva is othered by the Christian church: her insistence on burying Bela

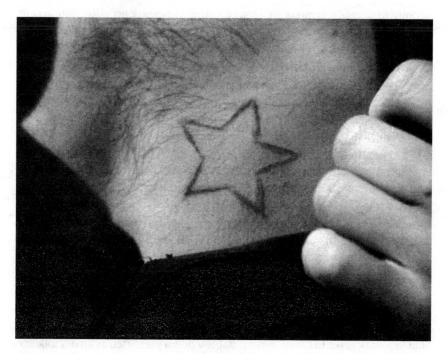

7.4 Larry (Lon Chaney Jr.) discovers the sign of the werewolf over his heart in *The Wolf Man*.

according to Roma customs is denounced by a priest as antireligious, a primitive regression to superstition akin to Satanism. The Christian townspeople tend to see the Gypsies the way they see Larry—as strangers who do not belong, as others who cannot be trusted—so the Gypsies carry the burden of figurative Jewishness in the film as well.

The Wolf Man's use of the Gypsies as racial others that highlight Larry's own figurative Jewishness is augmented by history and casting. The Nazis considered the Roma, like the Jews, to be racial inferiors who must be subjected to social persecution and ultimately extermination during the Holocaust.[33] Official Nazi persecution of the Roma began in 1935, so, again, it is possible that Siodmak was aware of this when he wrote *The Wolf Man*. Siodmak had personal experience meeting the Roma during his childhood, recalling in his memoir how the Roma's visits to Dresden were part of his exposure to that city's cosmopolitanism as a "center of art, musicians, painters, the hub of theater culture." This is where Siodmak saw Roma and Blacks alongside Jews as well as his first movies (*Wolf Man's Maker*, 11).

The two featured Gypsy characters in *The Wolf Man* are played by prominent immigrant actors: Bela Lugosi and Maria Ouspenskaya. Lugosi's Hungarian accent, first made famous in *Dracula*, and Ouspenskaya's Russian accent, which had helped her to earn Academy Award nominations for her roles in *Dodsworth* (William Wyler, 1936) and *Love Affair* (Leo McCarey, 1939), are deployed here to emphasize Gypsy otherness. Like Larry, though, the Gypsies are portrayed not as a threat but as the potentially threatened; when they pack up hurriedly after learning that there is a werewolf in their midst, they seem to be more fearful about being blamed by the Christian townspeople for the werewolf's violence than being attacked by the werewolf. Of course, they are right.

The Wolf Man insists again and again that the Gypsies should be listened to, not feared. Bela warns Jenny to run from him so she might save her life, while Maleva expresses far more genuine parental concern both for her own son and for Larry than Sir John can ever muster. When Larry suffers the fate of a hunted animal (his leg caught in the vise of a trap, his senses frightened by the sounds of barking dogs and gun-toting townspeople out for his blood), it is Maleva who comforts and saves him by enabling his transformation from wolf into man. The words she speaks over him, repeated several times in the film with small variations, include these lines: "The way you walk is thorny, through no fault of your own. But as the rain enters the soil, the river enters the sea, so tears run to a predestined end." These lines are similar to but not as famous as others that Siodmak gives to Gwen, most notably a poem presented as an old folk saying but actually invented by Siodmak: "Even a man who is pure in heart and says his prayers by night may become a wolf when the wolfbane blooms and the autumn moon is bright." What Siodmak focuses on in this poem and the previous lines spoken by Maleva is how the curse of the werewolf is not a monstrous otherness of subhuman animality but a tragic otherness of human victimization. For Siodmak, *anyone* can become a werewolf, through no fault of their own, even if they say their prayers at night. So even if it is the Jew or the Gypsy or the Black who is victimized and made to carry the curse of the other, they do not *deserve* to; their suffering is our potential suffering, their otherness is our potential otherness.

In *The Wolf Man*, the essence of transformative otherness is captured in an approach to on-screen transformation that underlines not self/other discontinuity and division but self–other continuity and union. The film's most spectacular transformation scene is not the conversion of man into wolf but the metamorphosis of wolf into man. When Larry undergoes the transformation that turns him into a werewolf, we see only his feet and legs change from human to animal as they become progressively hairier and more muscular through a series of dissolves; his werewolf face is presented only after his transformation, not during it. But at the film's end, when Larry is killed in his werewolf form, we witness his face change slowly from wolf into man (fig. 7.5). The hair and the fangs gradually fade until it is only Larry's face that we see. We are forced

7.5 Larry, now dead, transforms from wolf into man in *The Wolf Man*.

to acknowledge, along with Larry's stubbornly disbelieving father, that the other was never entirely an other at all, that Larry's otherness was never without a self, his self never without an other.

What's more, because the transformation itself is fleeting, we are left with the haunting visual implication that we may have projected an illusory otherness onto Larry that has now disappeared without a trace. This implication becomes even more disturbing when those who actually know and care for Larry seize upon it not to recognize his entwined self–otherness but to deny it. With the important exception of Maleva, who has always seen Larry clearly, all of these characters remain silent when Chief Constable Paul Montford (Ralph Bellamy) rationalizes Larry's death as caused by the attack of a wolf. No one— not Sir John, who has killed his own son, and not Gwen, who retreats into the arms of her fiancé as if to repudiate the specter of miscegenation in her love for Larry—says anything about what they and we know full well: Larry was never only a wolf, nor was he ever only a man. He was always a wolf/man, a self/other, an American/Englishman, a native/immigrant, a literal Gentile/figurative Jew. This refusal to acknowledge the transformative otherness embodied by Larry means that at the film's conclusion the killer has not been caught, that the "wolf" is still loose, and that the "wolf" is finally not a monster at all but our desire to divorce self from other, to turn human into subhuman so that we might deny the humanity of others and the inhumanity in ourselves.

This is the horror crystallized by Siodmak's Jewish werewolf—a horror at the very roots of this cinematic genre whose branches include not just direct, Jewish-inflected offshoots such as *An American Werewolf in London* (John Landis, 1981) and *The Beast Within* (Philippe Mora, 1982) but also horror's entire minority vocabulary as articulated so forcefully by Ira Levin and Jordan Peele as a language of transformative otherness. When in 1993 Siodmak wrote about his screenplay, "I'm convinced that *The Wolf Man* will survive me,"[34] he could not have known how understated his claim would turn out to be.

AFTERWORD

Horror and Otherness in Anguished Times

Although much of the research and initial writing of *Horror Film and Otherness* was completed years earlier, the book itself was born in October 2018, following the anti-Semitic Tree of Life killings in Pittsburgh described in the introduction. It was completed during the spring and summer of 2020, in the age of the COVID-19 virus and the national as well as international upheaval following the racist murder of George Floyd at the hands of the police in Minneapolis. So it feels appropriate to conclude with a brief, personal meditation on Jewish/Black otherness in the horror film that grows out of this book's previous chapter as well as on the anguished times that frame my project.

This book presents an account of transformative otherness in the horror film—transformative in the sense that divisions between self and other are resisted in favor of ongoing metamorphoses that unify these categories, so that we are confronted with the continuities that bind other to self rather than with the discontinuities that keep them separate. My own account of horror's transformative otherness is anchored in critical conversation with Robin Wood's landmark criticism on the horror film, particularly "An Introduction to the American Horror Film" (1979). Wood's focus in that essay, like mine in this book, centers on the generation of American and English-language modern horror (including Canada and Great Britain) of the period 1968–1978, covering the now legendary auteurs David Cronenberg, Tobe Hooper, and George A. Romero.

But *Horror Film and Otherness* also moves beyond Wood by reaching back (to Curt Siodmak's *The Wolf Man* [1941] and *Donovan's Brain* [1942]; to the Jewish film theory of Sigmund Freud, Siegfried Kracauer, and Emmanuel Levinas), reaching forward (to the less canonical and/or post-1978 films of Cronenberg, Hooper, and Romero; to Jennifer Kent's Australian film *The Babadook* [2014] and Jordan Peele's *Get Out* [2017]), and reaching around (to Jerzy Skolimowski's British film *The Shout* [1978]; Marina de Van's French film *In My Skin* [2002]; Ira Levin's work, from *Rosemary's Baby* [1967] to *The Boys from Brazil* [1976]; and Stephanie Rothman's *The Velvet Vampire* [1971], mentioned by Wood but elevated here to the station it deserves as essential modern horror alongside the work of Cronenberg, Hooper, and Romero). Because Wood's criticism has been so influential for making scholarly study of the horror film possible, *Horror Film and Otherness* functions as both a history of horror studies and a map charting potential future directions in horror studies. If Wood made us aware that the horror film matters, then I have attempted to provide a new explanation for the horror film's social significance. My account of horror reimagines the genre's relation to social otherness, including those underacknowledged forms of otherness attached to ethnographic surrealism, aging, economics, gender, race, and Jewishness. My hope is that this book, concurrent with my work involving the George A. Romero Foundation and the University of Pittsburgh (including the establishment of the world's first Horror Studies Archive, founded through Pitt's acquisition of the George A. Romero Collection in 2019), can contribute toward making horror studies the scholarly field it deserves to be: a widely respected, rigorously pursued, conceptually ambitious, and curricularly instituted discipline on par with film and media studies, literary studies, cultural studies, and other recognized humanistic fields from which it emerges and that it continues to affect.

In my introduction to *Horror Film and Otherness*, I described how this book came to be during the fiftieth anniversary of Romero's *Night of the Living Dead* (1968) and in response to the Tree of Life tragedy. In this conclusion, I reflect on the echoes of those events that I hear in the work of a filmmaker who embodies the present and future of horror perhaps more influentially than any other right now: Jordan Peele. I devoted much of chapter 7 to Peele's breakthrough debut feature *Get Out*, but I turn here to one of the many projects that Peele has pursued after *Get Out*—the television series *Hunters* (David Weil and Nikki Toscano, 2020–).

Peele is not the writer or director of *Hunters* but one of its executive producers. For many other filmmakers, their credits as producers or executive producers are not nearly as significant as their credits as writers or directors. But one of Peele's emerging trademarks (with *Get Out* and the equally impressive horror film *Us* [2019] as his only two features to date, his career is still very much near its beginning, although already proceeding at warp speed) is a commitment to getting off the ground other people's projects that reflect his own investments in having minority voices heard in an entertainment industry often dismissive or hostile to them. Peele, as an African American filmmaker, is clearly aware of and responsible toward his ability to lift social others from ignored silence to acknowledged speech. *Hunters* is particularly striking in this group of projects that Peele has supported because, like his work as a producer on Spike Lee's *BlacKkKlansman* (2018), it extends the project of shared Black/Jewish otherness begun with *Get Out*. Neither *BlacKkKlansman* nor *Hunters* is a horror genre project like *Get Out* and *Us*, but they participate in the workings of transformative otherness that this book has analyzed in relation to horror.

Hunters is set in America during the 1970s. It follows Jonah Heidelbaum (Logan Lerman), a young Jewish man who loses his overprotective but beloved grandmother in a mysterious homicide. As Jonah learns more about his grandmother's hidden life—her experiences as both a Holocaust survivor and a relentless researcher of Nazis in America—he becomes drawn into the activities of a group of Nazi hunters led by Meyer Offerman (Al Pacino). Jonah's ambivalence about joining Offerman's hunters—they fulfill his desires for revenge and for belonging, yet they participate in acts of violence and murder that also disturb him—changes as the Nazis are revealed as the killers of his grandmother, a mortal threat to his friends, and the architects of a planned Fourth Reich.

David Weil, the creator of *Hunters* and its coshowrunner with Nikki Toscano, credits Peele with bringing the series into being. Weil explains, "I brought *Hunters* to Jordan Peele, as soon as it was done, and he saw something in it that he really responded to and really loved, so he came on as an executive producer. He's been the most unbelievable partner and champion."[1] Given *Get Out's* inspiration from Ira Levin and its explorations of shared Black/Jewish otherness through Levin's work explicitly and Curt Siodmak's work implicitly (see chapter 7), it is no surprise that Peele became the project's champion. *Hunters* is indebted to Levin's *The Boys from Brazil* in particular because both Levin's novel and Weil's series pursue the fantastical premise that the world is on the brink of a Fourth Reich due to the evil schemes of an organized network of Nazis who survived the war. But this fantastical premise is shot through with Weil's personal story as a Jew whose grandmother was a Holocaust survivor, just as *Get Out* pulses with Peele's own personal resemblances to his African American protagonist, Chris, even amid the far-fetched plot regarding the conspiratorial replacement of Black people's brains.

What is most remarkable about *Hunters* and feels like the dimension of the series that owes the most to Peele, whether in terms of conception or execution, is its multiracial, multicultural, multigendered, multigenerational band of Nazi hunters. They are men, women, Jews, Blacks, Asians, Christians, elder Holocaust survivors and people too young to have experienced the Holocaust. Even beyond the hunters, the series gives a prominent role to a Black lesbian FBI agent. The sheer boldness and hopefulness of this utopian vision with which the hunters are imagined is strong enough to carry the series even when it runs into plot holes that threaten to swallow it. The series seems to understand, in a way that feels hard to conceive without Peele's involvement, that the *desire* for the hunters to exist as this utopian collective of others is far more important than the *plausibility* of their existence in the 1970s or even now. What matters is the commitment to imagining this collective of others in ways that make their socially translated existence in the future (in terms of personal and political alliances, not literal vigilantism) something we can envision and strive for.

Perhaps I am particularly moved by this vision of collective otherness because I am writing these words during the spring and summer of 2020—anguished times of virus lockdown, economic meltdown, murderous racism, presidential failure, international upheaval. In many ways, we have never been more separate, more riven by the medical requirements of social distancing during a deadly pandemic and by the rage that social othering still results in the lethal refusal to acknowledge that Black lives matter. While sheltering in place in Pittsburgh, my family and I were unable to go to New Jersey to attend the funeral of my wife's grandfather, who succumbed to COVID-19 at ninety-five years of age. Yakov Kreychman lived one of the most remarkable lives I have ever encountered personally, surviving Hitler, Stalin, Chernobyl, and then immigration to the United States from Ukraine while in his sixties. He was a survivor in the deepest sense, a proud Jew who spoke many languages but loved Yiddish best of all. Yet he could not survive COVID-19, and in the midst of a pandemic lockdown he was buried like an other, without his family and friends surrounding him.

Rarely have I felt so desolate, so othered myself on someone else's behalf, as when I watched Yakov's funeral on a cell phone screen. The trembling hand of my wife's sister showed the masked rabbi, the empty cemetery, the gravediggers forbidden by law to approach the gravesite before the tiny group of masked, gloved, and socially distanced mourners retreated to their cars. In that moment, my inability to be there felt as if I had been othered from my own family in ways that recalled my othering from my own city and my own country during the Tree of Life killings. Where am I? Who am I? Do I belong here? Did I ever belong here? Will I ever belong here?

In this book, I have tried to stake a claim for my own belonging alongside the need for others such as Yakov to belong. No matter how othered I might feel, even as a Jew in the shadow of the Tree of Life tragedy, even separated from my family as COVID-19 kills a loved one, I do indeed belong as much as Yakov belongs to all of us. The horror film gives me the language to say that. Horror allows me, as it has allowed so many others, to transform otherness in ways that make the past knowable, the present survivable, and the future—somehow, someway—hopeful.

NOTES

Introduction: Situating Horror and Otherness: Tree of Life, *Night of the Living Dead*, Pittsburgh

1. Adam Lowenstein, "*Night of the Living Dead* at 50," *Pittsburgh Jewish Chronicle*, October 26, 2018, 15.
2. A few landmarks in the theorization of otherness that have influenced my own understanding of it, selected from a nearly infinite array of possible examples, include Simone de Beauvoir, *The Second Sex*, ed. and trans. H. M. Parshley (1953; reprint, New York: Vintage, 1989; orig. pub. in French in 1949); Homi K. Bhabha, "The Other Question: Stereotype, Discrimination, and the Discourse of Colonialism" (1992), in *The Location of Culture* (London: Routledge, 1994), 66–84; Johannes Fabian, *Time and the Other: How Anthropology Makes Its Object* (1983; reprint, New York: Columbia University Press, 2002); Frantz Fanon, *Black Skin, White Masks*, trans. Richard Philcox (New York: Grove Press, 2008; orig. pub. in French in 1952); Alexandre Kojève, *Introduction to the Reading of Hegel*, ed. Allan Bloom, trans. James H. Nichols Jr. (Ithaca, NY: Cornell University Press, 1996; orig. pub. in French in 1947); Julia Kristeva, *Strangers to Ourselves*, trans. Leon S. Roudiez (New York: Columbia University Press, 1991; orig. pub. in French in 1988); Jacques Lacan, "The Freudian Thing, or the Meaning of the Return to Freud in Psychoanalysis" (orig. pub. in French in 1956), in *Écrits: A Selection*, trans. Alan Sheridan (1966; reprint, New York: Norton, 1977), 114–45; Emmanuel Levinas, *Totality and Infinity: An Essay on Exteriority*, trans. Alphonso Lingis (1969; reprint, Pittsburgh: Duquesne University Press, 2015; orig. pub. in French in 1961); Jean-Paul Sartre, *Being and Nothingness: An Essay on Phenomenological Ontology*, trans. Hazel E. Barnes (London: Routledge, 2015; orig. pub. in French in 1943). Especially inspirational for me has been Toni Morrison, *The Origin of Others* (Cambridge, MA: Harvard University Press, 2017).

3. Morrison, *The Origin of Others*, 15.
4. Morrison, *The Origin of Others*, 83. Morrison does not mention the film adaptation of *Beloved* produced by Oprah Winfrey and directed by Jonathan Demme in 1998, so I will just offer in passing that my own sense of that film's limitations has everything to do with decisions that distance the project from the novel's investments in horror.
5. Morrison, *The Origin of Others*, 82, 91.
6. Robin Wood, "An Introduction to the American Horror Film" (1979), in *Robin Wood on the Horror Film: Collected Essays and Reviews*, ed. Barry Keith Grant (Detroit, MI: Wayne State University Press, 2018), 83 ("Monster" is capitalized in the original publication but not in the reprint). This essay is subsequently cited in the text as "An Introduction" followed by the page number. For the original version of this essay, see Robin Wood, "An Introduction to the American Horror Film," in *The American Nightmare: Essays on the Horror Film*, ed. Robin Wood and Richard Lippe (Toronto: Festival of Festivals, 1979), 7–28.
7. Italics in the original publication but missing in the reprint.
8. Chapter 1 offers further discussion of spectacle horror, but see also Adam Lowenstein, "Spectacle Horror and *Hostel*: Why 'Torture Porn' Does Not Exist," *Critical Quarterly* 53, no. 1 (April 2011): 42–60.
9. Robin Wood, "Neglected Nightmares" (1980), in *Robin Wood on the Horror Film*, 191.
10. Wood, "Neglected Nightmares," 195.
11. Robin Wood, "Cronenberg: A Dissenting View" (1983), in *Robin Wood on the Horror Film*, 245, italics in the original publication but missing in the reprint.
12. Wood, "Neglected Nightmares," 194.
13. Italics in the original publication but missing in the reprint.
14. George A. Romero, interview in *The American Nightmare* (Adam Simon, 2000), DVD, (New York: Independent Film Channel, 2003). See also Adam Lowenstein, "Living Dead: Fearful Attractions of Film," *Representations* 110 (Spring 2010): 105–28.
15. Robin Wood, "Apocalypse Now: Notes on the Living Dead" (1979), in *Robin Wood on the Horror Film*, 161.
16. Robin Wood, "Responsibilities of a Gay Film Critic" (1978), in *Out in Culture: Gay, Lesbian, and Queer Essays on Popular Culture*, ed. Corey K. Creekmur and Alexander Doty (Durham, NC: Duke University Press, 1995), 12–24.
17. As this list of fields suggests, there is no way to summarize the scholarly development of horror studies through a comprehensive inventory of examples. For a sampling of recent anthologies that is far from exhaustive but offers some useful critical landmarks, see Stacey Abbott and Lorna Jowett, eds., *Global TV Horror* (Cardiff: University of Wales Press, 2021); Stacey Abbott, Adam Lowenstein, Roger Luckhurst, and Kristopher Woofter, eds., *The Routledge Companion to Horror* (London: Routledge, forthcoming); Simon Bacon, ed., *Horror: A Companion* (New York: Peter Lang, 2019); Harry M. Benshoff, ed., *A Companion to the Horror Film* (Oxford: Wiley-Blackwell, 2017); Aviva Briefel and Sam J. Miller, eds., *Horror After 9/11: World of Fear, Cinema of Terror* (Austin: University of Texas Press, 2011); Glennis Byron and Dale Townshend, eds., *The Gothic World* (London: Routledge, 2013); Darren Elliott-Smith and John Edgar Browning, eds., *New Queer Horror Film and Television* (Cardiff: University of Wales Press, 2020); Ken Gelder, ed., *The Horror Reader* (London: Routledge, 2000); Barry Keith Grant, ed., *The Dread of Difference: Gender and the Horror Film*, 2nd ed. (Austin: University of Texas Press, 2015); Barry Keith Grant and Christopher Sharrett, eds., *Planks of Reason: Essays on the Horror Film*, rev. ed. (Lanham, MD: Scarecrow, 2004); Mark Jancovich, ed., *Horror, the Film Reader* (London: Routledge, 2002);

Dawn Keetley, ed., *Jordan Peele's* Get Out: *Political Horror* (Columbus: Ohio State University Press, 2020); Murray Leeder, ed., *Cinematic Ghosts: Haunting and Spectrality from Silent Cinema to the Digital Era* (New York: Bloomsbury, 2015); Richard Nowell, ed., *Merchants of Menace: The Business of Horror Cinema* (New York: Bloomsbury, 2014); Stephen Prince, ed., *The Horror Film* (New Brunswick, NJ: Rutgers University Press, 2004); Steven Jay Schneider and Daniel Shaw, eds., *Dark Thoughts: Philosophic Reflections on Cinematic Horror* (Lanham, MD: Scarecrow, 2003); Steven Jay Schneider and Tony Williams, eds., *Horror International* (Detroit, MI: Wayne State University Press, 2005); as well as Sophia Siddique and Raphael Raphael, eds., *Transnational Horror Cinema: Bodies of Excess and the Global Grotesque* (London: Palgrave Macmillan, 2016).

18. See Wood, "Cronenberg," and Robin Wood, "King Meets Cronenberg" (1984), in *Robin Wood on the Horror Film*, 253–57. In the latter article, Wood professes his admiration for Cronenberg's *The Dead Zone* (1983) but in terms that emphasize how Wood sees Stephen King's source novel as freeing Cronenberg from his usual reactionary inclinations.

19. See Wood, "Apocalypse Now" and "Neglected Nightmares" as well as Robin Wood, "The Woman's Nightmare: Masculinity in *Day of the Dead*" (1986), "George Romero" (2000), "Fresh Meat: *Diary of the Dead*" (2008), and "What Lies Beneath?" (2004), all in *Robin Wood on the Horror Film*, 319–29, 373–75, 377–83, and 399–405.

20. Wood, "What Lies Beneath?," 404 (italics in the original publication but missing in the reprint).

1. A Reintroduction to the American Horror Film: Revisiting Robin Wood and 1970s Horror

1. Robin Wood, "An Introduction to the American Horror Film" (1979), in *Robin Wood on the Horror Film: Collected Essays and Reviews*, ed. Barry Keith Grant (Detroit, MI: Wayne State University Press, 2018), 79, italics in the original publication but missing in the reprint. This essay is subsequently cited in the text as "An Introduction" followed by the page number. For the original version of this essay, see Robin Wood, "An Introduction to the American Horror Film," in *The American Nightmare: Essays on the Horror Film*, ed. Robin Wood and Richard Lippe (Toronto: Festival of Festivals, 1979), 7–28.

2. For an illuminating account of the genesis of Robin Wood's commitment to the horror film and the organization of "The American Nightmare," see Richard Lippe, "Preface: The Journey from *Psycho* to *The American Nightmare*; or, Why Should We Take the Horror Film Seriously?," in Wood, *Robin Wood on the Horror Film*, xi–xvii.

3. Italics in the original publication but missing in the reprint.

4. "Other" is capitalized in the original publication but not in the reprint.

5. "Monster" is capitalized in the original publication but not in the reprint.

6. Italics in the original publication but missing in the reprint.

7. For further context on auteurism, see Barry Keith Grant, ed., *Auteurs and Authorship: A Film Reader* (Oxford: Wiley-Blackwell, 2008).

8. Robin Wood, *Hitchcock's Films Revisited*, rev. ed. (New York: Columbia University Press, 2002), 57.

9. For further discussion of Tobe Hooper's auteurist status, see chapter 3 as well as Kristopher Woofter and Will Dodson, eds., *American Twilight: The Cinema of Tobe Hooper* (Austin: University of Texas Press, 2021).

10. For further context on the *Screen* moment in film theory, see Philip Rosen, ed., *Narrative, Apparatus, Ideology: A Film Theory Reader* (New York: Columbia University Press, 1986).

11. Gad Horowitz, *Repression: Basic and Surplus Repression in Psychoanalytic Theory: Freud, Reich, and Marcuse* (Toronto: University of Toronto Press, 1977).

12. Italics in the original publication but missing in the reprint.

13. Italics in the original publication but missing in the reprint.

14. See Adam Lowenstein, *Shocking Representation: Historical Trauma, National Cinema, and the Modern Horror Film* (New York: Columbia University Press, 2005), 154–64.

15. Italics in the original publication but missing in the reprint.

16. Carol J. Clover, "Her Body, Himself: Gender in the Slasher Film," *Representations* 20 (1987): 187–228; and *Men, Women, and Chain Saws: Gender in the Modern Horror Film* (Princeton, NJ: Princeton University Press, 1992), which is subsequently cited in the text as *Men, Women,* followed by the page number. In the wake of Clover, scholarship on the slasher film has grown significantly. See, for example, Murray Leeder, *Halloween* (Leighton Buzzard, UK: Auteur, 2014); Adam Lowenstein, "A Detroit Landscape with Figures: The Subtractive Horror of *It Follows*," *Discourse* 40, no. 3 (Fall 2018): 358–69; Richard Nowell, *Blood Money: A History of the First Teen Slasher Film Cycle* (New York: Continuum, 2011); and Jeffrey Sconce, "Spectacles of Death: Identification, Reflexivity, and Contemporary Horror," in *Film Theory Goes to the Movies*, ed. Jim Collins, Hilary Radner, and Ava Preacher Collins (London: Routledge, 1993), 103–19.

17. Laura Mulvey, "Visual Pleasure and Narrative Cinema" (1975), in *Narrative, Apparatus, Ideology*, ed. Rosen, 203.

18. Mulvey, "Visual Pleasure and Narrative Cinema," 205.

19. See Adam Lowenstein, "The Master, the Maniac, and *Frenzy*: Hitchcock's Legacy of Horror," in *Hitchcock: Past and Future*, ed. Richard Allen and Sam Ishii-Gonzáles (London: Routledge, 2004), 179–92.

20. For further discussion of *The Last House on the Left*, see Lowenstein, *Shocking Representation*, 111–43. For further discussion of *Friday the 13th*, see Adam Lowenstein, "The Giallo/Slasher Landscape: *Ecologia del delitto*, *Friday the 13th*, and Subtractive Spectatorship," in *Italian Horror Cinema*, ed. Stefano Baschiera and Russ Hunter (Edinburgh: Edinburgh University Press, 2016), 127–44.

21. Tom Gunning, "The Cinema of Attractions: Early Film, Its Spectator, and the Avant-Garde," in *Early Cinema: Space—Frame—Narrative*, ed. Thomas Elsaesser, with Adam Barker (London: British Film Institute, 1990), 58–59. For further discussion of Gunning's work in relation to the horror film, see Adam Lowenstein, "Living Dead: Fearful Attractions of Film," *Representations* 110 (Spring 2010): 105–28.

22. Lowenstein, *Shocking Representation*, 2.

23. John D'Emilio and Estelle B. Freedman, *Intimate Matters: A History of Sexuality in America* (New York: Harper and Row, 1988), 331.

24. For research on children of divorce, see Elizabeth Marquardt, *Between Two Worlds: The Inner Lives of Children of Divorce* (New York: Three Rivers, 2005).

25. Robin Wood, "What Lies Beneath?" (2004), in *Robin Wood on the Horror Film*, 404, italics in the original publication but missing in the reprint.

26. Wood, "What Lies Beneath?," 405.

2. The Surrealism of Horror's Otherness: Listening to *The Shout*

1. Robin Wood, "An Introduction to the American Horror Film" (1979), in *Robin Wood on the Horror Film: Collected Essays and Reviews*, ed. Barry Keith Grant (Detroit, MI: Wayne State University Press, 2018), 83, italics in the original publication but missing in the reprint; subsequently cited in the text as "An Introduction" followed by the page number. For the original version of this essay, see Robin Wood, "An Introduction to the American Horror Film," in *The American Nightmare: Essays on the Horror Film*, ed. Robin Wood and Richard Lippe (Toronto: Festival of Festivals, 1979), 7–28.

2. See Jean Ferry, "Concerning *King Kong*" (orig. pub. in French in 1934), in *The Shadow and Its Shadow: Surrealist Writings on the Cinema*, 3rd ed., ed. and trans. Paul Hammond (San Francisco: City Lights, 2000), 161–65. For Breton on *Nosferatu*, see Adam Lowenstein, *Dreaming of Cinema: Spectatorship, Surrealism, and the Age of Digital Media* (New York: Columbia University Press, 2015), 181–82. For Bataille on *Nosferatu*, see Adam Lowenstein, *Shocking Representation: Historical Trauma, National Cinema, and the Modern Horror Film* (New York: Columbia University Press, 2005), 20.

3. See José de la Colina and Tomás Pérez Turrent, *Objects of Desire: Conversations with Luis Buñuel*, ed. and trans. Paul Lenti (New York: Marsilio, 1992), 45.

4. Alfred Hitchcock, "Why I Am Afraid of the Dark" (1960), in *Hitchcock on Hitchcock: Selected Writings and Interviews*, ed. Sidney Gottlieb (Berkeley: University of California Press, 1995), 142.

5. For further discussion of Franju, see Lowenstein, *Shocking Representation*, 17–54. For Wood on Franju, see Robin Wood, "Terrible Buildings: The World of Georges Franju," *Film Comment* 9, no. 6 (1973): 43–46.

6. See Jean-Michel Rabaté, "Loving Freud Madly: Surrealism Between Hysterical and Paranoid Modernism," *Journal of Modern Literature* 25, nos. 3–4 (2002): 60–61.

7. A major exception is Ado Kyrou, whose foundational work *Le surréalisme au cinéma* (Paris: Arcanes, 1953) still remains unavailable in English. For other exceptions in this regard, see James Leo Cahill, *Zoological Surrealism: The Nonhuman Cinema of Jean Painlevé* (Minneapolis: University of Minnesota Press, 2019); Graeme Harper and Rob Stone, eds., *The Unsilvered Screen: Surrealism on Film* (London: Wallflower, 2007); Rudolf E. Kuenzli, ed., *Dada and Surrealist Film* (Cambridge, MA: MIT Press, 1996); Lowenstein, *Dreaming of Cinema*; and Linda Williams, *Figures of Desire: A Theory and Analysis of Surrealist Film* (Berkeley: University of California Press, 1992).

8. James Clifford, "On Ethnographic Surrealism," in *The Predicament of Culture: Twentieth-Century Ethnography, Literature, and Art* (Cambridge, MA: Harvard University Press, 1988), 117, subsequently cited in the text as "Ethnographic Surrealism" followed by the page number.

9. See, for example, Joan Hawkins, *Cutting Edge: Art-Horror and the Horrific Avant-Garde* (Minneapolis: University of Minnesota Press, 2000); and Lowenstein, *Shocking Representation*.

10. For further discussion of Skolimowski's career, see Ewa Mazierska, *Jerzy Skolimowski: The Cinema of a Nonconformist* (New York: Berghahn, 2010).

11. "Monster" capitalized in the original publication but not in the reprint.

12. Italics in the original publication but missing in the reprint.

13. David Bordwell, "The Art Cinema as a Mode of Film Practice," *Film Criticism* 4, no. 1 (Fall 1979): 60. For further discussion of the definition of art cinema, see Lowenstein, *Dreaming of Cinema*, 44–48.

14. André Breton, "Manifesto of Surrealism" (orig. pub. in French in 1924), in *Manifestoes of Surrealism*, trans. Richard Seaver and Helen R. Lane (Ann Arbor: University of Michigan Press, 1994), 14, italics in original.

15. For scholarship that connects film and ethnography, see, for example, Alison Griffiths, *Wondrous Difference: Cinema, Anthropology, and Turn-of-the-Century Visual Culture* (New York: Columbia University Press, 2002); Fatimah Tobing Rony, *The Third Eye: Race, Cinema, and Ethnographic Spectacle* (Durham, NC: Duke University Press, 1996); and Catherine Russell, *Experimental Ethnography: The Work of Film in the Age of Video* (Durham, NC: Duke University Press, 1999). For scholarship in visual anthropology, see, for example, David MacDougall, *The Corporeal Image: Film, Ethnography, and the Senses* (Princeton, NJ: Princeton University Press, 2006); David MacDougall, *Transcultural Cinema* (Princeton, NJ: Princeton University Press, 1998); and Lucien Taylor, ed., *Visualizing Theory: Selected Essays from V.A.R., 1990–1994* (New York: Routledge, 1994).

16. See Mazierska, *Jerzy Skolimowski*, 175.

17. Jerzy Skolimowski, quoted in Mazierska, *Jerzy Skolimowski*, 161.

18. For further reflection on these questions of representation's risks and rewards, especially in the Aboriginal Australian context, see Elizabeth A. Povinelli, *The Cunning of Recognition: Indigenous Alterities and the Making of Australian Multiculturalism* (Durham, NC: Duke University Press, 2002), as well as the films Povinelli made as a member of the Karrabing Film Collective. For related discussion concerning the anthropology of media, see Faye D. Ginsburg, Lila Abu-Lughod, and Brian Larkin, eds., *Media Worlds: Anthropology on New Terrain* (Berkeley: University of California Press, 2002).

3. Nightmare Zone: Aging as Otherness in the Cinema of Tobe Hooper

1. Robin Wood, "An Introduction to the American Horror Film" (1979), in *Robin Wood on the Horror Film: Collected Essays and Reviews*, ed. Barry Keith Grant (Detroit, MI: Wayne State University Press, 2018), 97.

2. Lynne Segal, "The Coming of Age Studies," *Age, Culture, Humanities* 1 (2014): 31–32.

3. Kathleen Woodward, introduction to *Figuring Age: Women, Bodies, Generations*, ed. Kathleen Woodward (Bloomington: Indiana University Press, 1999), ix.

4. Tobe Hooper, interview in *The American Nightmare* (Adam Simon, 2000), DVD (New York: Independent Film Channel, 2003).

5. See, for example, Noël Carroll, *The Philosophy of Horror, or Paradoxes of the Heart* (New York: Routledge, 1990); Barbara Creed, *The Monstrous-Feminine: Film, Feminism, Psychoanalysis* (New York: Routledge, 1993); and Andrew Tudor, *Monsters and Mad Scientists: A Cultural History of the Horror Movie* (Oxford: Basil Blackwell, 1989).

6. Jodi Brooks, "Performing Aging/Performance Crisis (for Norma Desmond, Baby Jane, Margo Channing, Sister George—and Myrtle)," in *Figuring Age*, ed. Woodward, 234.

7. For an illuminating history of the conjuncture between the female and the grotesque, see Mary Russo, *The Female Grotesque: Risk, Excess, and Modernity* (New York: Routledge, 1995).

8. Woodward, introduction to *Figuring Age*, xiii.

9. See E. Ann Kaplan, "Trauma and Aging: Marlene Dietrich, Melanie Klein, and Marguerite Duras," in *Figuring Age*, ed. Woodward, 171–94.

10. *Lifeforce* (Tobe Hooper, 1985), liner notes, DVD (Beverly Hills, CA: MGM Home Entertainment, 1998).

11. Christopher Sharrett, "The Idea of Apocalypse in *The Texas Chainsaw Massacre*," in *Planks of Reason: Essays on the Horror Film*, rev. ed., ed. Barry Keith Grant and Christopher Sharrett (Lanham, MD: Scarecrow, 2004), 315.

12. Vivian Sobchack, "Scary Women: Cinema, Surgery, and Special Effects," in *Figuring Age*, ed. Woodward, 205.

13. Sobchack, "Scary Women," 209.

14. Carol J. Clover, *Men, Women, and Chain Saws: Gender in the Modern Horror Film* (Princeton, NJ: Princeton University Press, 1992), 21–64.

15. For further discussion of *Poltergeist* around the Hooper versus Spielberg authorship debate, see Joan Hawkins, "*Poltergeist*: TV People and Suburban Rage Monsters," in *American Twilight: The Cinema of Tobe Hooper*, ed. Kristopher Woofter and Will Dodson (Austin: University of Texas Press, 2021), 16–28.

16. For an ambitious, enlightening reconsideration of Hooper's entire oeuvre and its significance, see Woofter and Dodson, *American Twilight*.

4. The Trauma of Economic Otherness: Horror in George A. Romero's *Martin*

1. See, for example, Ben Hervey, *Night of the Living Dead* (New York: Palgrave Macmillan, 2008); Sumiko Higashi, "*Night of the Living Dead*: A Horror Film About the Horrors of the Vietnam Era," in *From Hanoi to Hollywood: The Vietnam War in American Film*, ed. Linda Dittmar and Gene Michaud (New Brunswick, NJ: Rutgers University Press, 1990), 175–88; Adam Lowenstein, *Shocking Representation: Historical Trauma, National Cinema, and the Modern Horror Film* (New York: Columbia University Press, 2005), 153–64; and Adam Lowenstein, "Living Dead: Fearful Attractions of Film," *Representations* 110 (Spring 2010): 105–28.

2. Cathy Caruth, in conversation with Shoshana Felman, discusses how to "make an injustice that has previously seemed to occur on the individual level (even when it has involved millions of individuals) clearly recognizable as collective, public, or universal" through "creating a collective public story that can be told and heard." See Caruth, *Listening to Trauma: Conversations with Leaders in the Theory and Treatment of Catastrophic Experience* (Baltimore, MD: Johns Hopkins University Press, 2014), 332. Caruth's emphasis on the process of translating individual into collective trauma through narrative and representation intersects, at least in part, with Jeffrey C. Alexander's social theory of cultural trauma, where he asserts that "trauma is a socially mediated attribution" (*Trauma: A Social Theory* [Malden, MA: Polity, 2012], 13). The work of Caruth and Alexander influences my claims in this chapter, as does the long history of research in trauma studies that relates individual trauma and collective trauma. This history can be detected at least implicitly in Sigmund Freud's work connected to the shell-shocked soldiers of World War I in *Beyond the Pleasure Principle*, ed. and trans. James Strachey (1961; reprint, New York: Norton, 1989; orig. pub. in German in 1920), and more explicitly in Kai Erikson, *Everything in Its Path: Destruction of Community in the Buffalo Creek Flood* (New York: Simon and Schuster, 1976).

3. My own book *Shocking Representation* is organized largely, with the exception of its final chapter on David Cronenberg, around an understanding of historical trauma's

relation to the horror film as a matter of discrete events rather than unfolding processes. In this sense, the chapter here builds outward from that book's final chapter and in conjunction with recent work in film and trauma studies that attempts to imagine new temporal frames for our understanding of trauma through cinema. See, for example, William Guynn, *Unspeakable Histories: Film and the Experience of Catastrophe* (New York: Columbia University Press, 2016); E. Ann Kaplan, *Climate Trauma: Foreseeing the Future in Dystopian Film and Fiction* (New Brunswick, NJ: Rutgers University Press, 2016); and Bliss Cua Lim, *Translating Time: Cinema, the Fantastic, and Temporal Critique* (Durham, NC: Duke University Press, 2009).

4. Robin Wood, "Neglected Nightmares" (1980), in *Robin Wood on the Horror Film: Collected Essays and Reviews*, ed. Barry Keith Grant (Detroit, MI: Wayne State University Press, 2018), 197, 198, 199. Wood's volume includes a number of other essays where Wood addresses Romero's work, up to and including *Diary of the Dead* (2008).

5. Although *Martin* has attracted relatively little critical attention, several important critical accounts of the film note its striking commitment to realism of one kind or another without emphasizing its engagement with trauma. See Richard Lippe, "The Horror of *Martin*," in *The American Nightmare: Essays on the Horror Film*, ed. Robin Wood and Richard Lippe (Toronto: Festival of Festivals, 1979), 87–90; Tony Williams, *The Cinema of George A. Romero: Knight of the Living Dead*, 2nd ed. (London: Wallflower, 2015), 80–89; and Wood, "Neglected Nightmares," 197–200. For valuable information on *Martin*'s production history, see Paul R. Gagne, *The Zombies That Ate Pittsburgh: The Films of George A. Romero* (New York: Dodd, Mead, 1987), 71–81.

6. See Amy McKeever, "In the Shadow of the Steel Mill," *Topic* 14 (August 2018), https://www.topic.com/in-the-shadow-of-the-steel-mill. For a history of the American steel industry leading up to 1978, when *Martin* was released, see Paul A. Tiffany, *The Decline of American Steel: How Management, Labor, and Government Went Wrong* (Oxford: Oxford University Press, 1988); for the industry after *Martin* was released, see John P. Hoerr, *And the Wolf Finally Came: The Decline of the American Steel Industry* (Pittsburgh: University of Pittsburgh Press, 1988).

7. In fact, *Martin* began as Romero's first (and only) black-and-white film since *Night of the Living Dead*, but economic and marketing concerns necessitated a switch to color as well as a significant shortening of the film's first cut. Because many commentators, including Romero himself, had noted the black-and-white look of *Night of the Living Dead* as part of the film's gritty power and kinship with contemporary news coverage, it is likely that the "objective" connotations of black-and-white film were important to *Martin*'s production. See Gagne, *The Zombies That Ate Pittsburgh*, 78–79.

8. For further discussion (and interrogation) of these "damaged vet" stereotypes that continue to characterize Vietnam veterans, see Philip F. Napoli, *Bringing It All Back Home: An Oral History of New York City's Vietnam Veterans* (New York: Hill and Wang, 2014).

9. David P. Demarest Jr., afterword to Thomas Bell, *Out of This Furnace* (1941; reprint, Pittsburgh: University of Pittsburgh Press, 1976), 418. Demarest, a literary scholar at Pittsburgh's Carnegie Mellon University, was responsible for rediscovering *Out of This Furnace* and bringing it back into print in 1976—just around the time Romero was conceptualizing *Martin*.

10. Franco Moretti, "Dialectic of Fear" (orig. pub. in Italian in 1982), trans. David Forgacs, in *Signs Taken for Wonders: On the Sociology of Literary Forms* (London: Verso, 2005), 83–108.

11. Caruth, *Listening to Trauma*, 288.

12. Caruth, *Listening to Trauma*, 332.

13. Arthur S. Blank Jr., quoted in Caruth, *Listening to Trauma*, 293.

14. On Michael Powell, see Lowenstein, *Shocking Representation*, 55–82; the quote from Powell is given in the title of Elliott Stein, "'A Very Tender Film, a Very Nice One': Michael Powell's *Peeping Tom*," *Film Comment* 15, no. 5 (September–October 1979): 57–59.

15. See, for example, LaToya Ruby Frazier, *The Notion of Family* (New York: Aperture Foundation, 2014).

16. Racist redlining policies and discrimination against Black steelworkers were important features of Braddock's economic decline. See McKeever, "In The Shadow of the Steel Mill," as well as Ray Henderson and Tony Buba's documentary *Struggles in Steel: The Fight for Equal Opportunity* (1996).

17. One film that walks through that door is *The Transfiguration* (Michael O'Shea, 2017), a remarkable horror film featuring a young African American "vampire" imagined along lines very much indebted to *Martin*.

5. Therapeutic Disintegration: Jewish Otherness in the Cinema of David Cronenberg

1. Here and throughout this chapter, "Jewishness" is imagined as a sensibility born of social identity and cultural experience rather than as any particular religious commitment. For an illuminating study of Jewishness as a sensibility within a social and cultural frame, see Jeremy Dauber, *Jewish Comedy: A Serious History* (New York: Norton, 2017).

2. For a comprehensive survey of Cronenberg criticism, see Ernest Mathijs, *The Cinema of David Cronenberg: From Baron of Blood to Cultural Hero* (London: Wallflower, 2008).

3. Robin Wood, "An Introduction to the American Horror Film" (1979), in *Robin Wood on the Horror Film: Collected Essays and Reviews*, ed. Barry Keith Grant (Detroit, MI: Wayne State University Press, 2018), 77, 102. For the original version of this essay, see Robin Wood, "An Introduction to the American Horror Film," in *The American Nightmare: Essays on the Horror Film*, ed. Robin Wood and Richard Lippe (Toronto: Festival of Festivals, 1979), 7–28.

4. Wood, "An Introduction to the American Horror Film," 104–5, italics in the original publication but missing in the reprint.

5. For further discussion of Wood on Cronenberg, see this book's introduction and Adam Lowenstein, *Shocking Representation: Historical Trauma, National Cinema, and the Modern Horror Film* (New York: Columbia University Press, 2005), 145–75, esp. 154–64. See also Robin Wood, "Cronenberg: A Dissenting View" (1983) and "King Meets Cronenberg" (1984), both in *Robin Wood on the Horror Film*, 231–52, 253–57.

6. David Cronenberg, in Alicia Potter, "The eXistenZ of Life: A Talk with Director David Cronenberg," *Infoplease*, 1999, http://www.infoplease.com/spot/existenz1.html. For further discussion of *eXistenZ*, see Adam Lowenstein, *Dreaming of Cinema: Spectatorship, Surrealism, and the Age of Digital Media* (New York: Columbia University Press, 2015), 43–77.

7. David Cronenberg, in Chris Rodley, ed., *Cronenberg on Cronenberg*, rev. ed. (London: Faber and Faber, 1997), 3.

8. David Cronenberg, in William Beard and Piers Handling, "The Interview," in *The Shape of Rage: The Films of David Cronenberg*, ed. Piers Handling (Toronto: General Publishing, 1983), 175.

9. See, for example, Sam B. Girgus, *Levinas and the Cinema of Redemption: Time, Ethics, and the Feminine* (New York: Columbia University Press, 2010); and Orna Raviv, *Ethics of Cinematic Experience: Screens of Alterity* (New York: Routledge, 2020).

10. For Levinas on Judaism, see Emmanuel Levinas, *Difficult Freedom: Essays on Judaism*, trans. Seán Hand (1990; reprint, Baltimore, MD: Johns Hopkins University Press, 1997; orig. pub. in French in 1963).

11. Emmanuel Levinas, *Existence and Existents*, trans. Alphonso Lingis (1978; reprint, Pittsburgh: Duquesne University Press, 2014; orig. pub. in French in 1947), 55, 52.

12. Levinas, *Existence and Existents*, 98.

13. Emmanuel Levinas, *Totality and Infinity: An Essay on Exteriority*, trans. Alphonso Lingis (1969; reprint, Pittsburgh: Duquesne University Press, 2015; orig. pub. in French in 1961), 23.

14. Siegfried Kracauer, "The Bible in German" (orig. pub. in German in 1926), in *The Mass Ornament: Weimar Essays*, ed. and trans. Thomas Y. Levin (Cambridge, MA: Harvard University Press, 1995), 201.

15. For further discussion of Kracauer's debate with Buber and Rosenzweig, see editor Thomas Y. Levin's notes in Kracauer, *The Mass Ornament*, 368–70.

16. See editor Asher D. Biemann's notes in Martin Buber, *The Martin Buber Reader: Essential Writings*, ed. Asher D. Biemann (New York: Palgrave Macmillan, 2002), 188; and Eric L. Santner, *On the Psychotheology of Everyday Life: Reflections on Freud and Rosenzweig* (Chicago: University of Chicago Press, 2001).

17. Siegfried Kracauer, quoted in Miriam Bratu Hansen, *Cinema and Experience: Siegfried Kracauer, Walter Benjamin, and Theodor W. Adorno* (Berkeley: University of California Press, 2012), 291 n. 72. See also Johannes von Moltke, *The Curious Humanist: Siegfried Kracauer in America* (Berkeley: University of California Press, 2016). Von Moltke sheds new light on Kracauer's relationship not only with Arnheim but also with the circle of New York intellectuals (many of them Jewish) who influenced his work in America, including *Theory of Film*.

18. Hansen, *Cinema and Experience*, 20, 17–18, 17.

19. Hansen, *Cinema and Experience*, 22.

20. Siegfried Kracauer, *Theory of Film: The Redemption of Physical Reality* (1960; reprint, Princeton, NJ: Princeton University Press, 1997), 300, 159.

21. Kracauer, *Theory of Film*, 86–87.

22. Kracauer, *Theory of Film*, 306. See also Lowenstein, *Shocking Representation*, 21–22; and Hansen, *Cinema and Experience*, 253–79.

23. Franz Rosenzweig, *The Star of Redemption*, trans. William W. Hallo (New York: Holt, Rinehart and Winston, 1971; orig. pub. in German in 1921), 422.

24. Kracauer, *Theory of Film*, 306. See also Lowenstein, *Shocking Representation*, 12–16, 146, 183; and Hansen, *Cinema and Experience*, 257–59.

25. Cronenberg, in Beard and Handling, "The Interview," 179.

26. Cronenberg, in Beard and Handling, "The Interview," 173.

27. See Adam Lowenstein, "Transforming Horror: David Cronenberg's Cinematic Gestures After 9/11," in *Horror After 9/11: World of Fear, Cinema of Terror*, ed. Aviva Briefel and Sam J. Miller (Austin: University of Texas Press, 2011), 62–80.

28. Sigmund Freud, *Beyond the Pleasure Principle*, ed. and trans. James Strachey (1961; reprint, New York: Norton, 1989; orig. pub. in German in 1920), 66 n. 16.

29. Sigmund Freud, *Moses and Monotheism*, trans. Katherine Jones (New York: Vintage, 1967; orig. pub. in German in 1939), 69–70.
30. Freud, *Moses and Monotheism*, 3.

6. Gendered Otherness: Feminine Horror and Surrealism in Marina de Van, Stephanie Rothman, and Jennifer Kent

1. James Quandt, "Flesh and Blood: Sex and Violence in Recent French Cinema" (2004), in *The New Extremism in Cinema: From France to Europe*, ed. Tanya Horeck and Tina Kendall (Edinburgh: Edinburgh University Press, 2011), 18–19. For valuable context on the emergence of New French Extremity as a critical category, see Tim Palmer, *Brutal Intimacy: Analyzing Contemporary French Cinema* (Middletown, CT: Wesleyan University Press, 2011), 66–70; and Horeck and Kendall, *The New Extremism in Cinema*. For discussion of the related critical category "torture porn," see Adam Lowenstein, "Spectacle Horror and *Hostel*: Why 'Torture Porn' Does Not Exist," *Critical Quarterly* 53, no. 1 (April 2011): 42–60.
2. Here and throughout this book, I do not capitalize the word *surrealism*, as others may, in order to indicate my desire to consider the term and its influence within but also outside formal connections with the Surrealist Group led by André Breton and founded in 1924.
3. See the following essays in Barry Keith Grant, ed., *The Dread of Difference: Gender and the Horror Film*, 2nd ed. (Austin: University of Texas Press, 2015): Carol J. Clover, "Her Body, Himself: Gender in the Slasher Film," 68–115; Barbara Creed, "Horror and the Monstrous-Feminine: An Imaginary Abjection," 37–67; and Linda Williams, "When the Woman Looks," 17–36.
4. For an important study of horror films directed by women, see Sonia Lupher, "From Women's Cinema to Women's Horror Cinema: Genre and Gender in the Twenty-First Century," PhD diss., University of Pittsburgh, 2020, as well as Lupher's pioneering digital project Cut-Throat Women: A Database of Women Who Make Horror, https:// www.cutthroatwomen.org. I am indebted to many conversations with Lupher over the years on the subject of women and horror.
5. André Breton, "Manifesto of Surrealism" (orig. pub. in French in 1924), in *Manifestoes of Surrealism*, trans. Richard Seaver and Helen R. Lane (Ann Arbor: University of Michigan Press, 1994), 14, italics in the original. For the history of surrealism, see Gérard Durozoi, *History of the Surrealist Movement*, trans. Alison Anderson (Chicago: University of Chicago Press, 2002; orig. pub. in French in 1997). For a consideration of surrealism's history with a particular emphasis on film, see Adam Lowenstein, *Dreaming of Cinema: Spectatorship, Surrealism, and the Age of Digital Media* (New York: Columbia University Press, 2015).
6. For example, Rudolf Kuenzli states, "The surrealist movement . . . was a men's club. The surrealists lived in their own masculine world, with their eyes closed, the better to construct their male phantasms of the feminine. They did not see woman as a subject, but as a projection, an object of their own dreams of femininity" ("Surrealism and Misogyny," in *Surrealism and Women*, ed. Mary Ann Caws, Rudolf E. Kuenzli, and Gwen Raaberg [Cambridge, MA: MIT Press, 1991], 17–18).
7. For example, Tim Palmer embraces the New French Extremity as thoroughly as James Quandt bemoans it, but he, too, chooses not to discuss surrealism in any significant

way. See Palmer, *Brutal Intimacy*, 59. By comparison, Jonathan Romney gives more serious consideration to surrealism's connection to the New French Extremity, albeit within the bounds of a journalistic account. See Romney, "Le Sex and Violence," *Independent*, September 12, 2004, https://www.independent.co.uk/arts-entertainment /films/features/le-sex-and-violence-546083.html. On women and surrealism, see Whitney Chadwick, *Women Artists and the Surrealist Movement* (New York: Thames and Hudson, 1985); Ilene Susan Fort, Tere Arcq, and Terri Geis, eds., *In Wonderland: The Surrealist Adventures of Women Artists in Mexico and the United States* (New York: Prestel, 2012); and Penelope Rosemont, ed., *Surrealist Women: An International Anthology* (Austin: University of Texas Press, 1998).

8. Stephanie Rothman, interview by Adam Lowenstein via Zoom, May 20, 2021. This interview was recorded and will be made available through the Horror Studies Archive at the University of Pittsburgh. I am grateful to Stephanie Rothman for her generous conversation with me, which produced insights that influence my account of her work in this chapter. I am also grateful to Heidi Honeycutt, Sonia Lupher, and Delaney Greenberg for arranging and facilitating this interview.

9. Robin Wood, "Neglected Nightmares" (1980), in *Robin Wood on the Horror Film: Collected Essays and Reviews*, ed. Barry Keith Grant (Detroit, MI: Wayne State University Press, 2018), 194.

10. It is telling that Wood's frustration with Rothman's work is ultimately very similar to his antipathy toward David Cronenberg's films (see chapter 5 and this book's introduction, where I also note this connection). On the conclusion of Rothman's *The Velvet Vampire*, Wood writes, "But the kind of liberation Diane embodies—if indeed she can be said to embody any at all (but if she doesn't, then what is the film about?)—is by this time so unclear that the spectator scarcely knows how to react" ("Neglected Nightmares," 195). On the conclusion of Cronenberg's *Shivers* (1975), Wood writes, "And what, in any case, could we possibly make of a film that dramatized liberation like *that*?" (Robin Wood, "Cronenberg: A Dissenting View" [1983], in *Robin Wood on the Horror Film*, 245, italics in the original publication but missing in the reprint). My own readings of Rothman and Cronenberg seek to see in their films what Wood misses: transformative otherness.

11. Laura Mulvey, "Visual Pleasure and Narrative Cinema" (1975), in *Narrative, Apparatus, Ideology: A Film Theory Reader*, ed. Philip Rosen (New York: Columbia University Press, 1986), 203, italics in the original.

12. For influential accounts of these processes of exchange, see Gayle Rubin, "The Traffic in Women: Notes Toward a Political Economy of Sex," in *Toward an Anthropology of Women*, ed. Rayna Reiter (New York: Monthly Review, 1975), 157–210; and Eve Kosofsky Sedgwick, *Between Men: English Literature and Male Homosocial Desire* (New York: Columbia University Press, 1986).

13. On the homoerotics of vampirism, see Nina Auerbach, *Our Vampires, Ourselves* (Chicago: University of Chicago Press, 1995). One hesitates to lean too heavily on an unambiguous lesbian reading of *The Velvet Vampire*, but it is striking how Rothman orchestrates a series of looks in the film that are intriguingly similar to the "lesbian looks" that Judith Mayne finds in the cinema of the pioneering woman director Dorothy Arzner. See Mayne, *The Woman at the Keyhole: Feminism and Women's Cinema* (Bloomington: Indiana University Press, 1990), and *Directed by Dorothy Arzner* (Bloomington: Indiana University Press, 1994).

14. P. Adams Sitney, *Visionary Film: The American Avant-Garde 1943–1978*, 2nd ed. (New York: Oxford University Press, 1979), 33. Sitney places Deren as a founding figure of

the American avant-garde film in a surrealist lineage that includes Cocteau as well as Luis Buñuel and Salvador Dalí's *Un chien andalou* (1929). Rothman's own debts to *Un chien andalou* can be detected in *Blood Bath* (1966), an early film she codirected with Jack Hill that is mentioned later in this chapter. *Blood Bath* includes the image of an eye impaled on a metronome, a possible allusion to *Un chien andalou*'s famous image of an eye slit by a razor blade. For further discussion of *Un chien andalou* in relation to surrealism, see Lowenstein, *Dreaming of Cinema*, 43–77.

15. Maya Deren, quoted in Sitney, *Visionary Film*, 9.

16. Mulvey, "Visual Pleasure and Narrative Cinema," 201–2.

17. Rothman describes her involvement with *Blood Bath* as a work-for-hire favor for Roger Corman, with her contribution allowing Corman to complete Jack Hill's unfinished film rather than giving Rothman the chance to express her own authorial vision. Rothman speaks about her fascination with surrealism as deep and long-lasting, naming Cocteau and Dalí as especially influential artists for her. See Rothman, interview by Lowenstein.

18. Stephanie Rothman, quoted in Marjorie Baumgarten, "Exploitation's Glass Ceiling: Feminist Filmmaker Stephanie Rothman on Her Short but Brilliant Run Making B-Movies," *Austin Chronicle*, April 9, 2010, https://www.austinchronicle.com/screens /2010-04-09/990516/. See also Alicia Kozma, "Stephanie Rothman Does Not Exist: Narrating a Lost History of Women in Film," *Camera Obscura* 32, no. 1 (2017): 179–86.

19. See, for example, Alison Peirse, ed., *Women Make Horror: Filmmaking, Feminism, Genre* (New Brunswick, NJ: Rutgers University Press, 2020). Peirse's important volume includes a welcome corrective to the typical overlooking of Rothman's career; see, for example, Alicia Kozma, "Stephanie Rothman and Vampiric Film Histories," 24–32.

20. On self-mutilation from a clinical perspective, see Marilee Strong, *A Bright Red Scream: Self-Mutilation and the Language of Pain* (New York: Penguin, 2009).

21. Breton, "Manifesto of Surrealism," 15. Perhaps more to the point for the particular case of *In My Skin*, Breton and his fellow surrealists were also ardent admirers of two important women authors who contributed powerfully to the Gothic tradition: Ann Radcliffe and Emily Brontë. See Penelope Rosemont, "All My Names Know Your Leap: Surrealist Women and Their Challenge," introduction to *Surrealist Women*, ed. Rosemont, xli–xlii.

22. Chadwick, *Women Artists and the Surrealist Movement*, 12. It is worth noting that de Van, taking a position toward her own work that echoes Oppenheim's, "downplays" any feminist interpretation of *In My Skin* by "insisting that Esther's estrangement is corporeal and not gender specific" (quoted in Palmer, *Brutal Intimacy*, 83).

23. My account of Oppenheim's biography draws on Josef Helfenstein, "Against the Intolerability of Fame: Meret Oppenheim and Surrealism," in *Meret Oppenheim: Beyond the Teacup*, ed. Jacqueline Burckhardt and Bice Curiger (New York: Independent Curators, 1996), 23–34. See also Bice Curiger, *Meret Oppenheim: Defiance in the Face of Freedom* (Cambridge, MA: MIT Press, 1989).

24. Alfred H. Barr Jr., quoted in Helfenstein, "Against the Intolerability of Fame," 27.

25. The fact that Oppenheim's *Object* was originally exhibited alongside not only surrealist art but also found objects such as crystals and carnivorous plants and "cult articles, fetishes, and masks" from outside Europe emphasizes her art's connection to surrealism's fascination with ethnographic forms and practices. See Helfenstein, "Against the Intolerability of Fame," 26; James Clifford, "On Ethnographic Surrealism," in *The Predicament of Culture: Twentieth-Century Ethnography, Literature, and*

Art (Cambridge, MA: Harvard University Press, 1988), 117–51; and chapter 2 in this volume.

26. Meret Oppenheim, "Automatism at a Crossroads," trans. Myrna Bell Rochester (orig. pub. in French in 1955), in *Surrealist Women*, ed. Rosemont, 256. Oppenheim's formulation resembles, in fascinating ways worthy of further analysis, those of Roland Barthes's *punctum* and Jacques Lacan's *objet petit a*. Both Barthes and Lacan had significant intellectual encounters with surrealism during their lives. See Lowenstein, *Dreaming of Cinema*, 11–42, 57–59.

27. Marcel Jean, quoted in Helfenstein, "Against the Intolerability of Fame," 27.

28. Marina de Van, director's audio commentary, *In My Skin* (Marina de Van, 2002), DVD (New York: Wellspring Media, 2004), at 2:20–3:00.

29. Mulvey, "Visual Pleasure and Narrative Cinema," 203–4.

30. Just as Esther's wounded leg may be seen as evoking Catherine Deneuve's amputated leg in Buñuel's *Tristana* (1970).

31. For example, not only Buñuel but also Dalí (the film's coscreenwriter) appear in *Un chien andalou*, and Max Ernst plays a key role in *L'âge d'or* (Luis Buñuel, 1930). Valentine Penrose, a female poet and associate of the surrealists (married to the surrealist artist Roland Penrose, who would go on to remarry Lee Miller), can also be glimpsed in *L'âge d'or*.

32. Chadwick, *Women Artists and the Surrealist Movement*, 66.

33. According to Palmer, "*In My Skin* has its origins in an accident de Van had as an eight-year-old, when a car ran over her right leg" (*Brutal Intimacy*, 81). De Van's casting of herself as Esther (as well as in key roles in her earlier short films) also testifies to personal investment: "More than being an actor, I wanted to film myself" (quoted in Palmer, *Brutal Intimacy*, 80).

34. Leonora Carrington, "What Is a Woman?" (1970), in *Surrealist Women*, ed. Rosemont, 372–73.

35. Palmer, *Brutal Intimacy*, 156.

36. Germaine Dulac, the director of *The Seashell and the Clergyman* (*La coquille et le clergyman*, 1928), also merits mention here, but that film's complicated relation to surrealism (it was written by Antonin Artaud but attacked by the surrealists) requires more detailed explication than this chapter allows. See Sandy Flitterman-Lewis, *To Desire Differently: Feminism and the French Cinema* (New York: Columbia University Press, 1996), 47–140.

37. For more information on many of these directors and others, see Lupher's database *Cut-Throat Women* and Hannah Neurotica's fanzine *Ax Wound*.

38. See Lianne McLarty, " 'Beyond the Veil of the Flesh': Cronenberg and the Disembodiment of Horror," and Barry Keith Grant, "Taking Back the *Night of the Living Dead*: George Romero, Feminism, and the Horror Film," both in *The Dread of Difference*, ed. Grant, 259–80, 228–40.

39. It is worth noting here that Robin Wood has argued for a feminist-influenced interpretation of De Palma's horror films, especially *Sisters* (1973), even though many critics have disparaged much of the director's work as misogynistic. See Wood, *Hollywood from Vietnam to Reagan* (New York: Columbia University Press, 1986), 135–61. De Palma's influence on de Van can also be detected in her horror film *Dark Touch* (2013), which includes a number of similarities to De Palma's *Carrie* (1976).

40. Space does not permit a full discussion of global horror studies, but for useful critical landmarks in this rapidly expanding field of scholarship, see Stacey Abbott and Lorna Jowett, eds., *Global TV Horror* (Cardiff: University of Wales Press, 2021); Rosalind Galt,

Alluring Monsters: The Pontianak and Cinemas of Decolonization (New York: Columbia University Press, 2021); Steven Jay Schneider and Tony Williams, eds., *Horror International* (Detroit: Wayne State University Press, 2005); and Meheli Sen, *Haunting
Bollywood: Gender, Genre, and the Supernatural in Hindi Commercial Cinema* (Austin: University of Texas Press, 2017).

41. Jennifer Kent, quoted in Paul MacInnes, "*The Babadook*: 'I Wanted to Talk About the
Need to Face Darkness in Ourselves,'" *Guardian*, October 18, 2014, https://www
.theguardian.com/film/2014/oct/18/the-babadook-jennifer-kent.

42. See Lucy Fischer, "Birth Traumas: Parturition and Horror in *Rosemary's Baby*," in *The
Dread of Difference*, ed. Grant, 439–58. For an excellent discussion of *The Babadook*
in relation to maternal horror, see Aviva Briefel, "Parenting Through Horror: Reassurance in Jennifer Kent's *The Babadook*," *Camera Obscura* 32, no. 2 (2017): 1–27.

43. Quotes from John Paul Brammer and Alex Abad-Santos in Alex Abad-Santos, "How
the Babadook Became the LGBTQ Icon We Didn't Know We Needed," *Vox*, June 25,
2017, https://www.vox.com/explainers/2017/6/9/15757964/gay-babadook-lgbtq.

7. Racial Otherness: Horror's Black/Jewish Minority Vocabulary, from Jordan Peele to Ira Levin and Curt Siodmak

1. Jordan Peele, "*Get Out* Sprang from an Effort to Master Fear, Says Director Jordan
Peele," interview by Terry Gross, *Fresh Air*, National Public Radio, March 15, 2017,
https://www.npr.org/sections/codeswitch/2017/03/15/520130162/get-out-sprung-from
-an-effort-to-master-fear-says-director-jordan-peele. Ira Levin was a master of sus-
penseful, paranoia-inducing horror. During his remarkable and underappreciated
career, he also wrote the novels *The Boys from Brazil* (1976) and *Sliver* (1991) as well as
the Broadway smash *Deathtrap* (1978), among others.

2. One might add that *Deathtrap* could be read as a queer nightmare of sexual oppression, but space does not permit more thorough investigation of this argument here.

3. Ira Levin, *Rosemary's Baby* (New York: Random House, 1967), 206, subsequently cited
in the text by page number.

4. Robin Wood, "An Introduction to the American Horror Film" (1979), in *Robin Wood
on the Horror Film: Collected Essays and Reviews*, ed. Barry Keith Grant (Detroit, MI:
Wayne State University Press, 2018), 83, 80–81. "Monster" is capitalized in the origi-
nal publication but not in the reprint. For the original version of this essay, see Robin
Wood, "An Introduction to the American Horror Film," in *The American Nightmare:
Essays on the Horror Film*, ed. Robin Wood and Richard Lippe (Toronto: Festival of
Festivals, 1979), 7–28.

5. This claim condenses a number of issues that receive more thorough elaboration over
the course of this chapter. For relevant background context on the history of relations
between Blacks and Jews in America, see Eric J. Sundquist, *Strangers in the Land:
Blacks, Jews, Post-Holocaust America* (Cambridge, MA: Harvard University Press,
2005); on the history of relations between Blacks and Jews in Hollywood cinema,
see Michael Rogin, *Blackface, White Noise: Jewish Immigrants in the Hollywood
Melting Pot* (Berkeley: University of California Press, 1996); and on the history of
Black representation in the American horror film, see Robin R. Means Coleman,
Horror Noire: Blacks in American Horror Films from the 1890s to Present (New York:
Routledge, 2011).

6. It is also worth noting how the presence of William Castle as the producer of *Rosemary's Baby* for Paramount suggests an intersection between "high" and "low" horror traditions.

7. For context on Polanski's Jewishness, see Christopher Sandford, *Polanski: A Biography* (New York: Palgrave Macmillan, 2008).

8. Ira Levin, "'Stuck with Satan': Ira Levin on the Origins of *Rosemary's Baby*" (2003), in *Rosemary's Baby* (Roman Polanski, 1968), DVD, liner notes (New York: Criterion Collection, 2012), 17.

9. Ira Levin, *The Stepford Wives* (1972; reprint, New York: William Morrow, 2002), 13.

10. Levin's *Cantorial* is a dramatic-comedic variation on the famous dybbuk story of supernatural possession descended from Jewish folklore. I return to the figure of the dybbuk later in this chapter.

11. Ralph Ellison, "The Shadow and the Act" (1949), in *American Movie Critics: An Anthology from the Silents Until Now*, exp. ed., ed. Phillip Lopate (New York: Library of America, 2006), 194.

12. Ellison, "The Shadow and the Act," 197.

13. Toni Morrison, *The Origin of Others* (Cambridge, MA: Harvard University Press, 2017), 25–26.

14. Morrison, *The Origin of Others*, 24.

15. Morrison, *The Origin of Others*, 17. In this section of *Origin*, Morrison is drawing on Jolie A. Sheffer, *The Romance of Race: Incest, Miscegenation, and Multiculturalism in the United States, 1880–1930* (New Brunswick, NJ: Rutgers University Press, 2013).

16. See Adam Lowenstein, *Shocking Representation: Historical Trauma, National Cinema, and the Modern Horror Film* (New York: Columbia University Press, 2005), 1–16. My concept of the "allegorical moment" relates cinematic horror to the horrors of history, where "a shocking collision of film, spectator, and history" allows "registers of bodily space and historical time" to become "disrupted, confronted, and intertwined" (2).

17. Zadie Smith's thoughtful review of *Get Out* argues that the film stumbles when it resorts to a "Black versus white," "us versus them" logic. See Smith, "Getting In and Out: Who Owns Black Pain?," *Harper's Magazine*, July 2017, https://harpers.org/archive/2017/07/getting-in-and-out/.

18. Marie Myung-Ok Lee, "*Get Out* Shows That Even the Most Intelligent Films Can Fall Prey to Asian-American Stereotypes," *Quartz*, March 31, 2017, https://qz.com/945493/get-out-shows-that-even-the-most-intelligent-films-can-fall-prey-to-asian-american-stereotypes/.

19. Curt Siodmak, *Wolf Man's Maker: Memoir of a Hollywood Writer* (Lanham, MD: Scarecrow, 2001), x, subsequently cited by title and page number.

20. Curt Siodmak, *Donovan's Brain* (1942; reprint, London: Tandem, 1972), 190.

21. Siodmak, *Donovan's Brain*, 129–30.

22. Siodmak, *Donovan's Brain*, 190.

23. While discussing his debt to Ira Levin's approach to paranoia, Jordan Peele explains *Get Out* in autobiographical terms: "This movie is also about how we deal with race. As a Black man, sometimes you can't tell if what you're seeing has underlying bigotry, or it's a normal conversation and you're being paranoid. That dynamic in itself is unsettling. I admit sometimes I see race and racism when it's not there. It's very disorienting to be aware of certain dynamics." See Jason Zinoman, "Jordan Peele on a Truly Terrifying Monster: Racism," *New York Times*, February 16, 2017, https://www.nytimes.com/2017/02/16/movies/jordan-peele-interview-get-out.html.

24. For discussion of the dybbuk in a literary context, see Jeremy Dauber, *In the Demon's Bedroom: Yiddish Literature and the Early Modern* (New Haven, CT: Yale University Press, 2010); for the dybbuk in a cinematic context, see Lester D. Friedman, "'Canyons of Nightmare': The Jewish Horror Film," in *Planks of Reason: Essays on the Horror Film*, rev. ed., ed. Barry Keith Grant and Christopher Sharrett (Lanham, MD: Scarecrow, 2004), 82–106.

25. See Sarah Juliet Lauro, *The Transatlantic Zombie: Slavery, Rebellion, and Living Death* (New Brunswick, NJ: Rutgers University Press, 2015).

26. For further discussion of the *Get Out*–zombie connection, see Erin Casey-Williams, "*Get Out* and the Zombie Film," in *Jordan Peele's* Get Out: *Political Horror*, ed. Dawn Keetley (Columbus: Ohio State University Press, 2020), 63–71.

27. I am indebted to the Jewish writer-director Philippe Mora for speaking with me about Curt Siodmak's role in creating *The Wolf Man* and encouraging me to recognize Siodmak as a "Jew on the run." Mora's own fascinating filmography, which ranges from the pioneering Australian Western *Mad Dog Morgan* (1976) to horror films to documentaries reflecting on the experience of his parents as Holocaust survivors, deserves more attention than I can provide here.

28. Although space does not permit a full exploration of this claim here, it is worth noting in passing how each of the Universal horror series incorporates different forms of social otherness, most often in implicit or figurative guises: Blackness in *Frankenstein*, queerness in *Dracula*, the Arab in *The Mummy*, nonwhite races in *The Invisible Man*, Jewishness in *The Wolf Man*, and the Indigenous in *Creature from the Black Lagoon*. Given Siodmak's own contributions to nearly all of these series, it would be worthwhile to examine them more closely in relation to patterns of transformative otherness. The legacy of Universal's merging of horror and social otherness can still be felt today. See, for example, *The Shape of Water* as an echo of *Creature from the Black Lagoon*.

29. See Brian J. Frost, *The Essential Guide to Werewolf Literature* (Madison: University of Wisconsin Press, 2003).

30. For discussion of the Jewish werewolf's longer theological and philosophical history, see David I. Shyovitz, "Christians and Jews in the Twelfth-Century Werewolf Renaissance," *Journal of the History of Ideas* 75, no. 4 (2014): 521–43.

31. See J. Hoberman, *Bridge of Light: Yiddish Film Between Two Worlds* (Philadelphia: Temple University Press, 1995), 60–61. Paul Wegener, the star and producer of *The Student of Prague* and the director and star of three different versions of *The Golem*, eventually became an actor of the state under the Nazi regime and appeared in several Nazi propaganda films.

32. Contrary to much conventional wisdom, recent research has shown that knowledge of Nazi policies and practices toward Jews was available in the United States far earlier than usually assumed. For example, Joseph Goebbels was featured on the cover of *Time* magazine for the July 10, 1933, issue, along with this quote from his interview: "THE JEWS ARE TO BLAME!" See Lily Rothman, "'It's Not That the Story Was Buried': What Americans in the 1930s Really Knew About What Was Happening in Germany," *Time*, July 10, 2018, https://time.com/5327279/ushmm-americans-and-the-holocaust/.

33. See János Bársony and Ágnes Daróczi, *Pharrajimos: The Fate of the Roma During the Holocaust* (New York: International Debate Education Association, 2007).

34. Curt Siodmak, "Introduction to My Screenplay, *The Wolf Man*," in *The Wolf Man: The Original 1941 Shooting Script*, ed. Philip Riley (Absecon, NJ: MagicImage Filmbooks, 1993), 14.

Afterword: Horror and Otherness in Anguished Times

1. David Weil, in Christina Radish, "*Hunters* Creator David Weil on How He Landed Al Pacino and Jordan Peele's Involvement," *Collider*, March 1, 2020, https://collider.com /hunters-interview-david-weil-amazon-series/.

BIBLIOGRAPHY

Abad-Santos, Alex. "How the Babadook Became the LGBTQ Icon We Didn't Know We Needed." *Vox*, June 25, 2017. https://www.vox.com/explainers/2017/6/9/15757964/gay-babadook-lgbtq.

Abbott, Stacey, and Lorna Jowett, eds. *Global TV Horror*. Cardiff: University of Wales Press, 2021.

Abbott, Stacey, Adam Lowenstein, Roger Luckhurst, and Kristopher Woofter, eds. *The Routledge Companion to Horror*. London: Routledge, forthcoming.

Alexander, Jeffrey C. *Trauma: A Social Theory*. Malden, MA: Polity, 2012.

Auerbach, Nina. *Our Vampires, Ourselves*. Chicago: University of Chicago Press, 1995.

Bacon, Simon, ed. *Horror: A Companion*. New York: Peter Lang, 2019.

Bársony, János, and Ágnes Daróczi. *Pharrajimos: The Fate of the Roma During the Holocaust*. New York: International Debate Education Association, 2007.

Baumgarten, Marjorie. "Exploitation's Glass Ceiling: Feminist Filmmaker Stephanie Rothman on Her Short but Brilliant Run Making B-Movies." *Austin Chronicle*, April 9, 2010. https://www.austinchronicle.com/screens/2010-04-09/990516/.

Beard, William, and Piers Handling. "The Interview." In *The Shape of Rage: The Films of David Cronenberg*, edited by Piers Handling, 159–98. Toronto: General Publishing, 1983.

Bell, Thomas. *Out of This Furnace*. 1941. Reprint. Pittsburgh: University of Pittsburgh Press, 1976.

Benshoff, Harry M., ed. *A Companion to the Horror Film*. Oxford: Wiley-Blackwell, 2017.

Bhabha, Homi K. "The Other Question: Stereotype, Discrimination, and the Discourse of Colonialism" (1992). In *The Location of Culture*, 66–84. London: Routledge, 1994.

Bordwell, David. "The Art Cinema as a Mode of Film Practice." *Film Criticism* 4, no. 1 (Fall 1979): 56–64.

Breton, André. "Manifesto of Surrealism" (orig. pub. in French in 1924). In *Manifestoes of Surrealism*, translated by Richard Seaver and Helen R. Lane, 1–47. Ann Arbor: University of Michigan Press, 1994.

Briefel, Aviva. "Parenting Through Horror: Reassurance in Jennifer Kent's *The Babadook*." *Camera Obscura* 32, no. 2 (2017): 1–27.

Briefel, Aviva, and Sam J. Miller, eds. *Horror After 9/11: World of Fear, Cinema of Terror*. Austin: University of Texas Press, 2011.

Brooks, Jodi. "Performing Aging/Performance Crisis (for Norma Desmond, Baby Jane, Margo Channing, Sister George—and Myrtle)." In Woodward, *Figuring Age*, 232–47.

Buber, Martin. *The Martin Buber Reader: Essential Writings*. Edited by Asher D. Biemann. New York: Palgrave Macmillan, 2002.

Byron, Glennis, and Dale Townshend, eds. *The Gothic World*. London: Routledge, 2013.

Cahill, James Leo. *Zoological Surrealism: The Nonhuman Cinema of Jean Painlevé*. Minneapolis: University of Minnesota Press, 2019.

Carrington, Leonora. "What Is a Woman?" (1970). In Rosemont, *Surrealist Women*, 372–75.

Carroll, Noël. *The Philosophy of Horror, or Paradoxes of the Heart*. New York: Routledge, 1990.

Caruth, Cathy. *Listening to Trauma: Conversations with Leaders in the Theory and Treatment of Catastrophic Experience*. Baltimore, MD: Johns Hopkins University Press, 2014.

Casey-Williams, Erin. "*Get Out* and the Zombie Film." In Keetley, *Jordan Peele's Get Out*, 63–71.

Chadwick, Whitney. *Women Artists and the Surrealist Movement*. New York: Thames and Hudson, 1985.

Clifford, James. "On Ethnographic Surrealism." In *The Predicament of Culture: Twentieth-Century Ethnography, Literature, and Art*, 117–51. Cambridge, MA: Harvard University Press, 1988.

Clover, Carol J. "Her Body, Himself: Gender in the Slasher Film." *Representations* 20 (1987): 187–228. Reprinted in Grant, *The Dread of Difference*, 68–115.

——. *Men, Women, and Chain Saws: Gender in the Modern Horror Film*. Princeton, NJ: Princeton University Press, 1992.

Creed, Barbara. "Horror and the Monstrous-Feminine: An Imaginary Abjection." In Grant, *The Dread of Difference*, 37–67.

——. *The Monstrous-Feminine: Film, Feminism, Psychoanalysis*. New York: Routledge, 1993.

Curiger, Bice. *Meret Oppenheim: Defiance in the Face of Freedom*. Cambridge, MA: MIT Press, 1989.

Dauber, Jeremy. *In the Demon's Bedroom: Yiddish Literature and the Early Modern*. New Haven, CT: Yale University Press, 2010.

——. *Jewish Comedy: A Serious History*. New York: Norton, 2017.

De Beauvoir, Simone. *The Second Sex*. Edited and translated by H. M. Parshley. 1953. Reprint. New York: Vintage, 1989. Orig. pub. in French in 1949.

De la Colina, José, and Tomás Pérez Turrent. *Objects of Desire: Conversations with Luis Buñuel*. Edited and translated by Paul Lenti. New York: Marsilio, 1992.

Demarest, David P., Jr. Afterword to Thomas Bell, *Out of This Furnace* (1941), 415–23. Pittsburgh: University of Pittsburgh Press, 1976.

D'Emilio, John, and Estelle B. Freedman. *Intimate Matters: A History of Sexuality in America*. New York: Harper and Row, 1988.

De Van, Marina. Audio commentary in *In My Skin* (Marina de Van, 2002), DVD. New York: Wellspring Media, 2004.

Durozoi, Gérard. *History of the Surrealist Movement*. Translated by Alison Anderson. Chicago: University of Chicago Press, 2002. Orig. pub. in French in 1997.

Elliott-Smith, Darren, and John Edgar Browning, eds. *New Queer Horror Film and Television*. Cardiff: University of Wales Press, 2020.

Ellison, Ralph. "The Shadow and the Act" (1949). In *American Movie Critics: An Anthology from the Silents Until Now*, exp. ed., edited by Phillip Lopate, 192–97. New York: Library of America, 2006.

Erikson, Kai. *Everything in Its Path: Destruction of Community in the Buffalo Creek Flood.* New York: Simon and Schuster, 1976.

Fabian, Johannes. *Time and the Other: How Anthropology Makes Its Object.* 1983. Reprint. New York: Columbia University Press, 2002.

Fanon, Frantz. *Black Skin, White Masks.* Translated by Richard Philcox. New York: Grove, 2008. Orig. pub. in French in 1952.

Ferry, Jean. "Concerning *King Kong*" (orig. pub. in French in 1934). In *The Shadow and Its Shadow: Surrealist Writings on the Cinema*, 3rd ed., edited and translated by Paul Hammond, 161–65. San Francisco: City Lights, 2000.

Fischer, Lucy. "Birth Traumas: Parturition and Horror in *Rosemary's Baby.*" In Grant, *The Dread of Difference*, 439–58.

Flitterman-Lewis, Sandy. *To Desire Differently: Feminism and the French Cinema.* New York: Columbia University Press, 1996.

Fort, Ilene Susan, Tere Arcq, and Terri Geis, eds. *In Wonderland: The Surrealist Adventures of Women Artists in Mexico and the United States.* New York: Prestel, 2012.

Frazier, LaToya Ruby. *The Notion of Family.* New York: Aperture Foundation, 2014.

Freud, Sigmund. *Beyond the Pleasure Principle.* Edited and translated by James Strachey. 1961. Reprint. New York: Norton, 1989. Orig. pub. in German in 1920.

——. *Moses and Monotheism.* Translated by Katherine Jones. New York: Vintage, 1967. Orig. pub. in German in 1939.

Friedman, Lester D. "'Canyons of Nightmare': The Jewish Horror Film." In Grant and Sharrett, *Planks of Reason*, 82–106.

Frost, Brian J. *The Essential Guide to Werewolf Literature.* Madison: University of Wisconsin Press, 2003.

Gagne, Paul R. *The Zombies That Ate Pittsburgh: The Films of George A. Romero.* New York: Dodd, Mead, 1987.

Galt, Rosalind. *Alluring Monsters: The Pontianak and Cinemas of Decolonization.* New York: Columbia University Press, 2021.

Gelder, Ken, ed. *The Horror Reader.* London: Routledge, 2000.

Ginsburg, Faye D., Lila Abu-Lughod, and Brian Larkin, eds. *Media Worlds: Anthropology on New Terrain.* Berkeley: University of California Press, 2002.

Girgus, Sam B. *Levinas and the Cinema of Redemption: Time, Ethics, and the Feminine.* New York: Columbia University Press, 2010.

Grant, Barry Keith, ed. *Auteurs and Authorship: A Film Reader.* Oxford: Wiley-Blackwell, 2008.

——, ed. *The Dread of Difference: Gender and the Horror Film.* 2nd ed. Austin: University of Texas Press, 2015.

——. "Taking Back the *Night of the Living Dead*: George Romero, Feminism, and the Horror Film." In Grant, *The Dread of Difference*, 228–40.

Grant, Barry Keith, and Christopher Sharrett, eds. *Planks of Reason: Essays on the Horror Film.* Rev. ed. Lanham, MD: Scarecrow, 2004.

Griffiths, Alison. *Wondrous Difference: Cinema, Anthropology, and Turn-of-the-Century Visual Culture.* New York: Columbia University Press, 2002.

Gunning, Tom. 1986. "The Cinema of Attractions: Early Film, Its Spectator, and the Avant-Garde." In *Early Cinema: Space—Frame—Narrative*, edited by Thomas Elsaesser, with Adam Barker, 56–62. London: British Film Institute, 1990.

Guynn, William. *Unspeakable Histories: Film and the Experience of Catastrophe*. New York: Columbia University Press, 2016.

Hansen, Miriam Bratu. *Cinema and Experience: Siegfried Kracauer, Walter Benjamin, and Theodor W. Adorno*. Berkeley: University of California Press, 2012.

Harper, Graeme, and Rob Stone, eds. *The Unsilvered Screen: Surrealism on Film*. London: Wallflower, 2007.

Hawkins, Joan. *Cutting Edge: Art-Horror and the Horrific Avant-Garde*. Minneapolis: University of Minnesota Press, 2000.

——. "*Poltergeist*: TV People and Suburban Rage Monsters." In Woofter and Dodson, *American Twilight*, 16–28.

Helfenstein, Josef. "Against the Intolerability of Fame: Meret Oppenheim and Surrealism." In *Meret Oppenheim: Beyond the Teacup*, edited by Jacqueline Burckhardt and Bice Curiger, 23–34. New York: Independent Curators, 1996.

Hervey, Ben. *Night of the Living Dead*. New York: Palgrave Macmillan, 2008.

Higashi, Sumiko. "*Night of the Living Dead*: A Horror Film About the Horrors of the Vietnam Era." In *From Hanoi to Hollywood: The Vietnam War in American Film*, edited by Linda Dittmar and Gene Michaud, 175–88. New Brunswick, NJ: Rutgers University Press, 1990.

Hitchcock, Alfred. "Why I Am Afraid of the Dark" (1960). In *Hitchcock on Hitchcock: Selected Writings and Interviews*, edited by Sidney Gottlieb, 142–45. Berkeley: University of California Press, 1995.

Hoberman, J. *Bridge of Light: Yiddish Film Between Two Worlds*. Philadelphia: Temple University Press, 1995.

Hoerr, John P. *And the Wolf Finally Came: The Decline of the American Steel Industry*. Pittsburgh: University of Pittsburgh Press, 1988.

Hooper, Tobe. Interview in *The American Nightmare* (dir. Adam Simon, 2000). DVD. New York: Independent Film Channel, 2003.

Horeck, Tanya, and Tina Kendall, eds. *The New Extremism in Cinema: From France to Europe*. Edinburgh: Edinburgh University Press, 2011.

Horowitz, Gad. *Repression: Basic and Surplus Repression in Psychoanalytic Theory: Freud, Reich, and Marcuse*. Toronto: University of Toronto Press, 1977.

Jancovich, Mark, ed. *Horror, the Film Reader*. London: Routledge, 2002.

Kaplan, E. Ann. *Climate Trauma: Foreseeing the Future in Dystopian Film and Fiction*. New Brunswick, NJ: Rutgers University Press, 2016.

——. "Trauma and Aging: Marlene Dietrich, Melanie Klein, and Marguerite Duras." In Woodward, *Figuring Age*, 171–94.

Keetley, Dawn, ed. *Jordan Peele's* Get Out: *Political Horror*. Columbus: Ohio State University Press, 2020.

Kojève, Alexandre. *Introduction to the Reading of Hegel*. Edited by Allan Bloom. Translated by James H. Nichols Jr. Ithaca, NY: Cornell University Press, 1996. Orig. pub. in French in 1947.

Kozma, Alicia. "Stephanie Rothman and Vampiric Film Histories." In Peirse, *Women Make Horror*, 24–32.

——. "Stephanie Rothman Does Not Exist: Narrating a Lost History of Women in Film." *Camera Obscura* 32, no. 1 (2017): 179–86.

Kracauer, Siegfried. "The Bible in German" (orig. pub. in German in 1926). In Kracauer, *The Mass Ornament*, 189–201.

——. *The Mass Ornament: Weimar Essays*. Edited and translated by Thomas Y. Levin. Cambridge, MA: Harvard University Press, 1995.

——. *Theory of Film: The Redemption of Physical Reality.* 1960. Reprint. Princeton, NJ: Princeton University Press, 1997.

Kristeva, Julia. *Strangers to Ourselves.* Translated by Leon S. Roudiez. New York: Columbia University Press, 1991. Orig. pub. in French in 1988.

Kuenzli, Rudolf E., ed. *Dada and Surrealist Film.* Cambridge, MA: MIT Press, 1996.

——. "Surrealism and Misogyny." In *Surrealism and Women,* edited by Mary Ann Caws, Rudolf E. Kuenzli, and Gwen Raaberg, 17–26. Cambridge, MA: MIT Press, 1991.

Kyrou, Ado. *Le surréalisme au cinema.* Paris: Arcanes, 1953.

Lacan, Jacques. "The Freudian Thing, or the Meaning of the Return to Freud in Psychoanalysis" (orig. pub. in French in 1956). In *Écrits: A Selection,* translated by Alan Sheridan, 114–45. 1966. Reprint. New York: Norton, 1977.

Lauro, Sarah Juliet. *The Transatlantic Zombie: Slavery, Rebellion, and Living Death.* New Brunswick, NJ: Rutgers University Press, 2015.

Lee, Marie Myung-Ok. "*Get Out* Shows That Even the Most Intelligent Films Can Fall Prey to Asian-American Stereotypes." *Quartz,* March 31, 2017. https://qz.com/945493/get -out-shows-that-even-the-most-intelligent-films-can-fall-prey-to-asian-american -stereotypes/.

Leeder, Murray, ed. *Cinematic Ghosts: Haunting and Spectrality from Silent Cinema to the Digital Era.* New York: Bloomsbury, 2015.

——. *Halloween.* Leighton Buzzard, UK: Auteur, 2014.

Levin, Ira. *Rosemary's Baby.* New York: Random House, 1967.

——. *The Stepford Wives.* 1972. Reprint. New York: William Morrow, 2002.

——. "'Stuck with Satan': Ira Levin on the Origins of *Rosemary's Baby*" (2003). In *Rosemary's Baby* (Roman Polanski, 1968), DVD, liner notes, 14–17. New York: Criterion Collection, 2012.

Levinas, Emmanuel. *Difficult Freedom: Essays on Judaism.* Translated by Seán Hand. 1990. Reprint. Baltimore: Johns Hopkins University Press, 1997. Orig. pub. in French in 1963.

——. *Existence and Existents.* Translated by Alphonso Lingis. 1978. Reprint. Pittsburgh: Duquesne University Press, 2014. Orig. pub. in French in 1947.

——. *Totality and Infinity: An Essay on Exteriority.* Translated by Alphonso Lingis. 1969. Reprint. Pittsburgh: Duquesne University Press, 2015. Orig. pub. in French in 1961.

Lifeforce (Tobe Hooper, 1985). DVD, liner notes. Beverly Hills, CA: MGM Home Entertainment, 1998.

Lim, Bliss Cua. *Translating Time: Cinema, the Fantastic, and Temporal Critique.* Durham, NC: Duke University Press, 2009.

Lippe, Richard. "The Horror of *Martin.*" In Wood and Lippe, *The American Nightmare,* 87–90.

——. "Preface: The Journey from *Psycho* to *The American Nightmare*; or, Why Should We Take the Horror Film Seriously?" In Wood, *Robin Wood on the Horror Film,* xi–xvii.

Lowenstein, Adam. "A Detroit Landscape with Figures: The Subtractive Horror of *It Follows.*" *Discourse* 40, no. 3 (Fall 2018): 358–69.

——. *Dreaming of Cinema: Spectatorship, Surrealism, and the Age of Digital Media.* New York: Columbia University Press, 2015.

——. "The *Giallo*/Slasher Landscape: *Ecologia del delitto, Friday the 13th,* and Subtractive Spectatorship." In *Italian Horror Cinema,* edited by Stefano Baschiera and Russ Hunter, 127–44. Edinburgh: Edinburgh University Press, 2016.

——. "Living Dead: Fearful Attractions of Film." *Representations* 110 (Spring 2010): 105–28.

——. "The Master, the Maniac, and *Frenzy*: Hitchcock's Legacy of Horror." In *Hitchcock: Past and Future*, edited by Richard Allen and Sam Ishii-Gonzáles, 179–92. London: Routledge, 2004.

——. "*Night of the Living Dead* at 50." *Pittsburgh Jewish Chronicle*, October 26, 2018.

——. *Shocking Representation: Historical Trauma, National Cinema, and the Modern Horror Film*. New York: Columbia University Press, 2005.

——. "Spectacle Horror and *Hostel*: Why 'Torture Porn' Does Not Exist." *Critical Quarterly* 53, no. 1 (April 2011): 42–60.

——. "Transforming Horror: David Cronenberg's Cinematic Gestures After 9/11." In Briefel and Miller, *Horror After 9/11*, 62–80.

Lupher, Sonia, comp. Cut-Throat Women: A Database of Women Who Make Horror. https://www.cutthroatwomen.org.

——. "From Women's Cinema to Women's Horror Cinema: Genre and Gender in the Twenty-First Century." PhD diss., University of Pittsburgh, 2020.

MacDougall, David. *The Corporeal Image: Film, Ethnography, and the Senses*. Princeton, NJ: Princeton University Press, 2006.

——. *Transcultural Cinema*. Princeton, NJ: Princeton University Press, 1998.

MacInnes, Paul. "*The Babadook*: 'I Wanted to Talk About the Need to Face Darkness in Ourselves.'" *Guardian*, October 18, 2014. https://www.theguardian.com/film/2014/oct/18/the-babadook-jennifer-kent.

Marquardt, Elizabeth. *Between Two Worlds: The Inner Lives of Children of Divorce*. New York: Three Rivers, 2005.

Mathijs, Ernest. *The Cinema of David Cronenberg: From Baron of Blood to Cultural Hero*. London: Wallflower, 2008.

Mayne, Judith. *Directed by Dorothy Arzner*. Bloomington: Indiana University Press, 1994.

——. *The Woman at the Keyhole: Feminism and Women's Cinema*. Bloomington: Indiana University Press, 1990.

Mazierska, Ewa. *Jerzy Skolimowski: The Cinema of a Nonconformist*. New York: Berghahn, 2010.

McKeever, Amy. "In the Shadow of the Steel Mill." *Topic* 14 (August 2018). https://www.topic.com/in-the-shadow-of-the-steel-mill.

McLarty, Lianne. "'Beyond the Veil of the Flesh': Cronenberg and the Disembodiment of Horror." In Grant, *The Dread of Difference*, 259–80.

Means Coleman, Robin R. *Horror Noire: Blacks in American Horror Films from the 1890s to Present*. New York: Routledge, 2011.

Moretti, Franco. "Dialectic of Fear" (orig. pub. in Italian in 1982). Translated by David Forgacs. In Franco Moretti, *Signs Taken for Wonders: On the Sociology of Literary Forms*, 83–108. London: Verso, 2005.

Morrison, Toni. *The Origin of Others*. Cambridge, MA: Harvard University Press, 2017.

Mulvey, Laura. "Visual Pleasure and Narrative Cinema" (1975). In Rosen, *Narrative, Apparatus, Ideology*, 198–209.

Napoli, Philip F. *Bringing It All Back Home: An Oral History of New York City's Vietnam Veterans*. New York: Hill and Wang, 2014.

Nowell, Richard. *Blood Money: A History of the First Teen Slasher Film Cycle*. New York: Continuum, 2011.

——, ed. *Merchants of Menace: The Business of Horror Cinema*. New York: Bloomsbury, 2014.

Oppenheim, Meret. "Automatism at a Crossroads" (orig. pub. in French in 1955). Translated by Myrna Bell Rochester. In Rosemont, *Surrealist Women*, 256.

Palmer, Tim. *Brutal Intimacy: Analyzing Contemporary French Cinema*. Middletown, CT: Wesleyan University Press, 2011.

Peele, Jordan. "*Get Out* Sprang from an Effort to Master Fear, Says Director Jordan Peele." Interview by Terry Gross. *Fresh Air*, National Public Radio, March 15, 2017. https://www.npr.org/sections/codeswitch/2017/03/15/520130162/get-out-sprung-from-an-effort-to-master-fear-says-director-jordan-peele.

Peirse, Alison, ed. *Women Make Horror: Filmmaking, Feminism, Genre*. New Brunswick, NJ: Rutgers University Press, 2020.

Potter, Alicia. "The eXistenZ of Life: A Talk with Director David Cronenberg." *Infoplease*, 1999. http://www.infoplease.com/spot/existenz1.html.

Povinelli, Elizabeth A. *The Cunning of Recognition: Indigenous Alterities and the Making of Australian Multiculturalism*. Durham, NC: Duke University Press, 2002.

Prince, Stephen, ed. *The Horror Film*. New Brunswick, NJ: Rutgers University Press, 2004.

Quandt, James. "Flesh and Blood: Sex and Violence in Recent French Cinema" (2004). In Horeck and Kendall, *The New Extremism in Cinema*, 18–25.

Rabaté, Jean-Michel. "Loving Freud Madly: Surrealism Between Hysterical and Paranoid Modernism." *Journal of Modern Literature* 25, nos. 3–4 (2002): 58–74.

Radish, Christina. "*Hunters* Creator David Weil on How He Landed Al Pacino and Jordan Peele's Involvement." *Collider*, March 1, 2020. https://collider.com/hunters-interview-david-weil-amazon-series/.

Raviv, Orna. *Ethics of Cinematic Experience: Screens of Alterity*. New York: Routledge, 2020.

Rodley, Chris, ed. *Cronenberg on Cronenberg*. Rev. ed. London: Faber and Faber, 1997.

Rogin, Michael. *Blackface, White Noise: Jewish Immigrants in the Hollywood Melting Pot*. Berkeley: University of California Press, 1996.

Romero, George A. Interview in *The American Nightmare* (dir. Adam Simon, 2000). DVD. New York: Independent Film Channel, 2003.

Romney, Jonathan. "Le Sex and Violence." *Independent*, September 12, 2004. https://www.independent.co.uk/arts-entertainment/films/features/le-sex-and-violence-546083.html.

Rony, Fatimah Tobing. *The Third Eye: Race, Cinema, and Ethnographic Spectacle*. Durham, NC: Duke University Press, 1996.

Rosemont, Penelope. "All My Names Know Your Leap: Surrealist Women and Their Challenge." Introduction to Rosemont, *Surrealist Women*, xxix–lvii.

——, ed. *Surrealist Women: An International Anthology*. Austin: University of Texas Press, 1998.

Rosen, Philip, ed. *Narrative, Apparatus, Ideology: A Film Theory Reader*. New York: Columbia University Press, 1986.

Rosenzweig, Franz. *The Star of Redemption*. Translated by William W. Hallo. New York: Holt, Rinehart and Winston, 1971. Orig. pub. in German in 1921.

Rothman, Lily. "'It's Not That the Story Was Buried': What Americans in the 1930s Really Knew About What Was Happening in Germany." *Time*, July 10, 2018. https://time.com/5327279/ushmm-americans-and-the-holocaust/.

Rothman, Stephanie. Interview by Adam Lowenstein via Zoom, May 20, 2021.

Rubin, Gayle. "The Traffic in Women: Notes Toward a Political Economy of Sex." In *Toward an Anthropology of Women*, edited by Rayna Reiter, 157–210. New York: Monthly Review, 1975.

Russell, Catherine. *Experimental Ethnography: The Work of Film in the Age of Video*. Durham, NC: Duke University Press, 1999.

Russo, Mary. *The Female Grotesque: Risk, Excess, and Modernity*. New York: Routledge, 1995.

Sandford, Christopher. *Polanski: A Biography*. New York: Palgrave Macmillan, 2008.

Santner, Eric L. *On the Psychotheology of Everyday Life: Reflections on Freud and Rosenzweig*. Chicago: University of Chicago Press, 2001.

Sartre, Jean-Paul. *Being and Nothingness: An Essay on Phenomenological Ontology*. Translated by Hazel E. Barnes. London: Routledge, 2015. Orig. pub. in French in 1943.

Schneider, Steven Jay, and Daniel Shaw, eds. *Dark Thoughts: Philosophic Reflections on Cinematic Horror*. Lanham, MD: Scarecrow, 2003.

Schneider, Steven Jay, and Tony Williams, eds. *Horror International*. Detroit, MI: Wayne State University Press, 2005.

Sconce, Jeffrey. "Spectacles of Death: Identification, Reflexivity, and Contemporary Horror." In *Film Theory Goes to the Movies*, edited by Jim Collins, Hilary Radner, and Ava Preacher Collins, 103–19. London: Routledge, 1993.

Sedgwick, Eve Kosofsky. *Between Men: English Literature and Male Homosocial Desire*. New York: Columbia University Press, 1986.

Segal, Lynne. "The Coming of Age Studies." *Age, Culture, Humanities* 1 (2014): 31–34.

Sen, Meheli. *Haunting Bollywood: Gender, Genre, and the Supernatural in Hindi Commercial Cinema*. Austin: University of Texas Press, 2017.

Sharrett, Christopher. "The Idea of Apocalypse in *The Texas Chainsaw Massacre*." In Grant and Sharrett, *Planks of Reason*, 300–320.

Sheffer, Jolie A. *The Romance of Race: Incest, Miscegenation, and Multiculturalism in the United States, 1880–1930*. New Brunswick, NJ: Rutgers University Press, 2013.

Shyovitz, David I. "Christians and Jews in the Twelfth-Century Werewolf Renaissance." *Journal of the History of Ideas* 75, no. 4 (2014): 521–43.

Siddique, Sophia, and Raphael Raphael, eds. *Transnational Horror Cinema: Bodies of Excess and the Global Grotesque*. London: Palgrave Macmillan, 2016.

Siodmak, Curt. *Donovan's Brain*. 1942. Reprint. London: Tandem, 1972.

——. "Introduction to My Screenplay, *The Wolf Man*." In *The Wolf Man: The Original 1941 Shooting Script*, edited by Philip Riley, 13–14. Absecon, NJ: MagicImage Filmbooks, 1993.

——. *Wolf Man's Maker: Memoir of a Hollywood Writer*. Lanham, MD: Scarecrow, 2001.

Sitney, P. Adams. *Visionary Film: The American Avant-Garde 1943–1978*. 2nd ed. New York: Oxford University Press, 1979.

Smith, Zadie. "Getting In and Out: Who Owns Black Pain?" *Harper's Magazine*, July 2017. https://harpers.org/archive/2017/07/getting-in-and-out/.

Sobchack, Vivian. "Scary Women: Cinema, Surgery, and Special Effects." In Woodward, *Figuring Age*, 200–211.

Stein, Elliott. " 'A Very Tender Film, a Very Nice One': Michael Powell's *Peeping Tom*." *Film Comment* 15, no. 5 (September–October 1979): 57–59.

Strong, Marilee. *A Bright Red Scream: Self-Mutilation and the Language of Pain*. New York: Penguin, 2009.

Sundquist, Eric J. *Strangers in the Land: Blacks, Jews, Post-Holocaust America*. Cambridge, MA: Harvard University Press, 2005.

Taylor, Lucien, ed. *Visualizing Theory: Selected Essays from V.A.R., 1990–1994*. New York: Routledge, 1994.

Tiffany, Paul A. *The Decline of American Steel: How Management, Labor, and Government Went Wrong*. Oxford: Oxford University Press, 1988.

Tudor, Andrew. *Monsters and Mad Scientists: A Cultural History of the Horror Movie*. Oxford: Basil Blackwell, 1989.

Von Moltke, Johannes. *The Curious Humanist: Siegfried Kracauer in America*. Berkeley: University of California Press, 2016.

Williams, Linda. *Figures of Desire: A Theory and Analysis of Surrealist Film.* Berkeley: University of California Press, 1992.

——. "When the Woman Looks." In Grant, *The Dread of Difference,* 17–36.

Williams, Tony. *The Cinema of George A. Romero: Knight of the Living Dead.* 2nd ed. London: Wallflower, 2015.

Wood, Robin. "Apocalypse Now: Notes on the Living Dead" (1979). In Wood, *Robin Wood on the Horror Film,* 161–69.

——. "Cronenberg: A Dissenting View" (1983). In Wood, *Robin Wood on the Horror Film,* 231–52.

——. "Fresh Meat: *Diary of the Dead*" (2008). In Wood, *Robin Wood on the Horror Film,* 377–83.

——. "George Romero" (2000). In Wood, *Robin Wood on the Horror Film,* 373–75.

——. *Hitchcock's Films Revisited.* Rev. ed. New York: Columbia University Press, 2002.

——. *Hollywood from Vietnam to Reagan.* New York: Columbia University Press, 1986.

——. "An Introduction to the American Horror Film" (1979). In Wood and Lippe, *The American Nightmare,* 7–28. Reprinted in Wood, *Robin Wood on the Horror Film,* 73–110.

——. "King Meets Cronenberg" (1984). In Wood, *Robin Wood on the Horror Film,* 253–57.

——. "Neglected Nightmares." (1980). In Wood, *Robin Wood on the Horror Film,* 181–200.

——. "Responsibilities of a Gay Film Critic" (1978). In *Out in Culture: Gay, Lesbian, and Queer Essays on Popular Culture,* edited by Corey K. Creekmur and Alexander Doty, 12–24. Durham, NC: Duke University Press, 1995.

——. *Robin Wood on the Horror Film: Collected Essays and Reviews.* Edited by Barry Keith Grant. Detroit, MI: Wayne State University Press, 2018.

——. "Terrible Buildings: The World of Georges Franju." *Film Comment* 9, no. 6 (1973): 43–46.

——. "What Lies Beneath?" (2004). In Wood, *Robin Wood on the Horror Film,* 399–405.

——. "The Woman's Nightmare: Masculinity in *Day of the Dead*" (1986). In Wood, *Robin Wood on the Horror Film,* 319–29.

Wood, Robin, and Richard Lippe, eds. *The American Nightmare: Essays on the Horror Film.* Toronto: Festival of Festivals, 1979.

Woodward, Kathleen, ed. *Figuring Age: Women, Bodies, Generations.* Bloomington: Indiana University Press, 1999.

——. Introduction to Woodward, *Figuring Age,* ix–xxix.

Woofter, Kristopher, and Will Dodson, eds. *American Twilight: The Cinema of Tobe Hooper.* Austin: University of Texas Press, 2021.

Zinoman, Jason. "Jordan Peele on a Truly Terrifying Monster: Racism." *New York Times,* February 16, 2017. https://www.nytimes.com/2017/02/16/movies/jordan-peele-interview -get-out.html.

INDEX

FILM AND CULTURE

A series of Columbia University Press

Edited by John Belton

African Film and Literature: Adapting Violence to the Screen
Lindiwe Dovey

Film, A Sound Art
Michel Chion

Film Studies: An Introduction
Ed Sikov

Hollywood Lighting from the Silent Era to Film Noir
Patrick Keating

Levinas and the Cinema of Redemption: Time, Ethics, and the Feminine
Sam B. Girgus

Counter-Archive: Film, the Everyday, and Albert Kahn's Archives de la Planète
Paula Amad

Indie: An American Film Culture
Michael Z. Newman

Pretty: Film and the Decorative Image
Rosalind Galt

Film and Stereotype: A Challenge for Cinema and Theory
Jörg Schweinitz

Chinese Women's Cinema: Transnational Contexts
Edited by Lingzhen Wang

Hideous Progeny: Disability, Eugenics, and Classic Horror Cinema
Angela M. Smith

Hollywood's Copyright Wars: From Edison to the Internet
Peter Decherney

Electric Dreamland: Amusement Parks, Movies, and American Modernity
Lauren Rabinovitz

Where Film Meets Philosophy: Godard, Resnais, and Experiments in Cinematic Thinking
Hunter Vaughan

The Utopia of Film: Cinema and Its Futures in Godard, Kluge, and Tahimik
Christopher Pavsek

Hollywood and Hitler, 1933–1939
Thomas Doherty

Cinematic Appeals: The Experience of New Movie Technologies
Ariel Rogers

Continental Strangers: German Exile Cinema, 1933–1951
Gerd Gemünden

Deathwatch: American Film, Technology, and the End of Life
C. Scott Combs

After the Silents: Hollywood Film Music in the Early Sound Era, 1926–1934
Michael Slowik

"It's the Pictures That Got Small": Charles Brackett on Billy Wilder and Hollywood's Golden Age
Edited by Anthony Slide